I08101590

IMAGES of America

LUDINGTON CAR FERRIES

ON THE COVER: The image of the crew of the *Pere Marquette 22* was taken by Erhardt Peters about 1930. Peters was an amateur photographer who was employed as a wheelsman in 1925. Over the 10 years that Peters sailed the Great Lakes, he was able to document many aspects of the daily life aboard the largest car ferry fleet in the world. (Author's collection.)

IMAGES
of America

LUDINGTON CAR FERRIES

David K. Petersen

ARCADIA
PUBLISHING

ISBN 978-0-7385-6011-3

Published by Arcadia Publishing
Charleston, South Carolina

Printed in the United States of America

Library of Congress Control Number: 2009925355

For all general information contact Arcadia Publishing at:
Telephone 843-853-2070
Fax 843-853-0044
E-mail sales@arcadiapublishing.com
For customer service and orders:
Toll-Free 1-888-313-2665

Visit us on the Internet at www.arcadiapublishing.com

I dedicate this book to my wife, Sherri, whose love and indulgence of my obsession makes it possible.

Contents

ACKNOWLEDGMENTS

Over the years, I have been fortunate in that many families have allowed me to purchase or copy treasured family photographs. The families of Erhardt Peters, Harold Holmes, Ted Schultz, E. Ross Leedham, and Herman Schmock among many others come to mind, and I thank them for the trust they have placed in me to use their legacies wisely.

I would like to also thank my friends James F. Fay and Steven Elve for providing some of the images used in this book and Art Chavez for providing the forward as well as his time in reviewing the photographs and text prior to publication. I would also like to thank my editor, Anna Wilson, for her help and continued support through out this past year as I have endeavored to complete *Ludington Car Ferries*.

FOREWORD

Ludington's maritime history is rich and diverse, with far more activity than the railroad car ferries, the most publicly visible operation, would indicate. For over a century, generations of local families earned honorable and hard-fought livings aboard the fish tugs, lumber hookers, schooners, and coast guard craft that regularly entered and departed the magnificent protected harbor that is currently the home port of the SS *Badger*, a tourist destination in its own right, carrying passengers and their automobiles to Manitowoc.

For decades, Ludington was Michigan's busiest port on Lake Michigan, both in terms of tonnage and in the number of vessel arrivals and departures. The port was ranked third behind Chicago and Milwaukee, due primarily to the daily, year-round operations of the Pere Marquette Railroad's car ferry fleet carrying loaded boxcars of general merchandise, Gus Kitzinger's Pere Marquette Line Steamers hauling less-than-carload package freight, and, to a lesser extent, the lake schooners taking timber products destined to markets on the west shore of Lake Michigan.

In this volume, local historian David K. Petersen chronicles Ludington's maritime heritage through an impressive photographic collection that he has amassed over 20 years of research, placing him among other well-known Ludington-area historians, including Dr. William Anderson, James L. Cabot, Paul S. Peterson, and Ronald M. Wood. A variety of outstanding images were also loaned from the collections owned by Dave Carlson, Steve Elve, and Jim Fay.

Many exceptional scenes were taken by Erhardt Peters, a talented amateur photographer and crew member aboard the car ferries *Pere Marquette 22* and *32* during the 1920s and 1930s. Peters artfully captured much of Ludington's early-20th-century maritime activity through his camera's viewfinder while performing his shipboard duties as wheelsman and watchman. Dave Petersen rescued a portion of Erhardt Peters's treasured photographs, many of which had burned in a 1989 fire, from an estate sale. Sadly it was much of Peters's photographs, books, and newspaper collection that fueled the flames that ultimately cost him his life.

Dave Petersen's dedication to preserving the rapidly fading memories of Ludington's past is evident not only in this volume but also in two previously self-published works and his weekly history column in the *Ludington Daily News*. Through these outlets, an incredible number of individuals have come forward to share with Dave their cherished family possessions, including historic three-dimensional artifacts, maps, drawings, and photograph albums.

I remember fondly a recent research visit with Dave to the home of a woman related to the chief engineer lost in 1910 on the car ferry *Pere Marquette 18*. She recalled, with eyes gleaming with pride, his short life and the devotion of his widow, who never remarried and somehow managed to put her three children through college. Much of the region's local and maritime history is recorded in such ancestral recollections and mementos and is intertwined in the daily lives of countless families.

Everyday reminders include wall-hung portraits and old uniforms of brave steamer and ferry captains, engineers, surfboat men, and rugged sailors that lived out their lives, many in anonymity, on the city streets, country roads, and rolling waters around Ludington. It is to the memories of these hardy men and women that this book is written.

—Art Chavez,
Milwaukee, Wisconsin
September 27, 2009

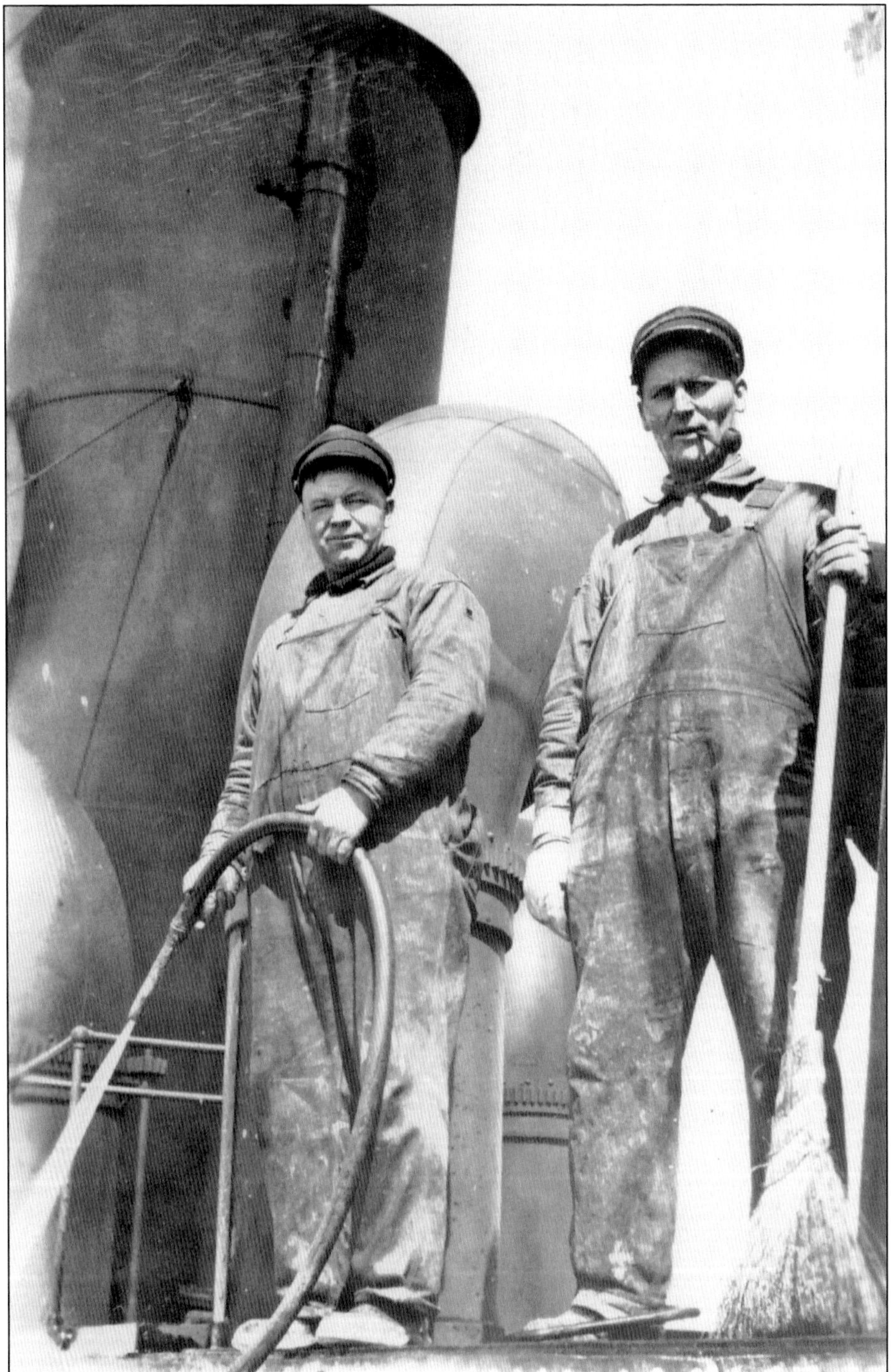

The whistles sound and the car ferry men and woken of the Great Lakes file in and prepare for another day and another trip across Lake Michigan. More than a job, they loved the lake and the ships that they sailed, and they left a great maritime history for all time. (Author's collection.)

INTRODUCTION

The Native Americans who lived on the shores of what would become known to us as the Pere Marquette Lake were the first mariners to travel along the Michigan lakeshore and also to cross the narrow and shallow harbor entrance that existed at the base of the hill coming down from the bluffs to the narrow strip of land eventually known as the Buttersville Peninsula.

Not a pe ka gon this area was called, which translates as "River with heads on sticks." This was the name given to the area by the Ottawa Indians after a fierce battle between the Ottawas and Mascoutens in the 17th century in which several thousand were killed. The victors then went about the task of severing the heads of the defeated Mascoutens and placed them on sticks along the river and lake as a warning to all who might come afterwards.

The next event of any historical nature involves Fr. Jacques Marquette. He was a Jesuit missionary who travelled by canoe throughout the Great Lakes to bring Christianity to the new world. On his way back to St. Ignace, he became ill and passed away on the shores of the lake that would eventually bear his name.

Early trappers and shingle makers made their way into the area by the lake route as early as 1835, with William Quevillion leading the way. They arrived in small schooners and travelled by canoe. Burr Caswell was the first permanent settler of European descent to arrive in 1847 with his family aboard the schooner *Eagle*.

The arrival of Burr Caswell and his family in 1847 marked the beginning of the settlement of the area and of our recorded maritime history. When Burr Caswell arrived, the area was a virtual wilderness, giant pines crowded the shores of the lake, wolves were common, and travel was hard. There were no roads to bring travelers to the new settlement that would begin to develop in the midst of the wilderness.

The only sure way to travel was by boat, whether it was by schooner or canoe. The alternative was to travel native paths and deer runs or along the beach, where each river and creek had to be crossed in some fashion.

In describing what met the family on their arrival, the 1882 edition of the *History of Manistee, Mason, and Oceana Counties* states, "Nothing could be wilder and more uncivilized then the surroundings of the first family of white settlers. Their home was in the midst of dense wilderness, their neighbors a tribe of Ottawa Indians. There were two or three white men at work up the river [making shingles] but there were no white settlers nearer then Manistee. The Indians introduced Mr. Caswell to the mysteries of their religious rites."

Sand, Sawdust, and Sawlogs, by Frances Caswell Hanna, relates the story of their arrival here in 1847. "On a balmy day in the late summer of 1847, The Eagle, a sailing schooner northbound from Chicago, with a family of six aboard, stood off the entrance to Pere Marquette Lake. Unable to sail through the shallow channel, the captain sent the family ashore in the yawl. Their oxen, cows, and pigs were forced overboard, and after circling the schooner once or twice, swam ashore. A year's provisions for the family were brought to land in row boats. Such was the dramatic arrival of the Burr Caswell family, first permanent white settlers in the region about Pere Marquette Lake. Burr was 40 years old, his wife, Hannah Green, a year or two younger. Of their four children, Mary was 15, George 13, Helen 10, and Edgar 7."

The history of the car ferries in Ludington begins much earlier then the completion of the first steel-hulled car ferry in 1897. Much work by many hands had to be accomplished in the early years of settlement in order to make that event possible. The tiny village that began to form up around the sawmills and crude buildings became known as the village of Pere Marquette.

The railroad, which had begun to extend from Flint, Michigan, towards the east coast of the state, was incorporated as the Flint and Pere Marquette. It was the railroad, which terminated in Ludington that chartered the first break-bulk ship to move goods for the railroad and solidified the need for an ever expanding fleet of boats, eventually creating the largest fleet of car ferries in the world.

Quoting from the pages of *Lumber, Lath, and Shingles*, by Luman Goodenough, "Lumber was the reason for the existence of the town. The mills scattered along the banks of the little lake were the means. A lake area two miles in length by half or three quarters of a mile in width afforded ample shore space for all the timber industries the adjacent forests could support or the river float in logs and bolts."

The development of the maritime industry in Ludington was directly related to the need to move goods to market and to move settlers and lumberjacks in search of work to remote areas that could only be easily accessible by water. The original trade and shipping routes were established to meet that need. The continued growth created the demand for bigger and better ships to carry both freight and passengers year-round across the lake.

Trappers arrived as early as 1835, shingle makers by the 1840s, and the first permanent settler in 1847. Change was happening, but by today's standards, it was coming slowly to the region. Traveling overland was difficult, as roads were nonexistent in Northern Michigan at the time.

The most efficient form of travel was by boat, and as lumbermen began to come into the area, the need was great to find a way to quickly move timber, supplies, and people. Large tracts of pine lands were being bought by men who had the vision to see the need and the future market for the seemingly unlimited pine forests. There were millions to be made for those willing to take the gamble and lives to be forged for immigrants willing to work long hours in the pinery.

Schooners and lumber hookers provided most of the transportation needs in those early years up to about 1865. Population growth was slow, and although it seemed that the lumbering concerns were moving a mountain of pine, they had in reality barely scratched the surface. Even by 1873, mammoth white pines crowded the shores of Pere Marquette Lake.

A man by the name of Ford purchased the land surrounding Pere Marquette Lake to establish a sawmill and had taken out a note with James Ludington, a Milwaukee businessman, to fund the construction and early operation of this enterprise. Around the same time, Eber Ward entered the game, as he purchased large tracts of pines in the Mason County area. Ward was Detroit's first millionaire and had been investing in lumber and mining through out the Midwest.

Ludington and Ward were captains of industry, both were forces to be reckoned with, and they were joined by yet another man who was a giant of the times, Charles Mears. Mears had already managed to secure the removal of the county seat from its former location on the peninsula to the village of Lincoln, which he controlled.

The next event of any consequence was the default of Ford in his note with James Ludington, who foreclosed and took possession of the properties owned by Ford. Much of the land that Ludington came to own in 1859 encompassed most of what would become known as the city of Ludington.

In 1859, there was a mill, some shanties, lumber shacks, a sawdust road, and very little else. Even the harbor entrance was too shallow, and this made it difficult to get the products to market.

The little lumbering community that had started to build up around the lake must have intrigued James Ludington; he wanted to build not just a business but a community. In 1859, the little village held the name Pere Marquette after the fallen Jesuit missionary who had died there centuries before and Ludington had his plans.

There were powerful men with powerful designs on the development of the area; a collision of giants was coming to the wilderness. Once James Ludington took possession of the sawmill at Pere Marquette, he needed someone to manage it. He made an offer of a two-year lease to Charles Mears to operate the mill in exchange for development of the channel.

Mears jumped at the chance to take control, but it was his biggest mistake, as that decision would ultimately lead to his financial and political demise. Over the next couple of years, Mears had the channel widened and deepened. Schooners could now navigate the channel much easier, and the commerce started to flow into Pere Marquette along with new families and lumbermen. When the lease was up, Ludington took back control of the mill and the new improved harbor.

Charles Mears was a Chicago businessman who had built mills at Pentwater in Oceana County, at the village of Lincoln, and at Hamlin in Mason County. He had successfully lobbied and won the vote to have the county seat of Mason County moved to the village of Lincoln, which he controlled. Mears had the hopes of being able to control every harbor and channel from north of Muskegon to Hamlin. In 1859, the village of Lincoln was on the move and was outdistancing the village of Pere Marquette in commerce and growth.

Mears originally entered all of the lands surrounding the Big and Little Sable Rivers because the land at Pere Marquette was taken by Joseph Boyden and the lands at Freesoil were taken by Wheeler and Harris. By 1860, Charles Mears employed about 500 in his operations; seasonally, other men and farmers in the county would also work for Mears in the woods.

In 1859, a group of Manitowoc residents came to Pere Marquette village aboard the steamer *Gazelle* to look into the possibilities of cross-lake shipping. The idea of cross-lake routes was on the minds of many early in the area's development. There were two ships that serviced the community of Lincoln on a regular basis: the *Charles Mears*, built in 1856, and the schooner *Blackhawk*.

Growth was slow during the war years of 1861 to 1865 but started to boom shortly thereafter. Veterans of the Civil War received their 40 acres, and many came to Mason County after the war to start a new life. Businesses were built, homes were constructed, and farms were established on newly cleared land. In a short time, the village of Lincoln was left holding its hands out as its population declined along with its political influence.

During these years, as the drama was unfolding between Mears and Ludington, Eber Ward was inching ever closer with the new railroad. It was a greatly anticipated event; everyone knew that having the railroad come to the village of Pere Marquette would benefit all.

When the time came for the village to have a post office, the paperwork was filled out with the name of Ludington. The village retained its name, but the post office was named for James Ludington. In 1865, Ludington started to plat out the city that would eventually bear his name. Ludington donated funds to promote almost every cause that would improve the social and economic growth of the village.

In 1869, James Ludington certainly must have felt that he had the upper hand in the negotiations with Eber Ward over a terminus in Ludington. While he had managed to get the upper hand over Charles Mears, he was about to find himself on the same end of the stick with which he knocked down Mears.

The crews of Ludington were cutting what was called a "round 40." What that meant is that in the areas where the lands of Ludington and Ward met, Ludington's crew was cutting trees down on the wrong side of the property line. Eber Ward probably did not care for how the negotiations were going with Ludington over a terminus for the railroad, and he was not a man to trifle with.

Ward knew that Ludington's crew was taking some of his lumber, and he waited until James Ludington came to Detroit to complete some business. When he arrived, he was arrested and jailed.

The result of this action was that James Ludington's health suffered greatly, and he was severely impacted by the loss of $650,000 from the subsequent lawsuit by Eber Ward against him. Ludington salvaged what he could. Ludington Lumber Company was formed with James Ludington as a stockholder but with the enterprise in control of others with whom he had previously conducted business.

The road was wide open now for Eber Ward to secure land for a terminus in Ludington on the Pere Marquette Lake. The newly formed Ludington Lumber Company donated the needed property, valued at $100,000, to the railroad. As a bonus, Ward secured some of the property for himself and constructed two sawmills on the lake to process the many thousands of acres of pines that he owned.

In 1873, when the village became chartered, Ludington offered to donate $5,000 to the city should it be named after him. It was a good year for the most part for Ludington—the city bore his name, it was growing in leaps and bounds, the railroad was almost here, and the county seat was moved from Lincoln to Ludington.

Several years before, Michael Engleman had prepared the way for cross-lake traffic by establishing his routes to Chicago and Wisconsin, and now there was nothing to stop Ward from moving forward in his plans to establish a permanent cross-lake link between Michigan and Wisconsin through the railroad. Eber Ward finished his railroad, established his mills at Ludington, and made arrangements to charter the side-wheel steamer *John Sherman* before he passed away on January 1, 1875. He did not live to see the creation of the car ferry fleet, but he played his part and set the stage for the cross-lake service that would change the region forever.

One

Early Shipping and Break-Bulk Boats

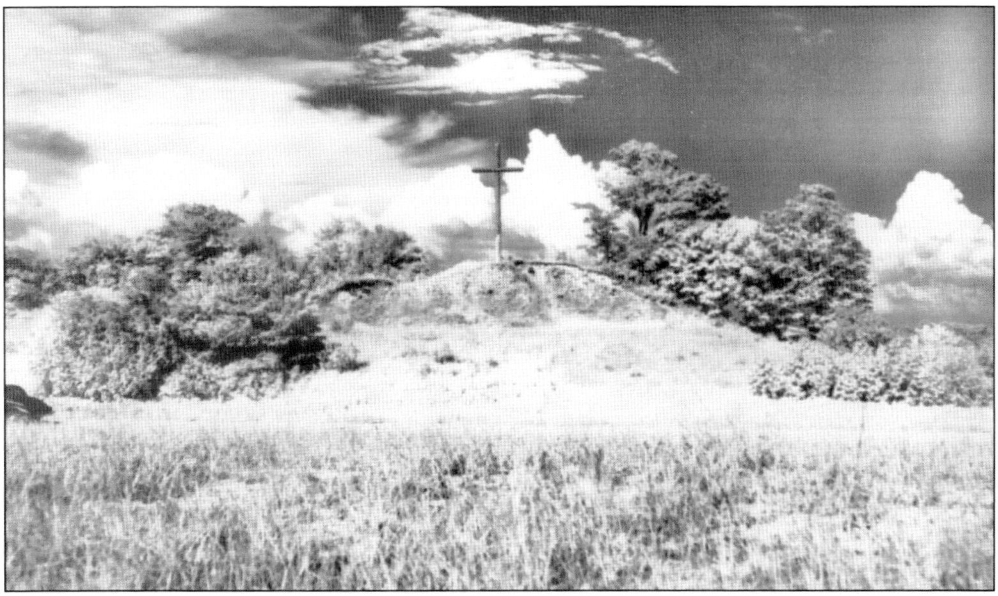

A simple wooden cross on the Buttersville Peninsula marks the spot at which Jesuit missionary Fr. Jacques Marquette passed away on his last trip to St. Ignace in 1687. The little knoll is situated on a sliver of dune separating Lake Michigan and the harbor at Ludington where the Pere Marquette car ferry fleet was based. (Photograph by Harold Holmes, author's collection.)

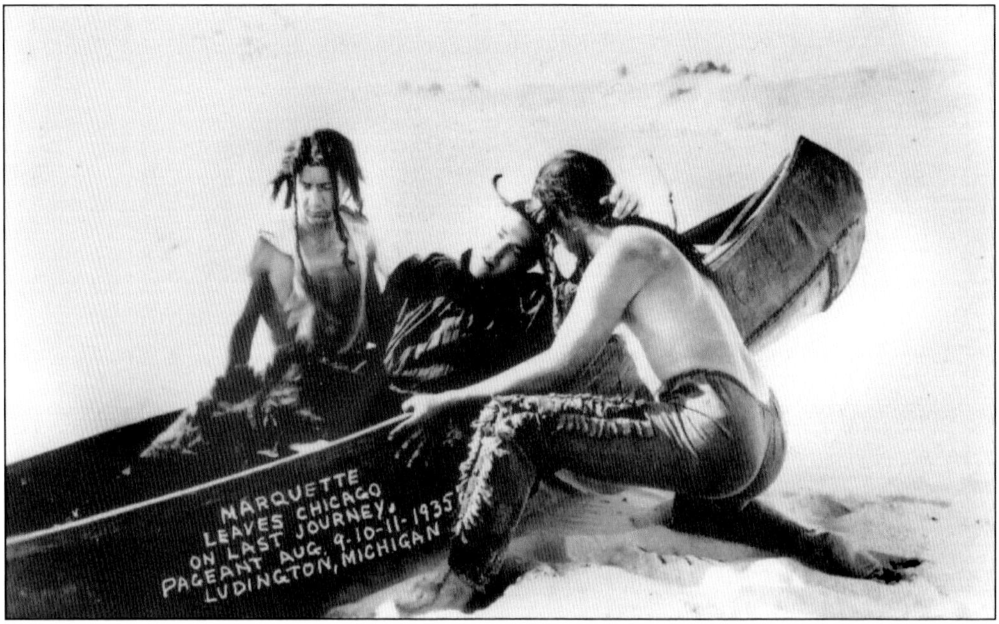

For many years, a reenactment of Father Marquette's trip was carried out by local residents in the Ludington area. This view is from a postcard depicting Father Marquette gravely ill and desperately trying to reach St. Ignace before he dies. Travel by canoe through the shallow harbor entrance was the first form of maritime traffic on the lake. (Courtesy of James F. Fay.)

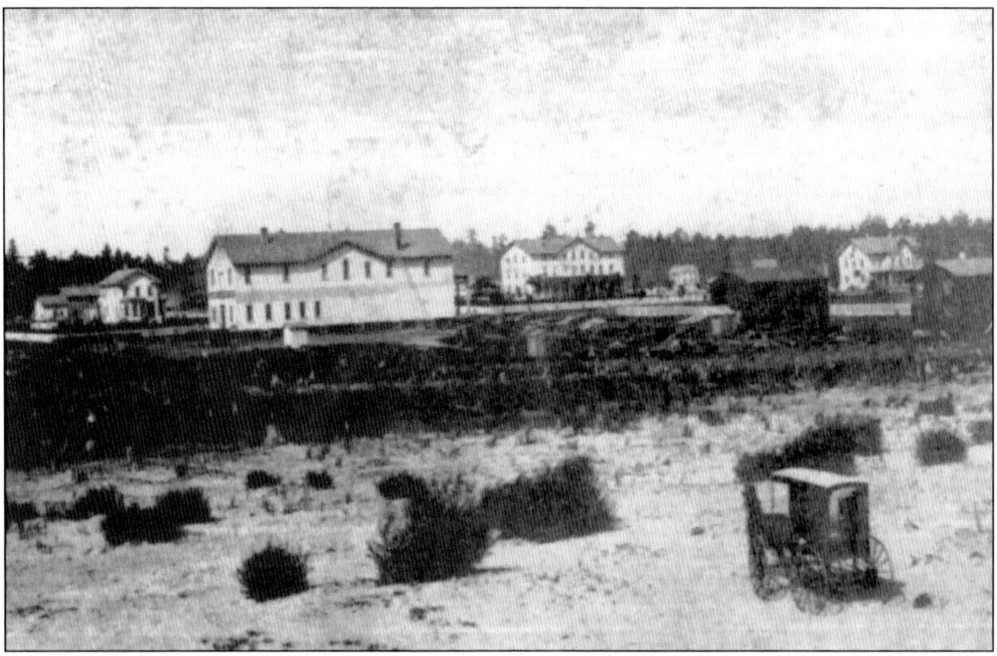

The first mill and shanties were built on the shore of northern Pere Marquette Lake. Just a short three blocks away from this site, there was nothing but swamp and wilderness. James Ludington's Big Store and the Filer House Hotel can be seen in this 1867 view. (Photograph by Harvey Silvers, author's collection.)

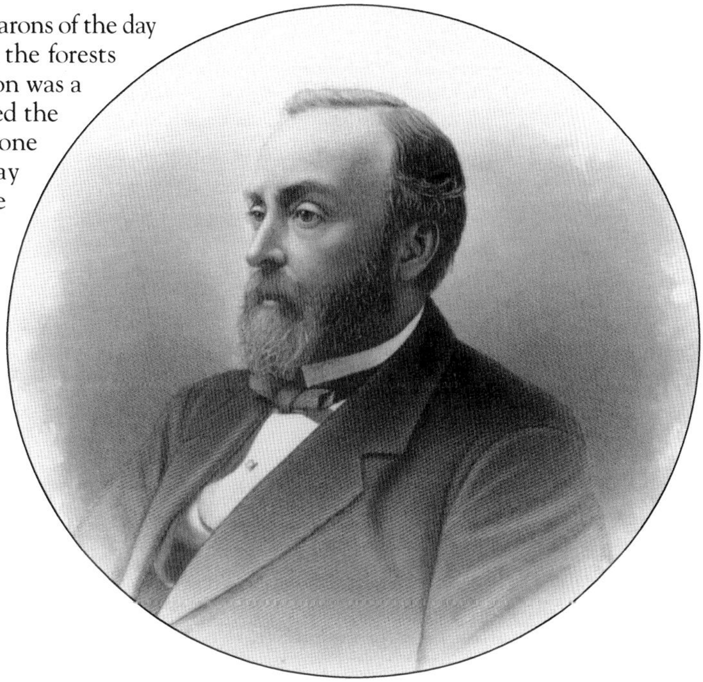

Unlike many of the lumber barons of the day who sought the riches that the forests would bring, James Ludington was a visionary in that he imagined the creation of a community—one that would not fade away but would withstand the harvesting of the great pine forests and continue to grow and prosper into the new century. (Author's collection.)

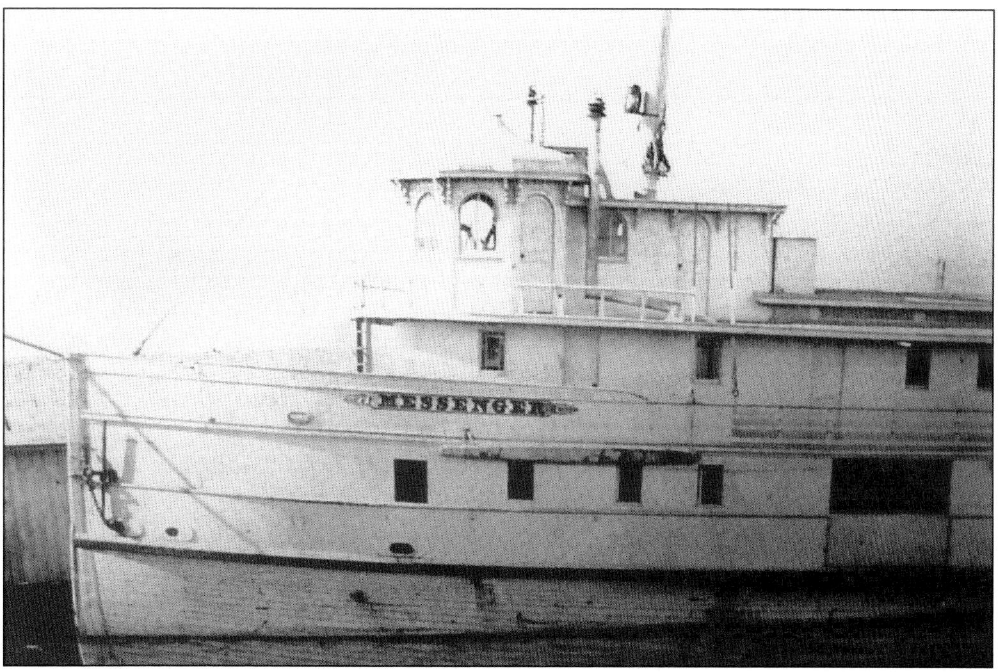

Prior to 1874, when the railroad arrived in Ludington, the Engleman line of ships, such as the *Manistee* and *Messenger* (pictured here), provided passenger and freight service along the shore. Michael Engleman came to America as a 16-year-old boy, and like those depicted in a Horatio Alger dime store novel, he rose from rags to riches to establish cross-lake shipping routes. (Courtesy of Mike Moblo.)

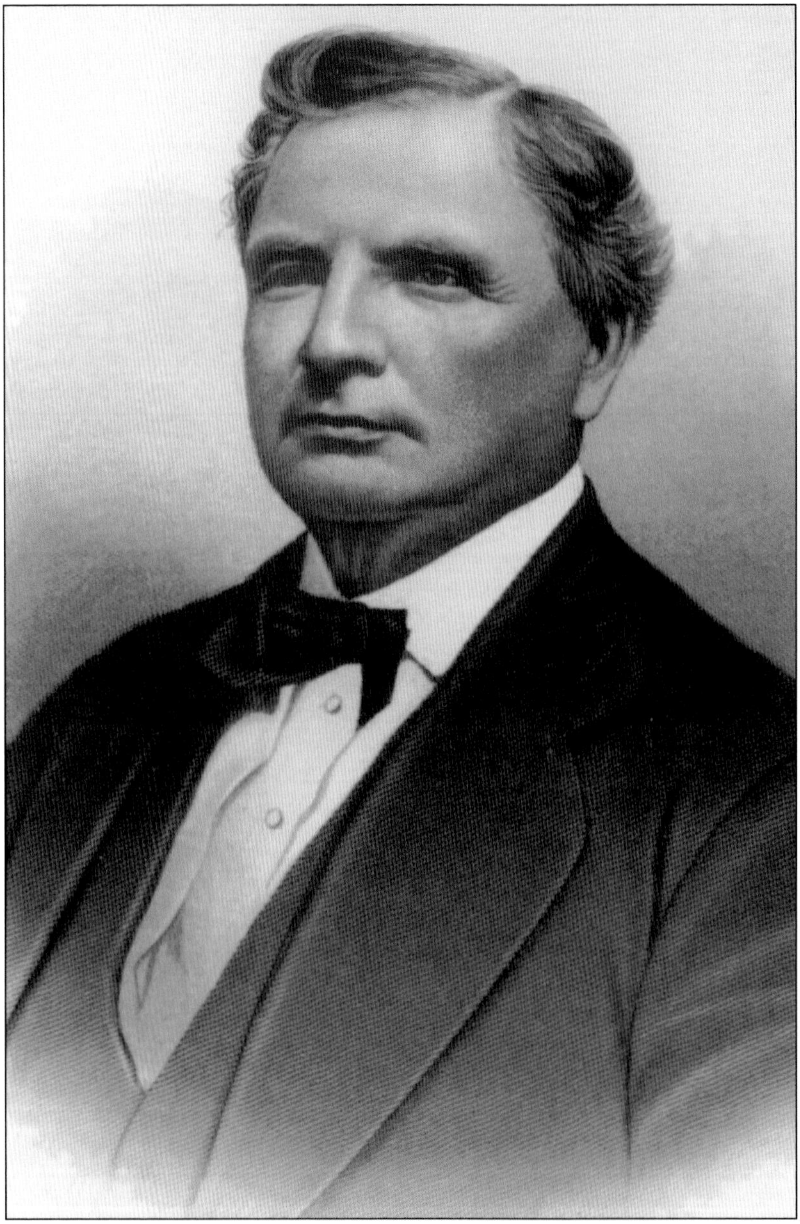

In 1860, Eber Ward had become president of the Flint and Pere Marquette Railroad, and he continued the plan to build a railroad all the way to the shores of Lake Michigan. Ward had purchased all of those thousands of acres of pine lands years before, and as an added bonus, the federal government gave his company 511,052 acres of land between 1862 and 1877 as an incentive to complete the railroad. There were millions of dollars waiting to be made, and Eber Ward was not going to let anything stand in the way of his goal of having a terminus at Pere Marquette, where he could ship his lumber to market in Detroit. To that end, in 1873, after securing his terminus at Ludington, Ward contracted with the railroad for a period of 15 years to ship 20 million feet of lumber annually to Detroit. A little more then a year later, Ward passed away, and his massive empire was sold off to satisfy debts. His wife, Catherine, took control of the Ward interests at Ludington, and her brother managed the mills. (Author's collection.)

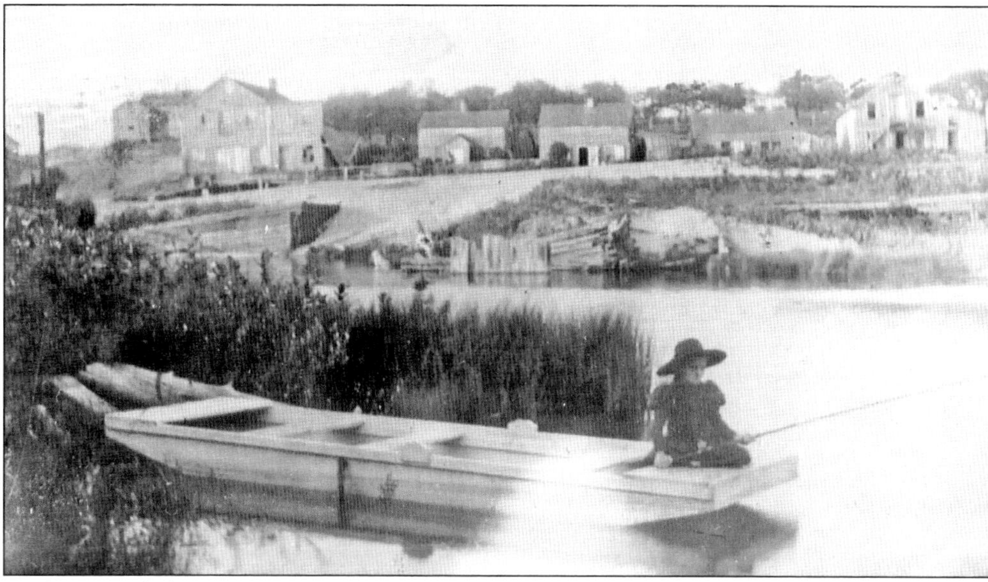

Looking north from Epworth Heights, the village of Lincoln unfolds. Mears named the village after his pick for president in 1860. The other mill at the site of the present Ludington State Park was named Hamlin, his choice for vice president. Lincoln River did not have the same potential as the harbor to the south at the village of Pere Marquette. The village of Lincoln gained short-lived control of the region in the early years of settlement. Once Mears improved the harbor and channel, Pere Marquette (soon to be known as Ludington) grew, prospered, and outdistanced its neighbor to the north. New townships of Riverton, Sherman, and Amber had formed in 1867, and by 1870, Charles Mears, admitting defeat if only to himself, relented and sold his lands and interests in Hamlin and Lincoln to Pardee and Cook in order to consolidate his business in Oceana County. (Both, author's collection.)

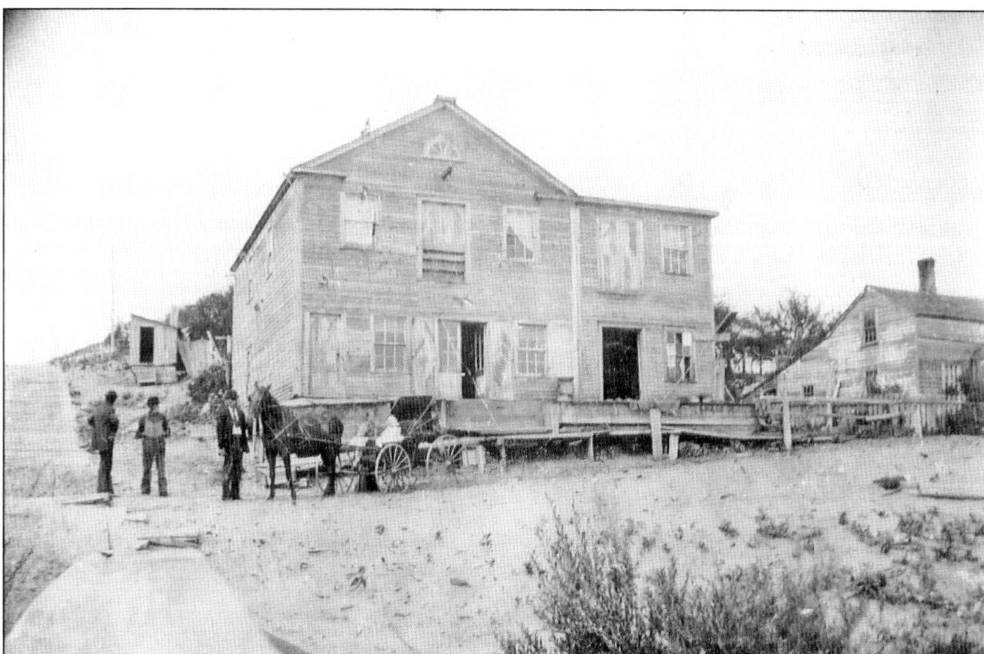

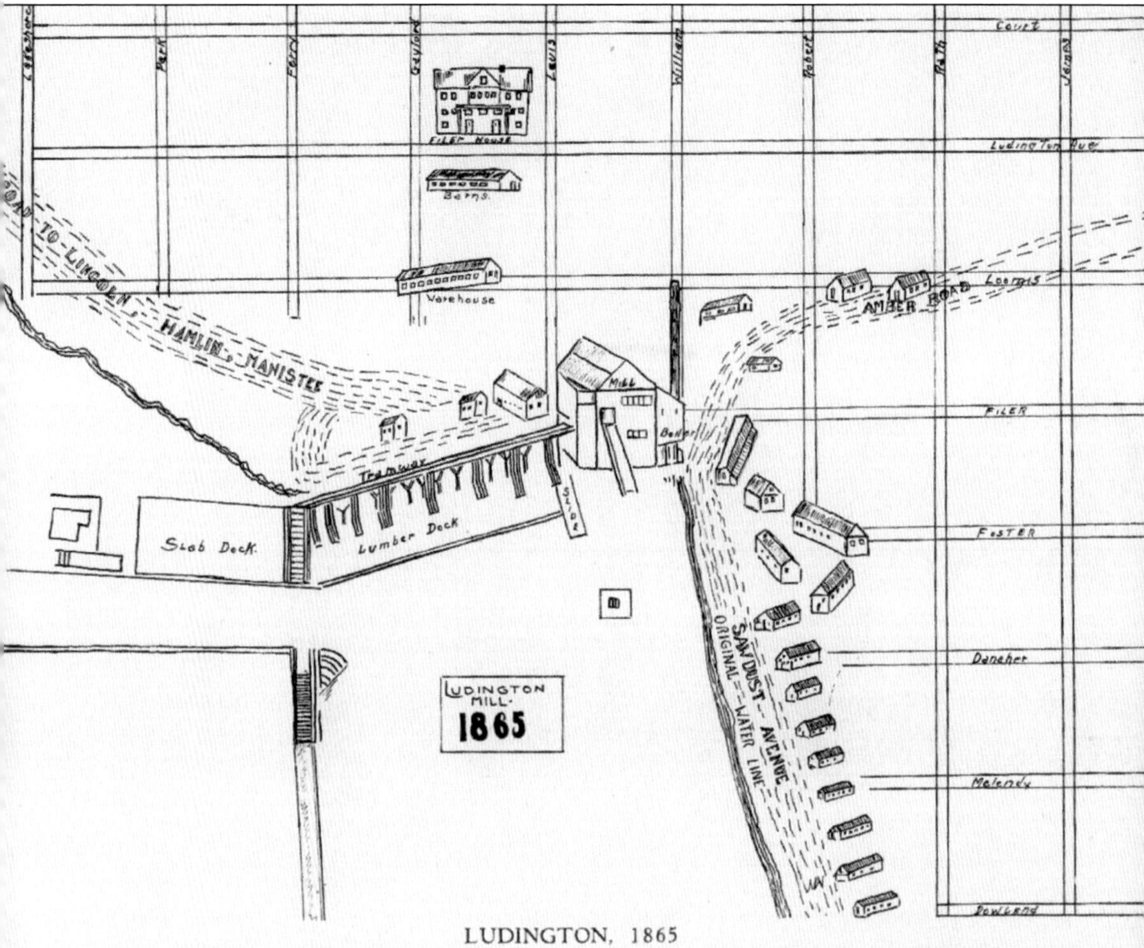

This 1865 map of Pere Marquette was drawn from memory by Charles Boerner about 1919 and was used as an illustration in the 1928 Ludington High School Oriole yearbook. According to notations on the original map, there was housing for about 150 people. The current streets of the city were laid in to illustrate where the buildings were located. The newly constructed Filer House was situated north of the mill and Sawdust Avenue, where most of the building and activity was taking place. The Filer House was probably considered in the boondocks by 1865 standards. In an 1870 letter to the *Detroit Free Press*, Delos Filer stated that the population of Ludington was about 1,200 people, with 800 having settled there in the past year. The population of the county was 846 in 1864 and by 1870 was over 3,000. (Author's collection.)

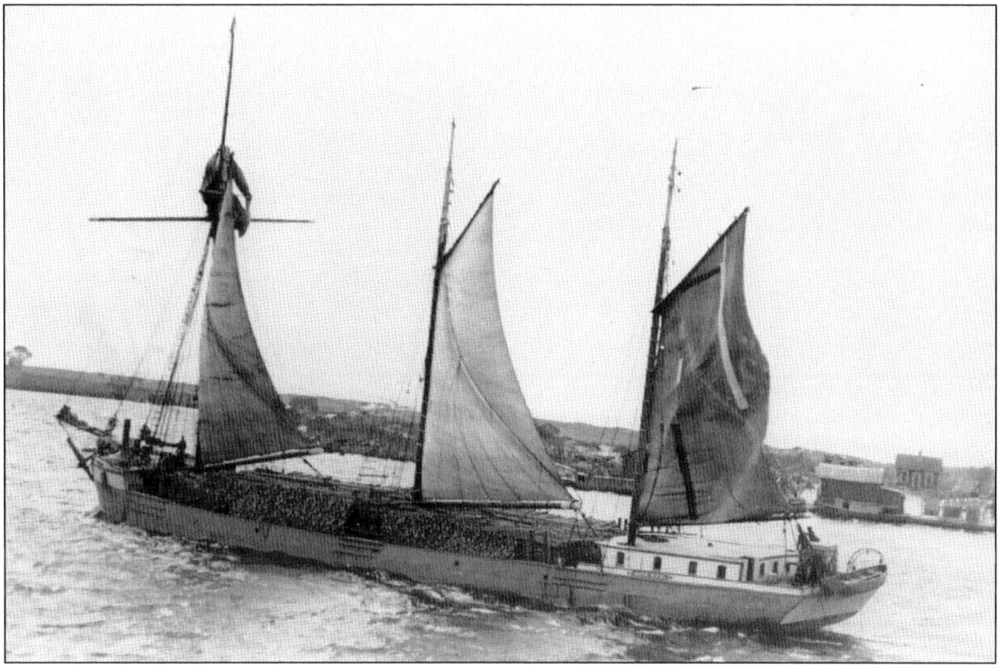

The schooner *Our Son* is seen here gliding into the Ludington Harbor past Finn Town, which is located on the Buttersville Peninsula where the Crosswind Condominiums are currently located. *Our Son* was the last commercial schooner on Lake Michigan and is seen here around 1930 loaded with lumber to be taken to market in Chicago. (Photograph by Erhardt Peters, author's collection.)

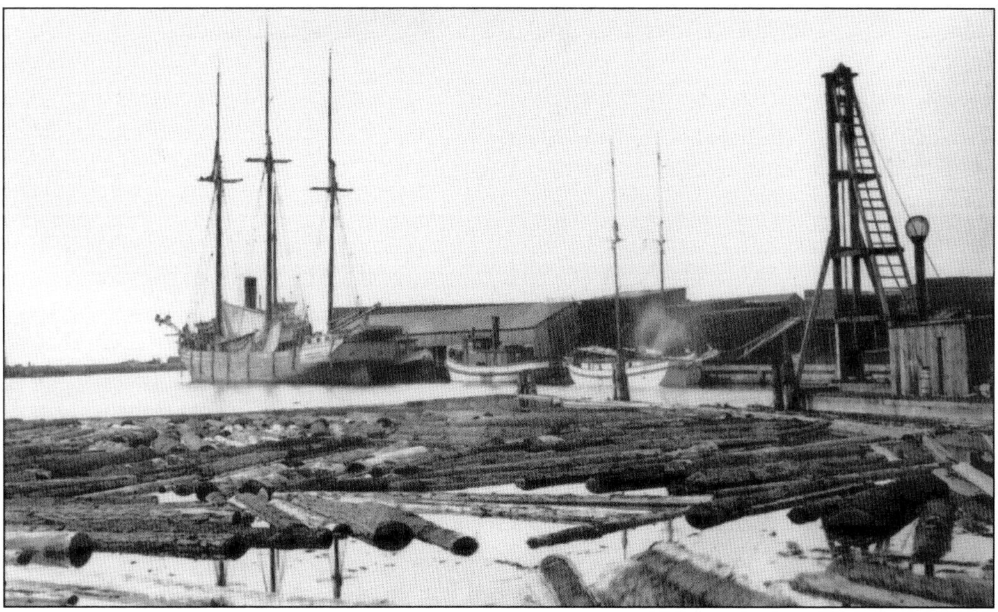

A three-masted schooner sits at the dock along Pere Marquette Lake about 1890. In the foreground is a lumber boom. Logs would be sent down the river, and upon reaching Pere Marquette Lake, they would be sorted by the log stamp indicating ownership. They were placed in the boom until they could be collected and were then moved to the mill for sawing and loaded on lumber hookers or barges at the dock. (Author's collection.)

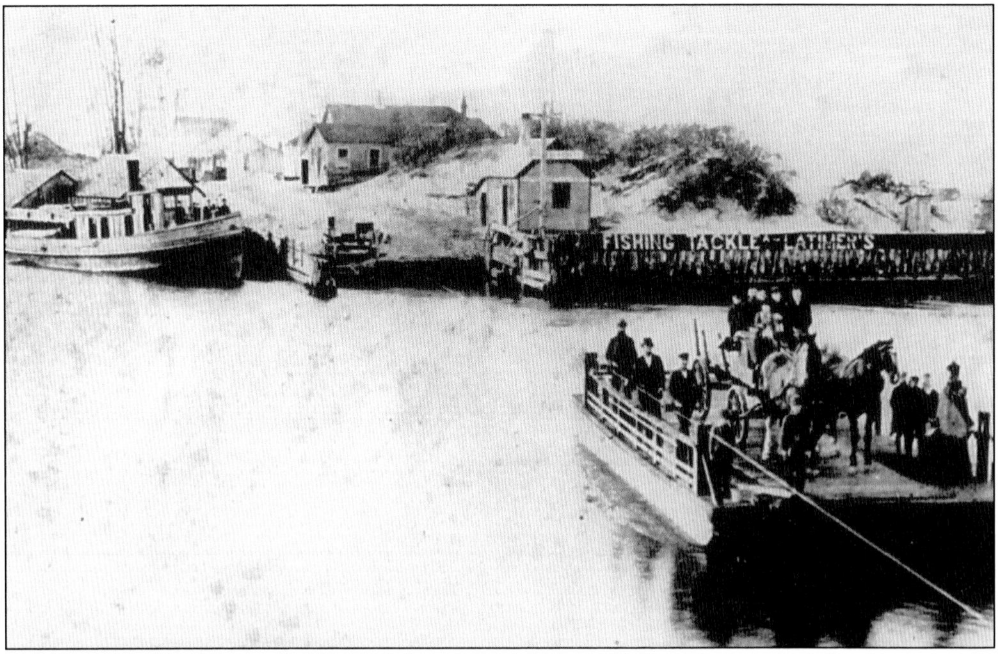

This view was taken about 1890 and illustrates the channel ferry that provided transportation between the Buttersville Peninsula and Ludington. Pictured are some of the fishing shacks at Finn Town, which is the present site of Crosswinds Condominiums. Passengers would help pull on the rope strung between the two shores to move the ferry back and forth. (Author's collection.)

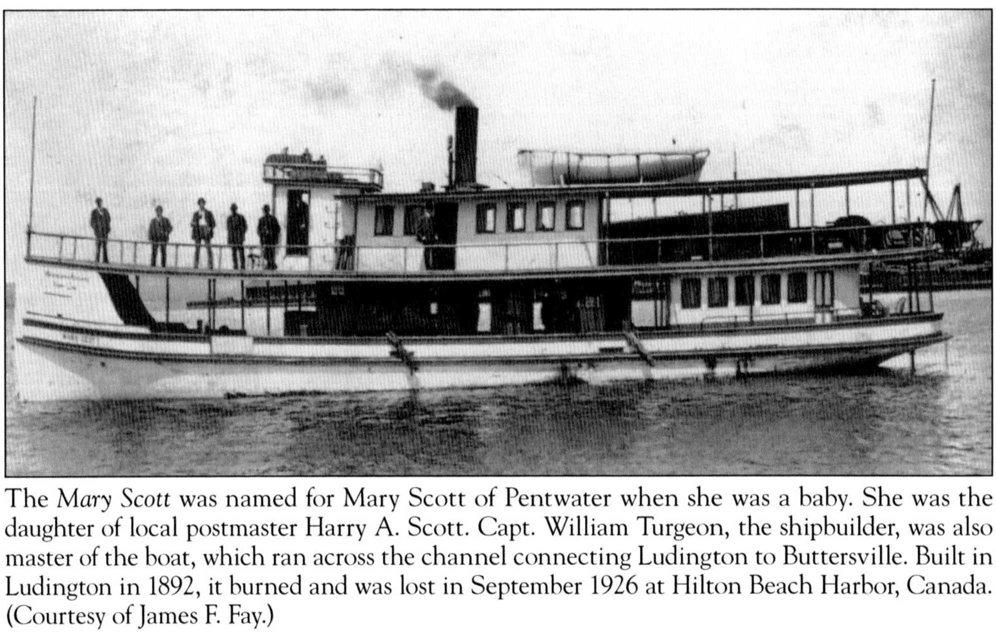

The *Mary Scott* was named for Mary Scott of Pentwater when she was a baby. She was the daughter of local postmaster Harry A. Scott. Capt. William Turgeon, the shipbuilder, was also master of the boat, which ran across the channel connecting Ludington to Buttersville. Built in Ludington in 1892, it burned and was lost in September 1926 at Hilton Beach Harbor, Canada. (Courtesy of James F. Fay.)

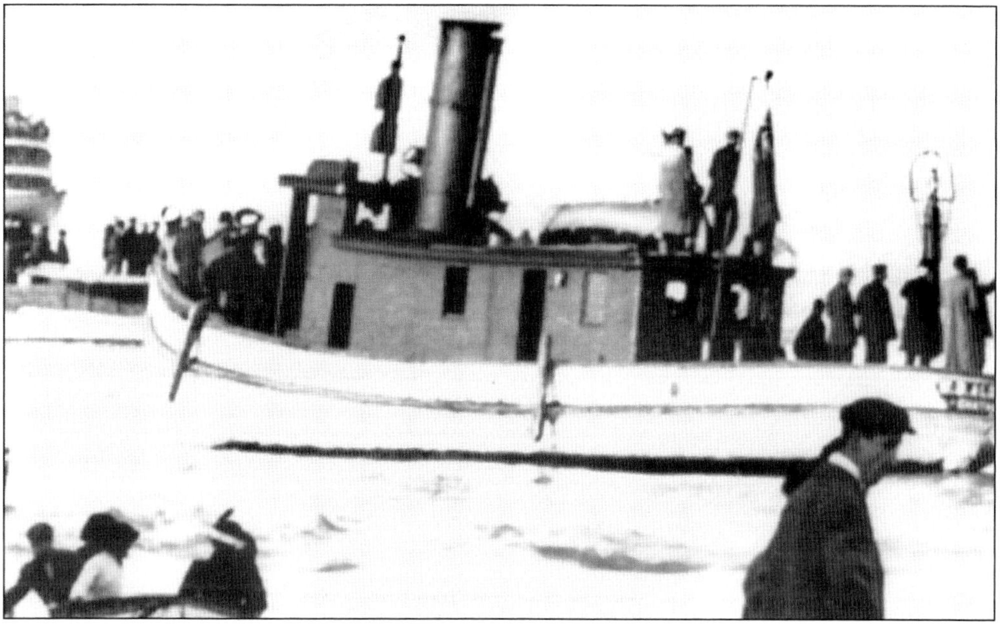

In 1867, Capt. Robert Caswell brought a tug named *Cyclone* from Chicago to Ludington for harbor towing. This tug, owned jointly by Captain Caswell and James Ludington, was built in Vermillion, Ohio, in 1866. After purchasing Ludington's share of the tug, Caswell formed a partnership with Capt. Amos Breinig and his tug *Aldrich* (built 1868 in Milwaukee) that lasted until Caswell's death in 1889. (Author's collection.)

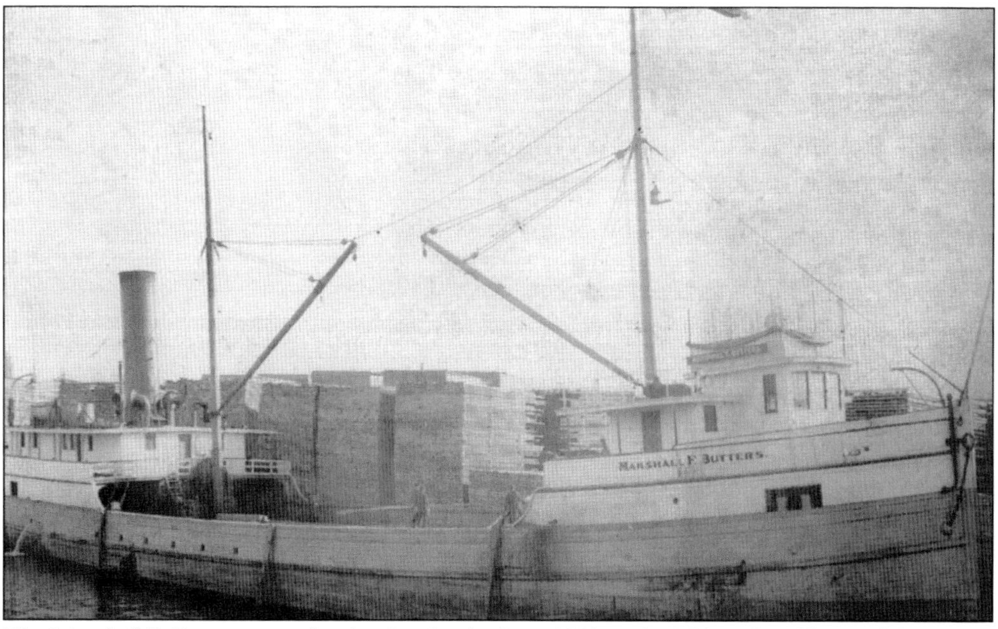

The *Marshall F. Butters* was a lumber hooker built in 1882 at the Milwaukee Shipyard Company for the Butters and Peters Salt and Lumber enterprises. The propeller-driven vessel, 164 feet long by 30 feet wide, was named after Horace Butter's son, Marshall. The ship served the Butters and Peters concern, transporting lumber and shingles, until it was sold to the Stearn's Salt and Lumber Company. (Courtesy of Dave Carlson.)

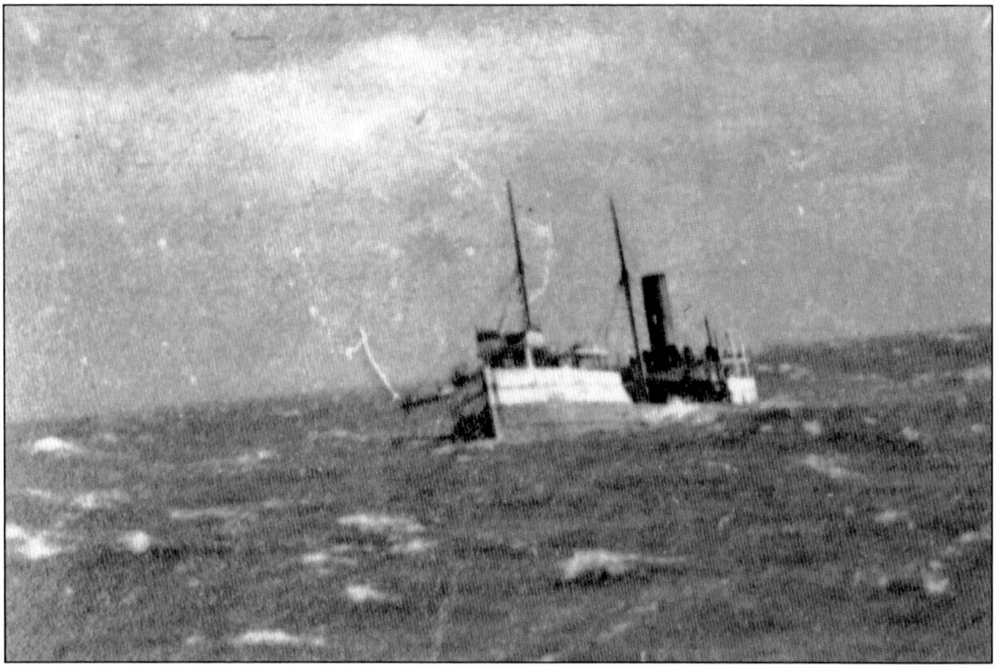

The *Marshall F. Butters* sank on October 20, 1916, on Lake Erie during a treacherous storm called Black Friday. The M. F. *Butters* was carrying a load of lumber and shingles to Cleveland at the time it was lost. This view of the *Marshall F. Butters* sinking in Lake Erie was taken by engineer Herman Schmock from the lifeboat prior to his rescue. (Author's collection.)

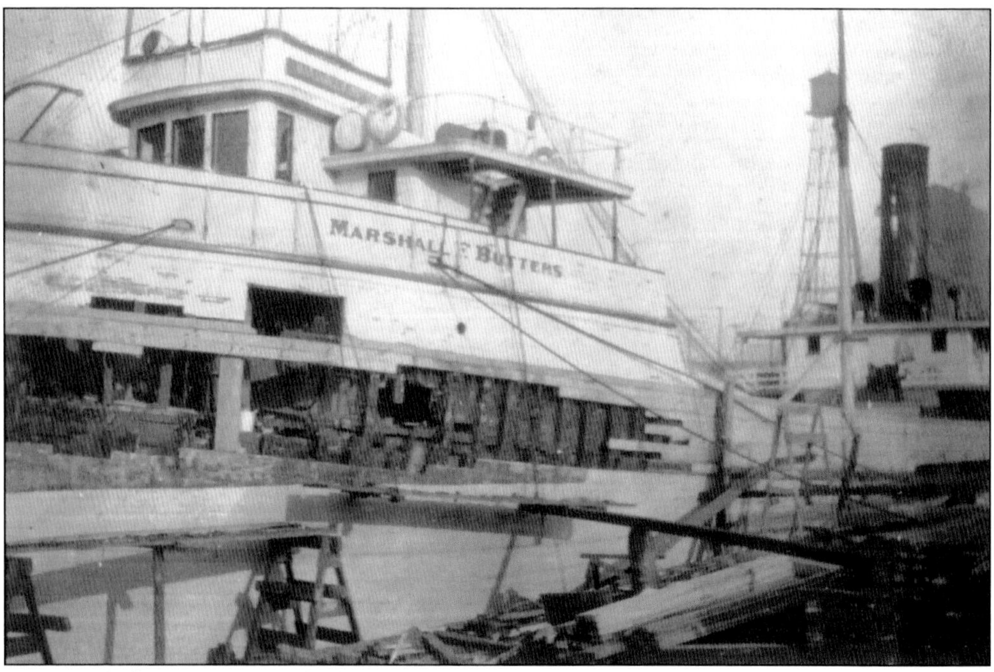

The *Marshall F. Butters* was luckier then the other ships lost during that raging storm, as the freighters *F. G. Hartwell* and *Frank R. Billings* arrived in time to rescue the crew of 13, a lucky number for them on that Black Friday. (Photograph by Herman Schmock, author's collection.)

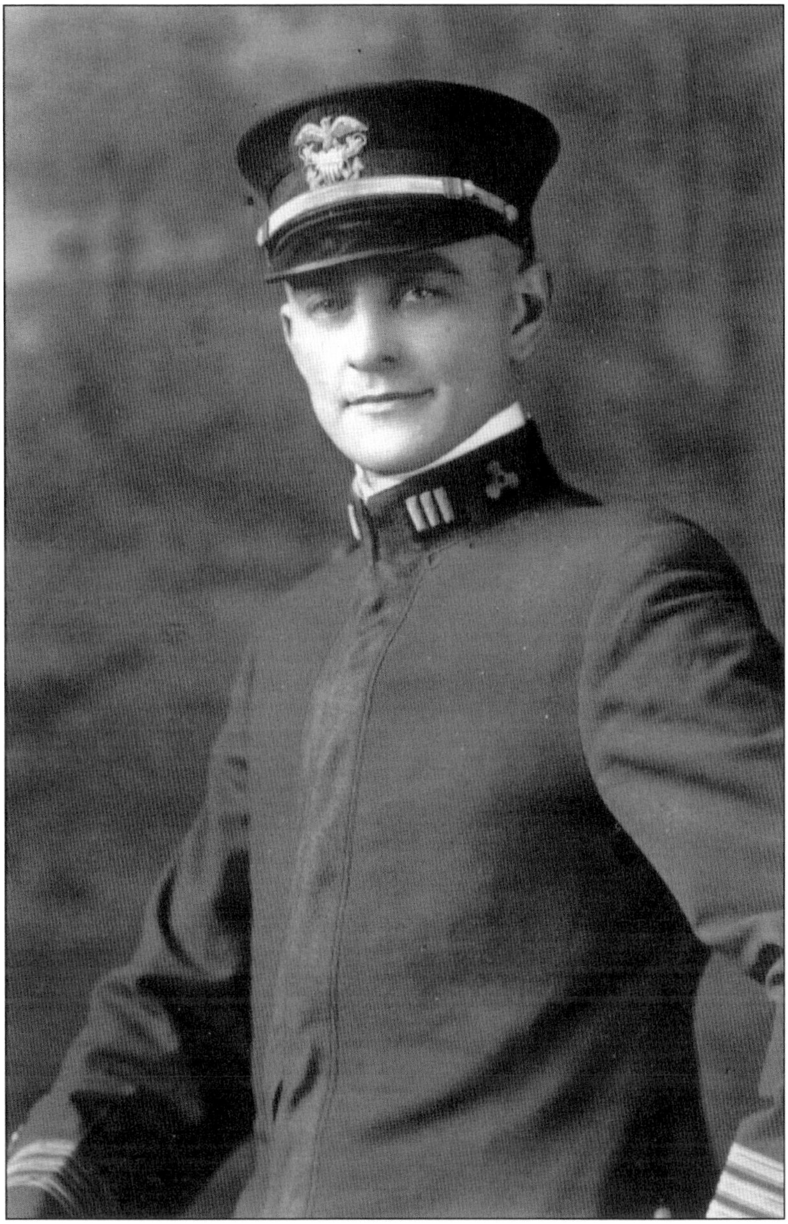

According to an interview in the October 26 edition of the *Ludington Chronicle*, Herman Schmock (pictured here) stated, "I went to my room, changed my clothes and filled my pockets with valuables. The seas washed into my room but I wanted to get a ring and watch-fob that a lady friend of mine had given me and for which I had rather go down than leave. After the boat was lowered on the starboard side ready to start anytime, I waded down the deck to the engine room after my pipe. I then enjoyed 'Sam,' (the name of his pipe) but in rather a nervous state. The steamer *Billings* came around a number of times and then the steamer *Hartwell* came, and the captain ordered us to come ahead. We reached the Hartwell after an exciting trip, the lifeboat nearly going on the steamers deck the first thing. Our intentions were to go back after the rest of the crew, but our boat was crushed before we got out." (Photograph by Herman Schmock, courtesy of Diane Solomon.)

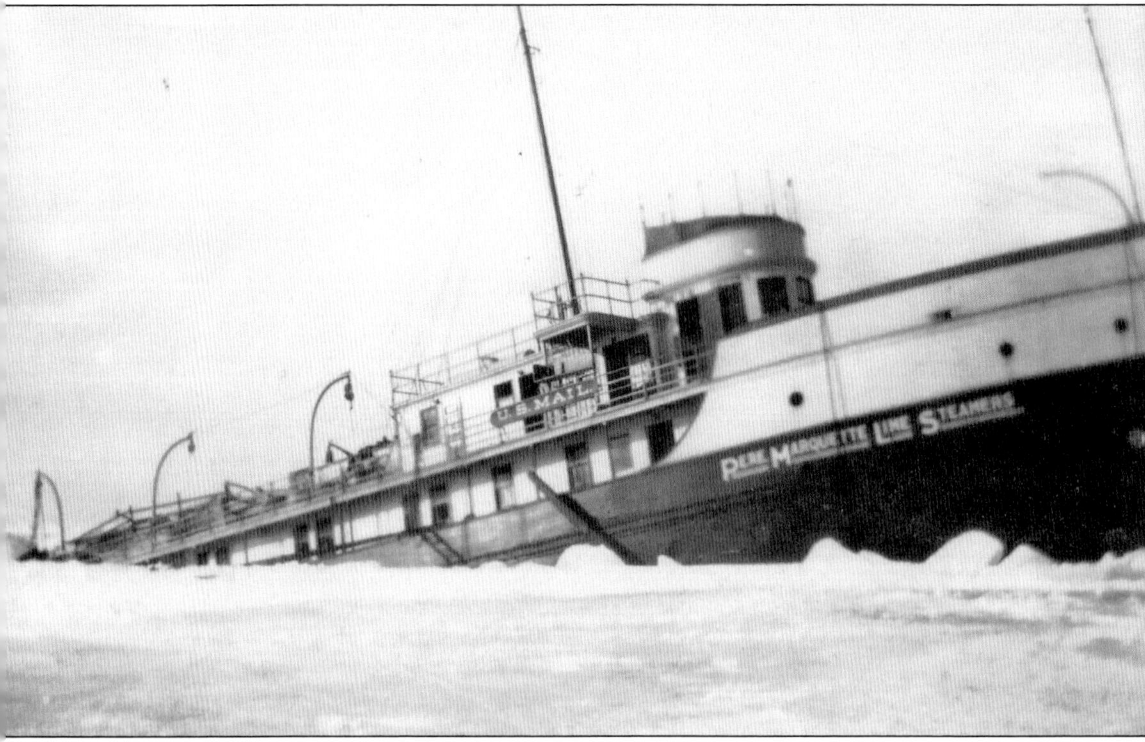

This image of the *Pere Marquette 3*, trapped and crushed in the ice, illustrates that winter travel on the lakes was not without problems. Engleman discovered this as well when two of his ships were caught in ice floes during the 1873 season. The *Messenger* was trapped for 65 days as it lay bound in a field of ice 5 to 9 feet deep. The *Manistee* was subject to the whims and mercies of the winds, which would push the ice fields up and down the lake from 1 to 18 miles out from shore from Big Point Sable to Whitehall for 52 days during the winter of 1873. The propeller-driven *Manistee* made its debut in the Ludington Harbor on April 1, 1868, as reported in the *Mason County Record*. "She came in with several colors flying and presented a beautiful and impressive sight." The *Manistee* joined the *Messenger*, *Bertschey*, and *Barber*, all boats of Engleman's Northern Steamship Line providing service to ports from Manistee, Ludington, Muskegon, Chicago, and Milwaukee. (Author's collection.)

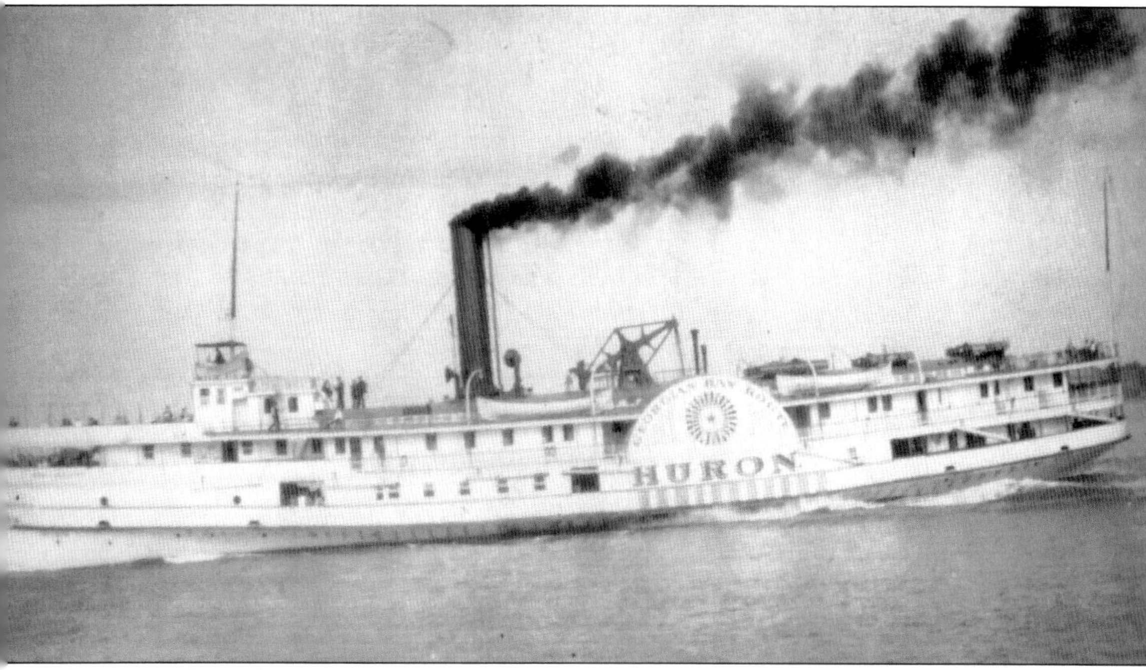

The *Huron*, shown here, was built in 1852 and was of similar size and construction as the *John Sherman*. The panic of Wall Street in 1873 and the resultant financial difficulties that it caused slowed the construction of the last 48 miles of track from Reed City to Ludington. The last spike was finally driven on December 1, 1874, and the first train arrived in Ludington on December 4, 1874. The Flint and Pere Marquette Railroad reached Ludington on December 18, 1874. The *John Sherman* was a small side-wheel ship that was contracted by the newly completed railroad in 1875 to move package freight from the Ludington Terminus to Sheboygan, Wisconsin. The *John Sherman*, under the command of Capt. John Steward, only operated for one season. It is nevertheless credited with being the start of continuous cross-lake car ferry service. The *Sherman* landed at a wooden dock on the west side of South Washington Avenue just north of the bridge to take on package freight. (Photograph by Herman Schmock, author's collection.)

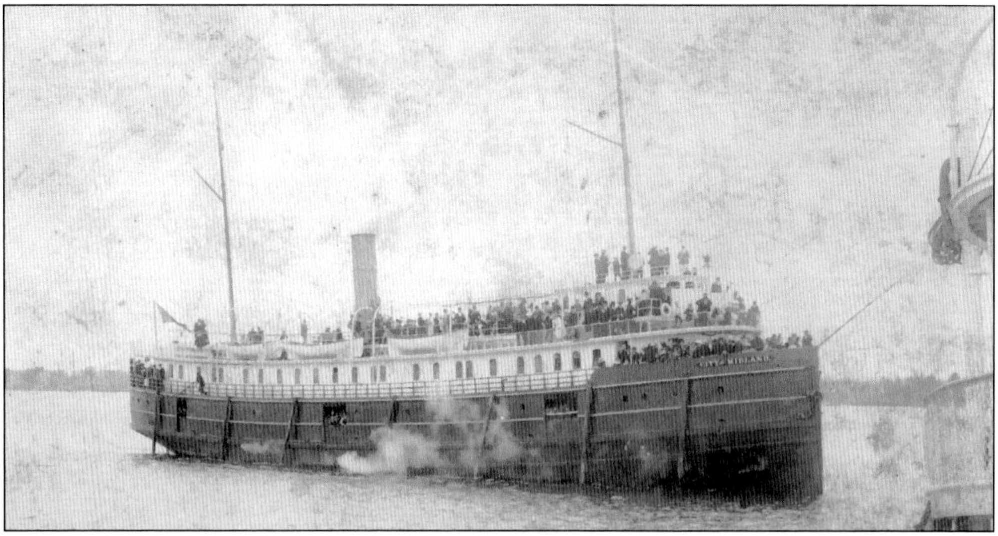

From 1875 to 1882, the Flint and Pere Marquette Railroad relied on contracted ships of the Goodrich Line to carry freight for the railroad. Initially the *Depere*, *Corona*, *City of Alpena*, and *Oconto* were given that task. The *City of Midland*, a similar-sized boat, is pictured here on a charter cruise to Sault Ste. Marie about 1885. The routes that the contracted ships ran were originally serviced by the Engleman Line out of Manistee. (Author's collection.)

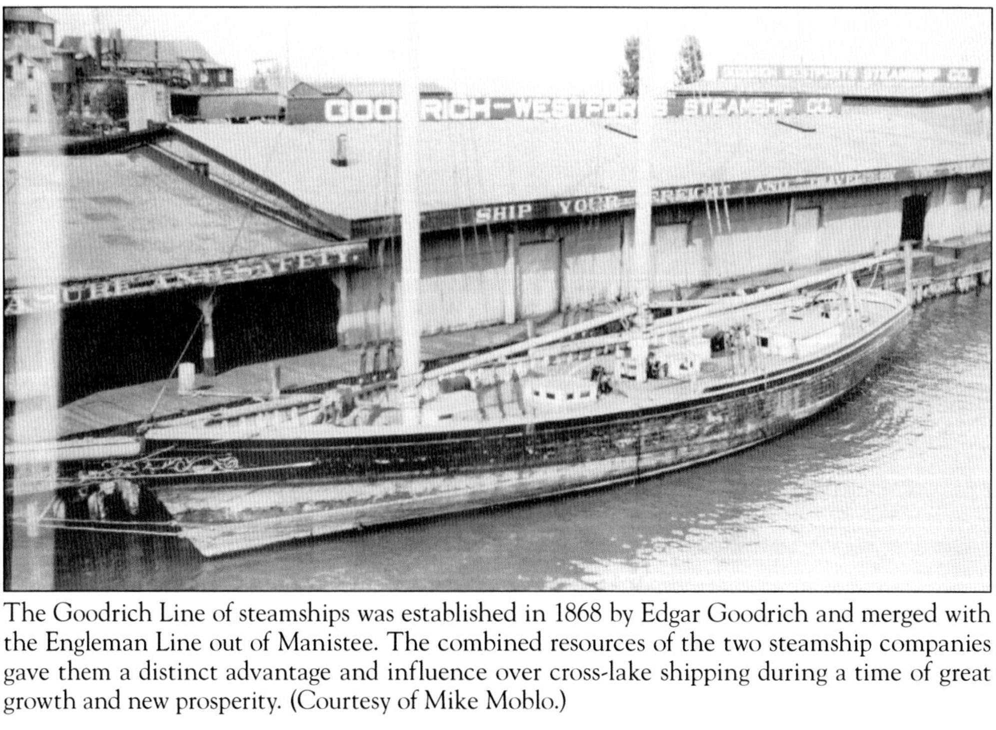

The Goodrich Line of steamships was established in 1868 by Edgar Goodrich and merged with the Engleman Line out of Manistee. The combined resources of the two steamship companies gave them a distinct advantage and influence over cross-lake shipping during a time of great growth and new prosperity. (Courtesy of Mike Moblo.)

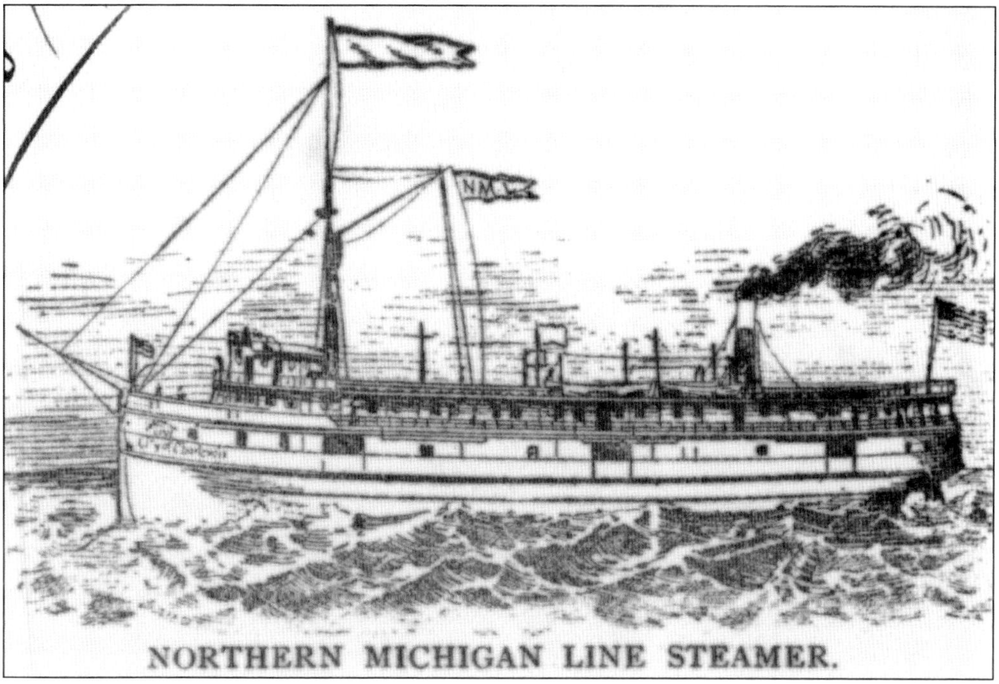

There were a number of break-bulk ships like the *Lawrence*, chartered by the Flint and Pere Marquette Railroad after the war of rates that happened between the Goodrich Line and the railroad. In January 1890, the *Osceola* and the *Colorado* were chartered, and a new route was established to exchange freight with the Wisconsin Central Railroad in Manitowoc. (Author's collection.)

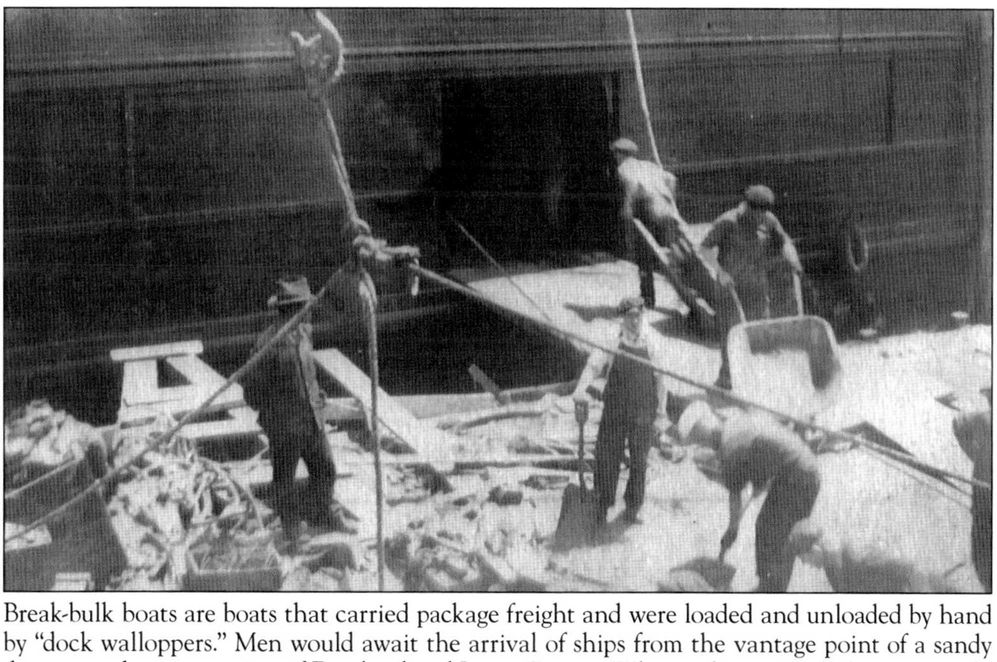

Break-bulk boats are boats that carried package freight and were loaded and unloaded by hand by "dock wallopers." Men would await the arrival of ships from the vantage point of a sandy dune near the intersection of Dowland and James Streets. When a ship arrived, the men would run down to the docks to hopefully be picked for a day's work and wages. (Photograph by Capt. Alan Hoxie, courtesy of James F. Fay.)

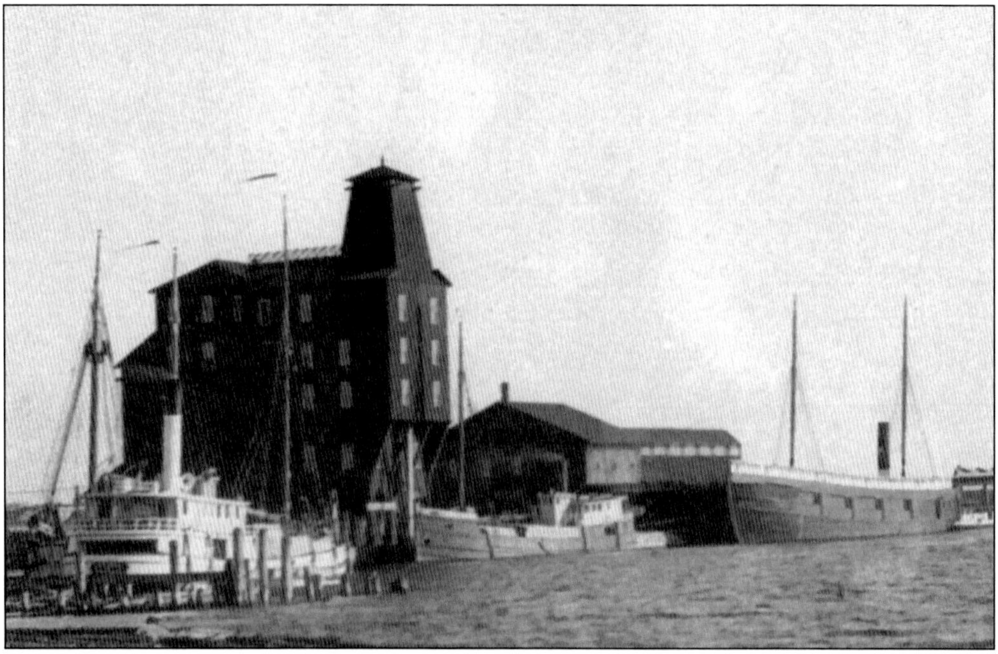

The original grain elevator, shown here, was built in 1877 and burned on July 7, 1899. Two of the Flint and Pere Marquette's black boats, *PM 2* and *PM 4* (named for the color of their hull), can be seen taking on a load of freight for the next trip across Lake Michigan. The freight shed was built in 1880 the same year that the Flint and Pere Marquette was reorganized. (Author's collection.)

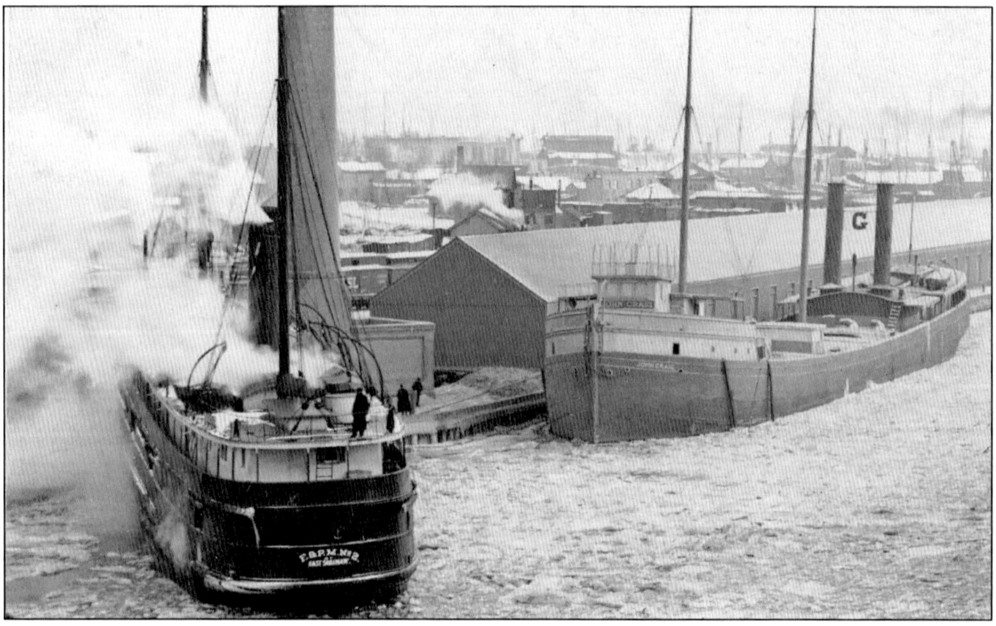

The railroad made the decision to build its own boats to handle the growing break-bulk trade. The *Flint and Pere Marquette No. 2*, at left is at Manitowoc about 1890. The railroad had relied on contracting for those services with the Goodrich Lines, which was mutually beneficial until a rate war ensued. The railroad had also contracted for a short time with the Northern Transit Company for the *City of Toledo* and *Nashua*. (Courtesy of Steve Elve.)

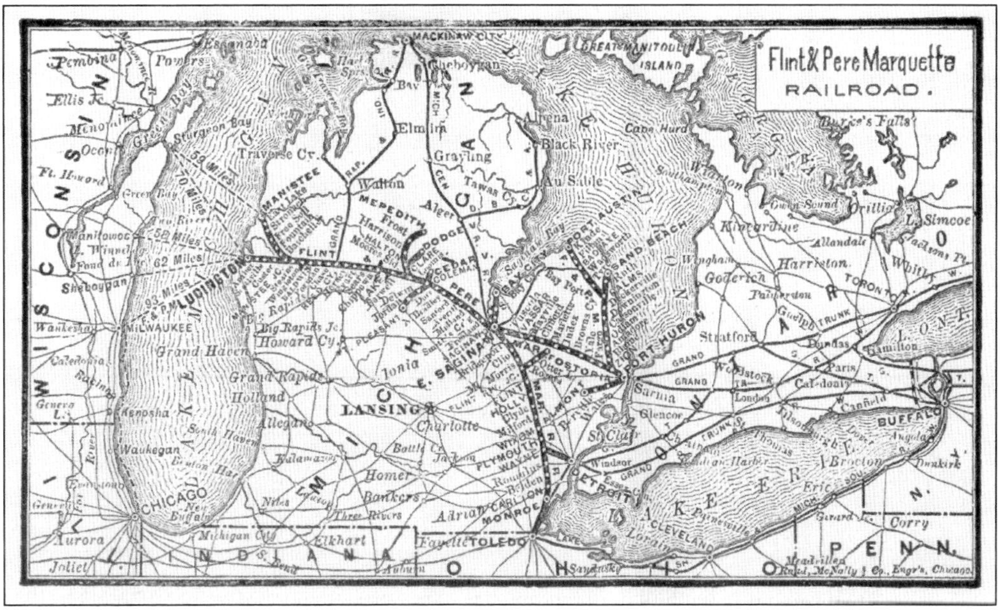

This 1890 map of the Flint and Pere Marquette Railroad illustrates the routes and terminals of the railroad just prior to the mergers, consolidations, and growth that would result in the creation of the Pere Marquette Railroad in 1900. The routes are clearly illustrated for Manitowoc, Milwaukee, Sheboygan, and Sturgeon Bay. (Author's collection.)

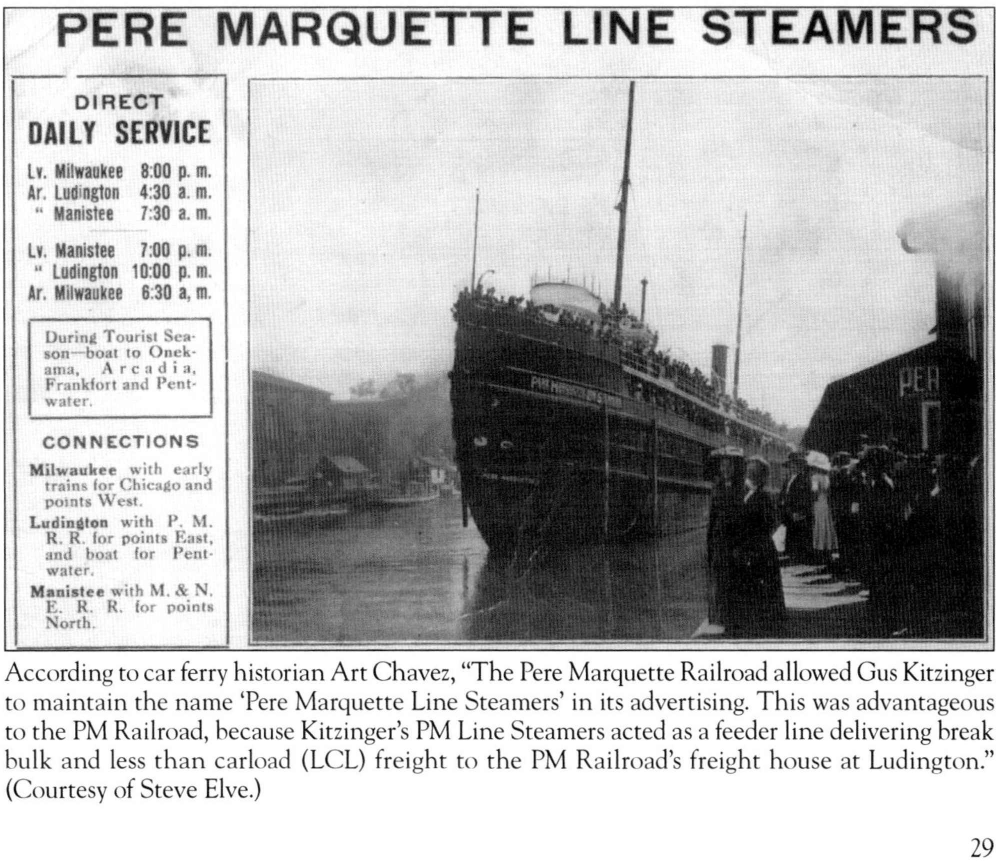

According to car ferry historian Art Chavez, "The Pere Marquette Railroad allowed Gus Kitzinger to maintain the name 'Pere Marquette Line Steamers' in its advertising. This was advantageous to the PM Railroad, because Kitzinger's PM Line Steamers acted as a feeder line delivering break bulk and less than carload (LCL) freight to the PM Railroad's freight house at Ludington." (Courtesy of Steve Elve.)

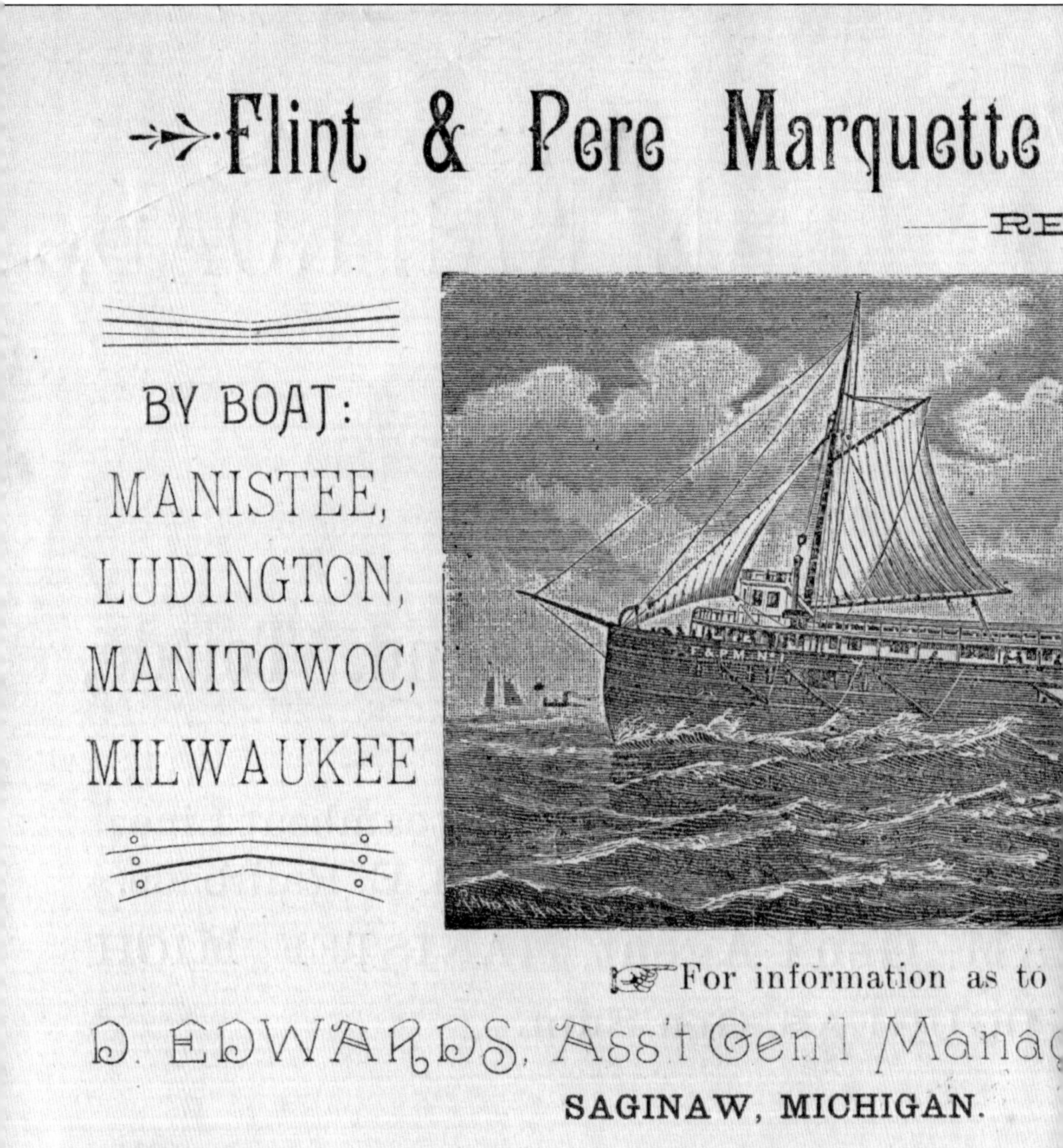

The Pere Marquette Line and the Pere Marquette Car Ferries, operated by the Pere Marquette Railway Company, were two separate business concerns that are often mixed up. The Flint and Pere Marquette Railroad initially authorized the construction of a total of five break-bulk boats to move freight across Lake Michigan and operated these vessels from 1882 to 1903. With three car ferries in operation, *Pere Marquette*, *PM 17*, and *PM 18*, the railroad decided to sell the break-bulk fleet. There was 4,721,291 tons of freight moved in and out of the port of Ludington. The new car

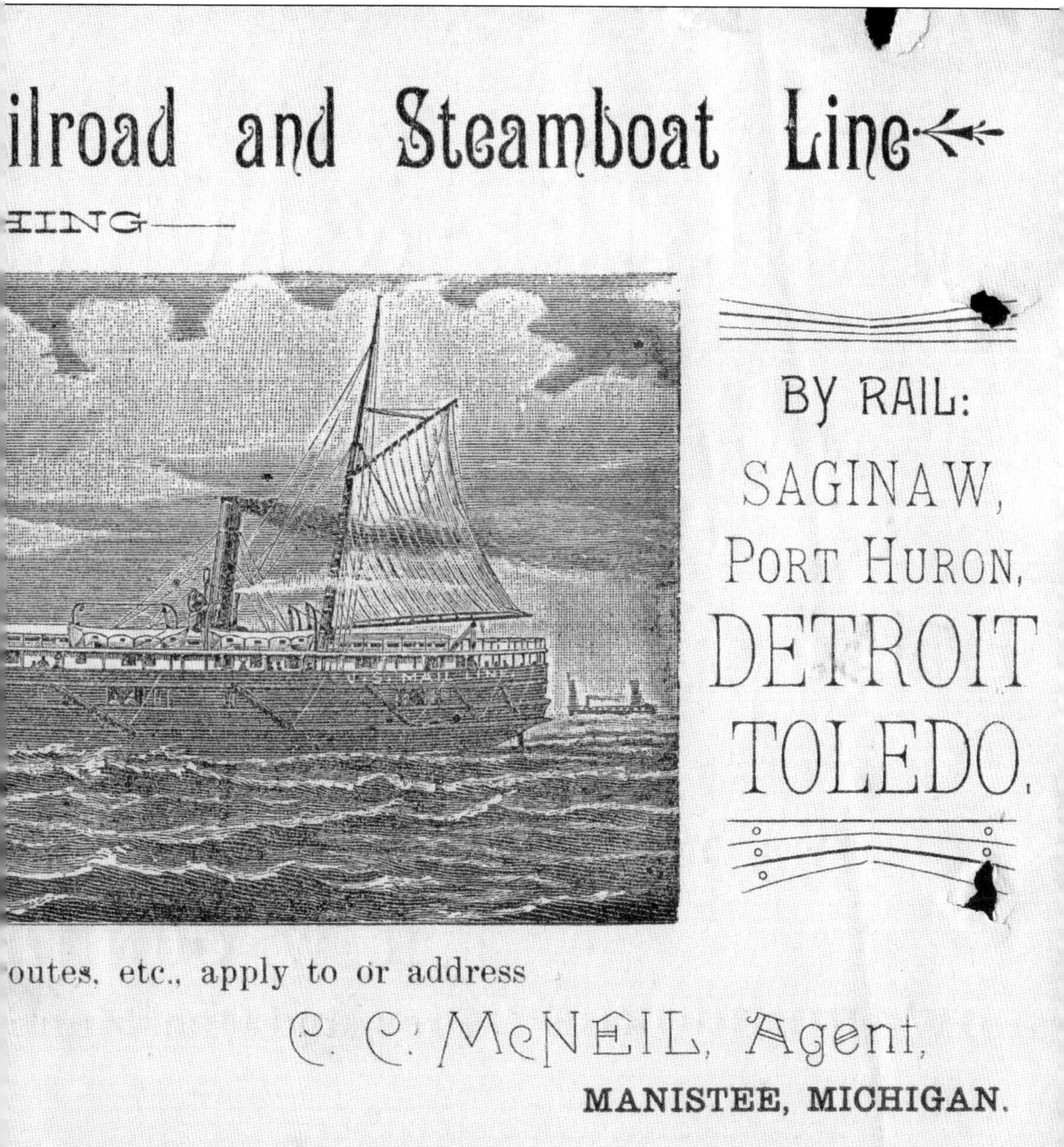

ferries afforded the opportunity to load railcars directly on to the boat saving an immense amount intensive labor. During the 1903 season, 1,955 arrivals and 1,981 departures were recorded. Gus Kitzinger purchased the *PM 2*, *3*, and *4* in 1903 and formed what would be known as the Pere Marquette Line Steamers of the Michigan Salt Transportation Company. The Pere Marquette Line of ships included the *Virginia*, *Nevada*, *Georgia*, *Mark B. Covell* (*Pere Marquette* 6), and others were often contracted for work by the Pere Marquette Railroad. (Author's collection.)

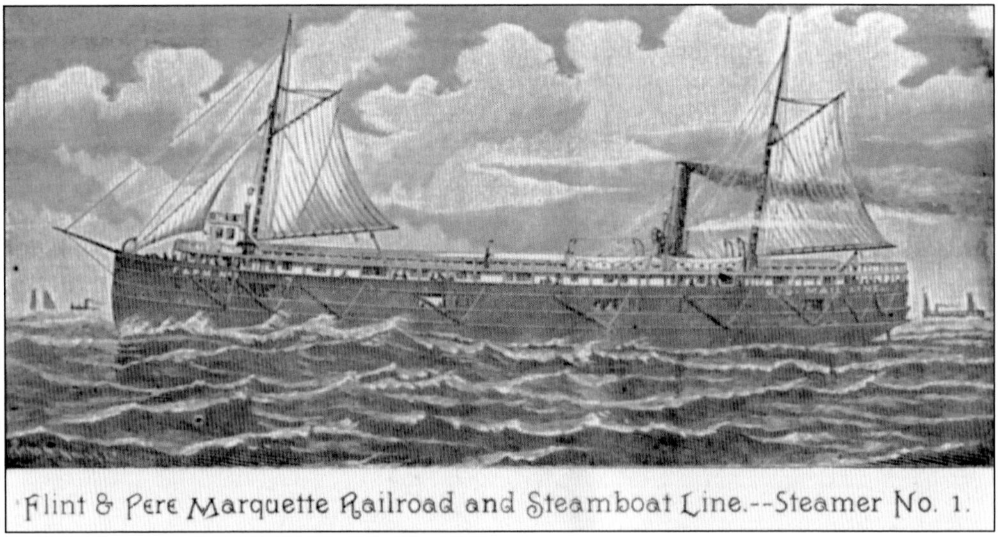

Both the *Flint and Pere Marquette No. 1* and *2* were schooners rigged and built by the Detroit Dry Dock Company in 1882. Originally built at a length of 145 feet, it was discovered early that the boats needed to be larger, and the next year, 36 feet were added to the length of both boats. The *No. 1* sank at the Ludington Harbor entrance on December 31, 1884, and was raised and repaired. (Author's collection.)

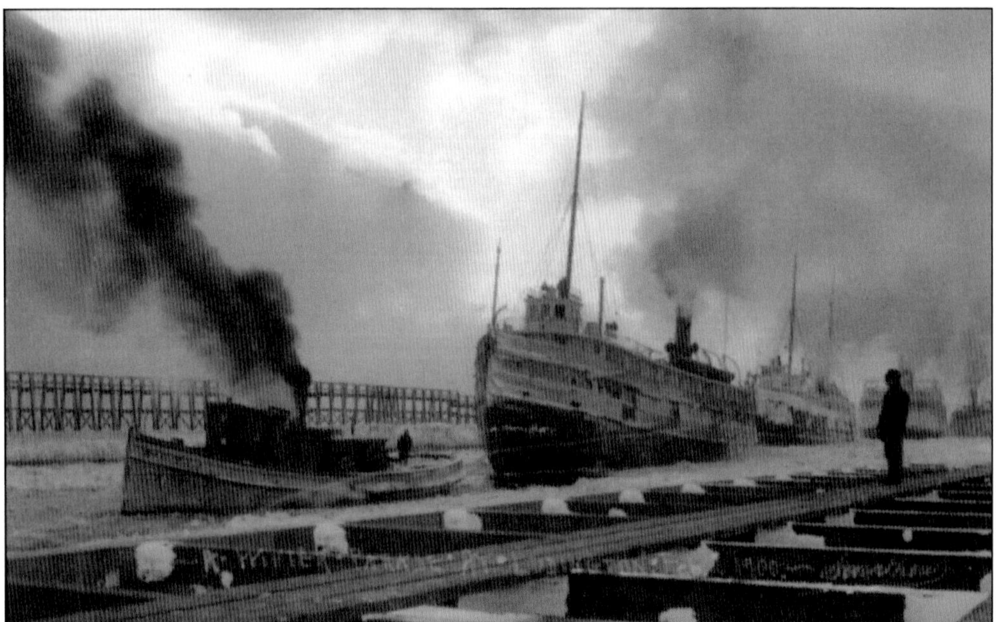

The *Pere Marquette 2*, *3*, *15*, and *4* can be seen in this 1904 photograph by Swarthout Studio being led into the Ludington Harbor behind the icebreaking tug *Frank Canfield*. The winter of 1904 was particularly disruptive to shipping, as most of Lake Michigan froze. The boats ran year-round, but there were times when assistance was required to make the dock. (Author's collection.)

Excursions were popular at a time when travel on poorly maintained roads was difficult. Trips to Manistee and other port towns were regular features generating passenger fares to help augment the income from break-bulk package service. The *Pere Marquette 2* was operated by Gus Kitzinger from 1901 to 1906. The boat was sold to a Canadian firm and renamed the *Dundern*; it sank in 1919 with two lives lost. (Courtesy of Steve Elve.)

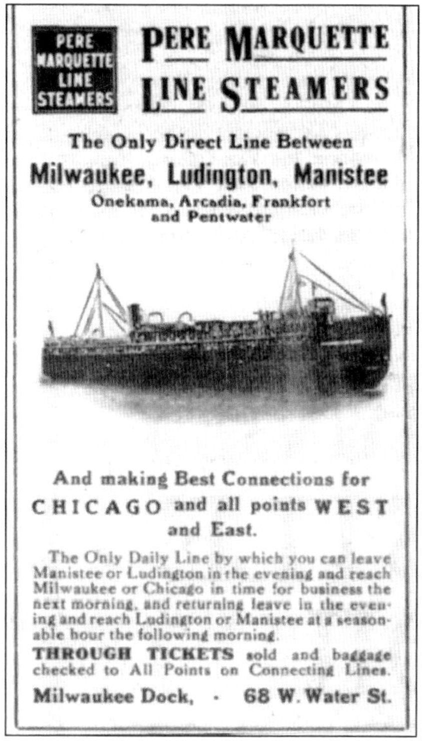

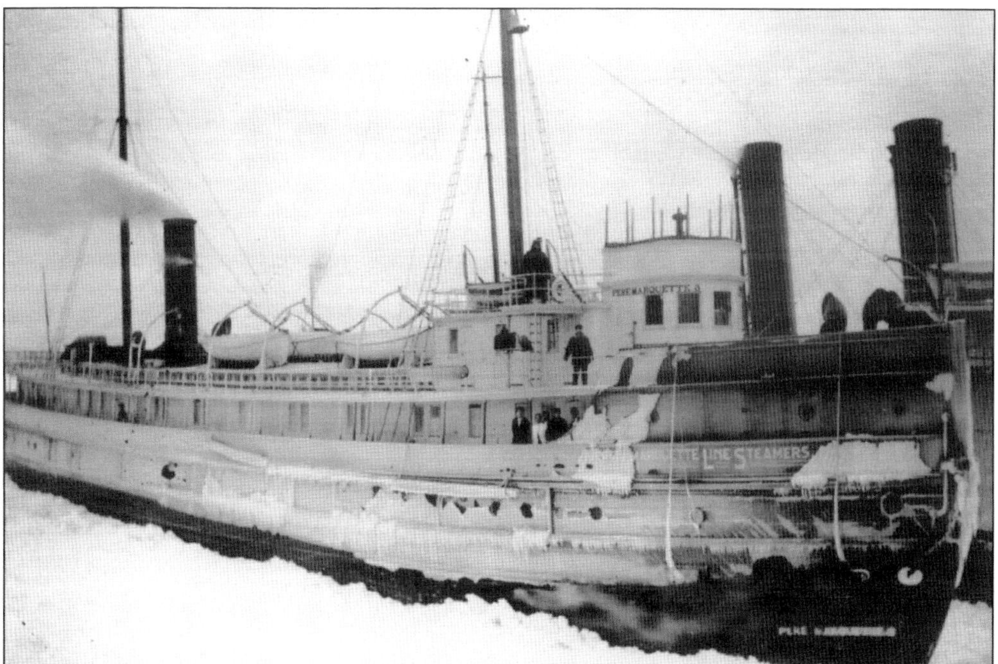

The *Flint and Pere Marquette No. 3*, pictured here at Ludington, was built in 1887 by the Detroit Dry Dock Company at 190 feet in length to assist in the growing freight business. The ship quickly became known as the "Hoodoo" ship because of the numerous accidents and mishaps that occurred, earning itself a place in *Ripley's Believe it or Not.* (Author's collection.)

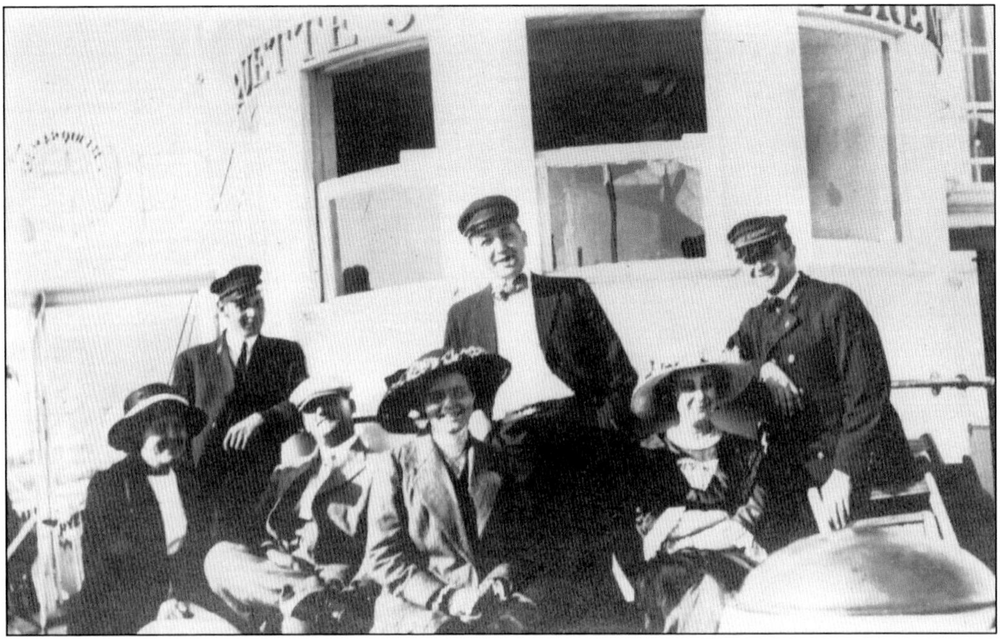

Alan Hoxie was a locally popular ship captain. He went to work for the Pere Marquette Line in 1910 as captain of the *Pere Marquette 4*, and from that point on, he always sailed as a ship's master. He was master of the *Pere Marquette 4* from 1910 to 1913 and again in 1920, after the loss and sinking of the *Pere Marquette 3* on March 7, 1920. (Author's collection.)

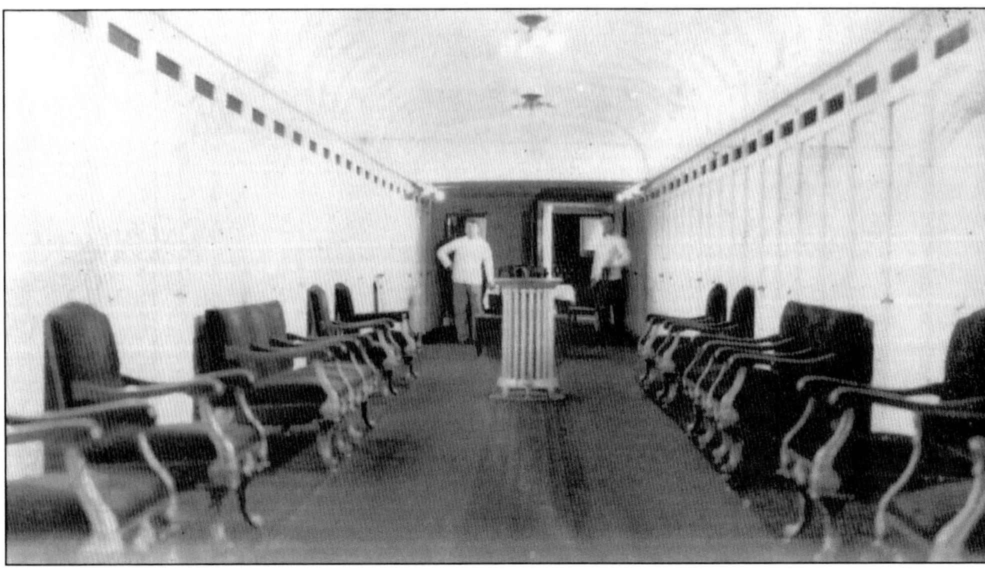

This view shows the elegant interior of the *Pere Marquette 3*. Hoxie was named captain of the ship in 1913 and on March 7, 1920, was on vacation for a month when his substitute, Capt. Cornelius McCauley, took the ship out, and it was caught in a field of ice just outside of Ludington along with the *Pere Marquette 17* and *18*. (Author's collection.)

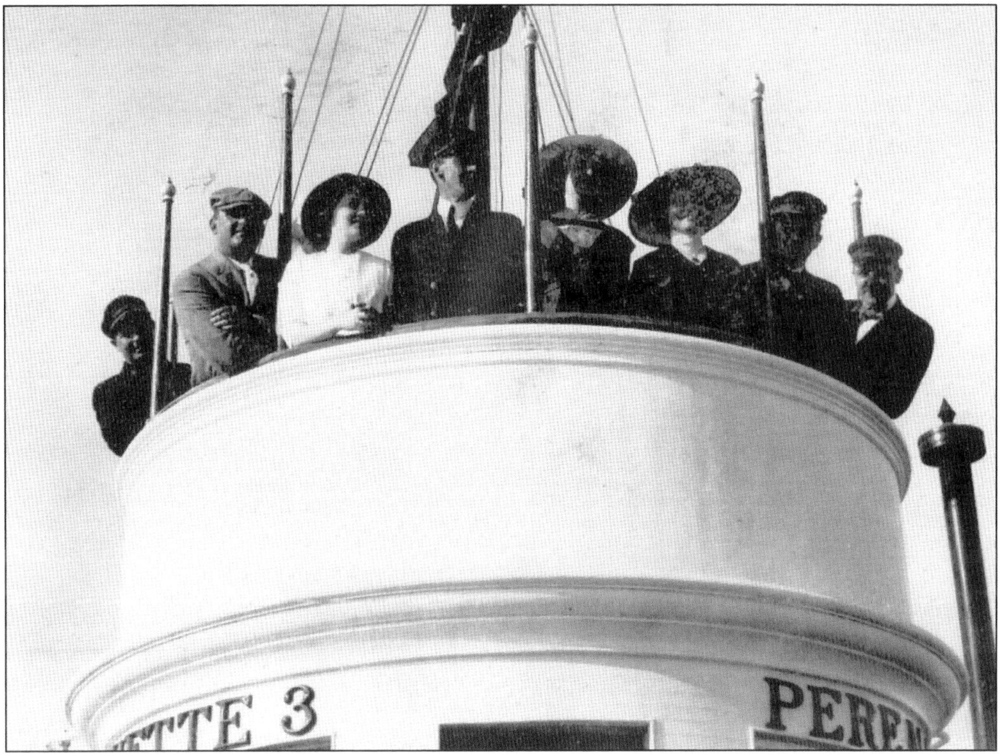

Captain Hoxie and friends look out from the *PM 3*. This was the only vacation the captain ever took when his ship was in operation, and afterwards, the ships under his command never left port without him. Hoxie is quoted as saying "I never lost a life or a ship." (Courtesy of Steve Elve.)

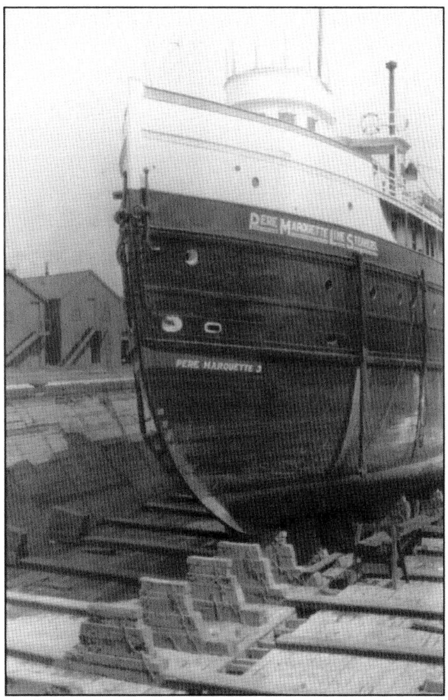

The *Pere Marquette 3* is in drydock for inspection and repair in 1915. The loss of the ship and cargo reportedly almost put Gus Kitzinger, owner of the Pere Marquette Line, out of business. The *Pere Marquette 3* was raised and the machinery salvaged, but this was the end of the hoodoo ship of the Pere Marquette Line. (Author's collection.)

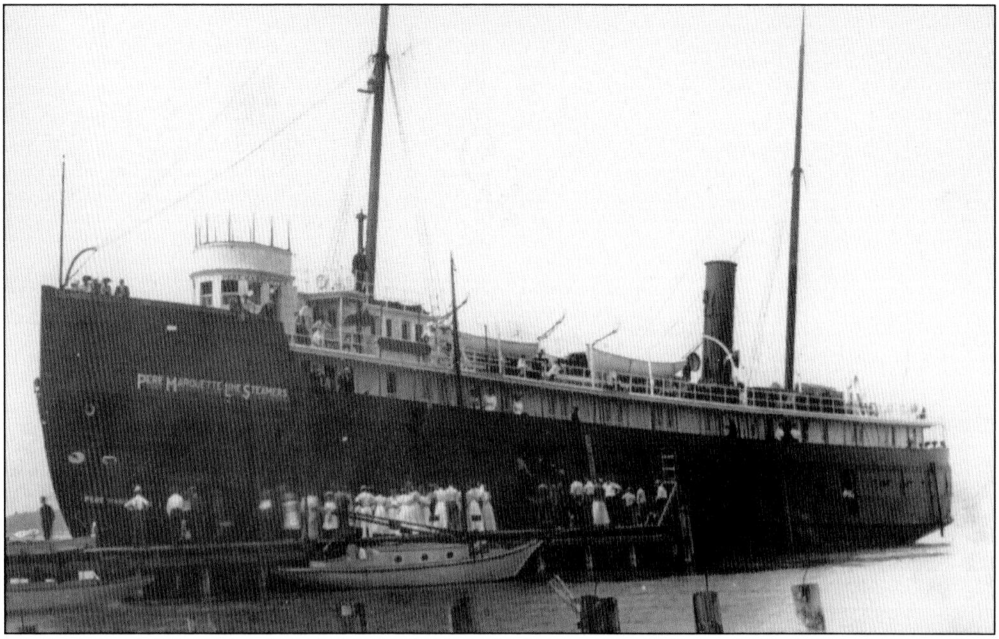

The *Pere Marquette 3* is taking on a load of passengers, most likely for a Sunday excursion along the lakeshore. Note the number of women in their white "Sunday best" dresses. Excursions for the day were popular in the early 1900s as a social event and often included stops for shopping or picnics at popular destinations. (Courtesy of Steve Elve.)

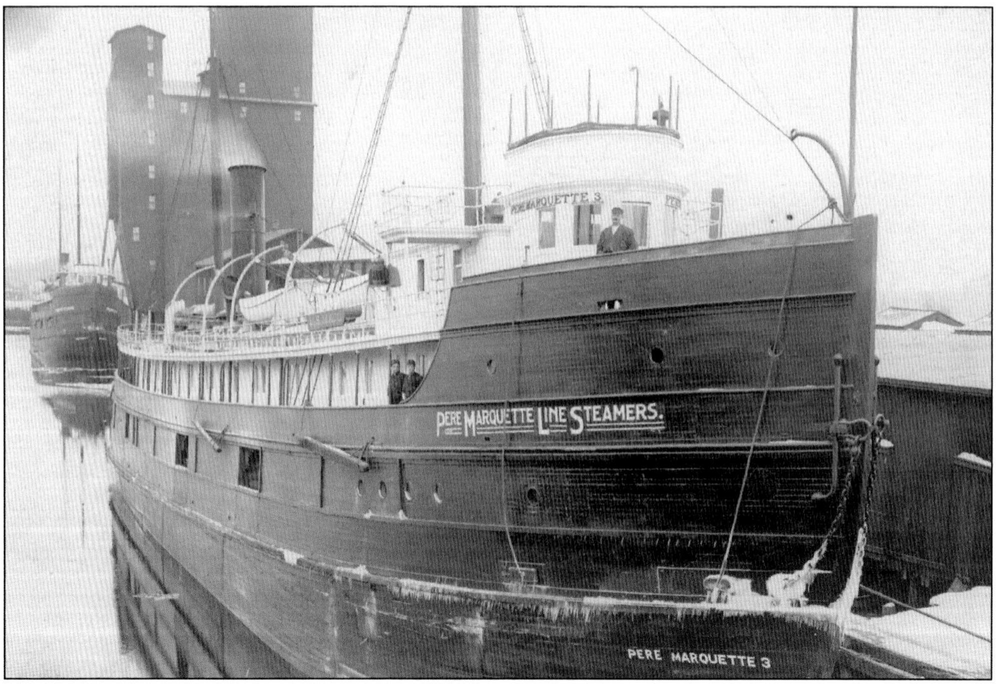

A great close-up view shows the *Pere Marquette 3* as it is docked in front of the freight shed at Ludington. Several unidentified crewmen are checking out the photographer as he captures this view while the boat is taking on freight loaded by the dock wallopers. (Courtesy of Steve Elve.)

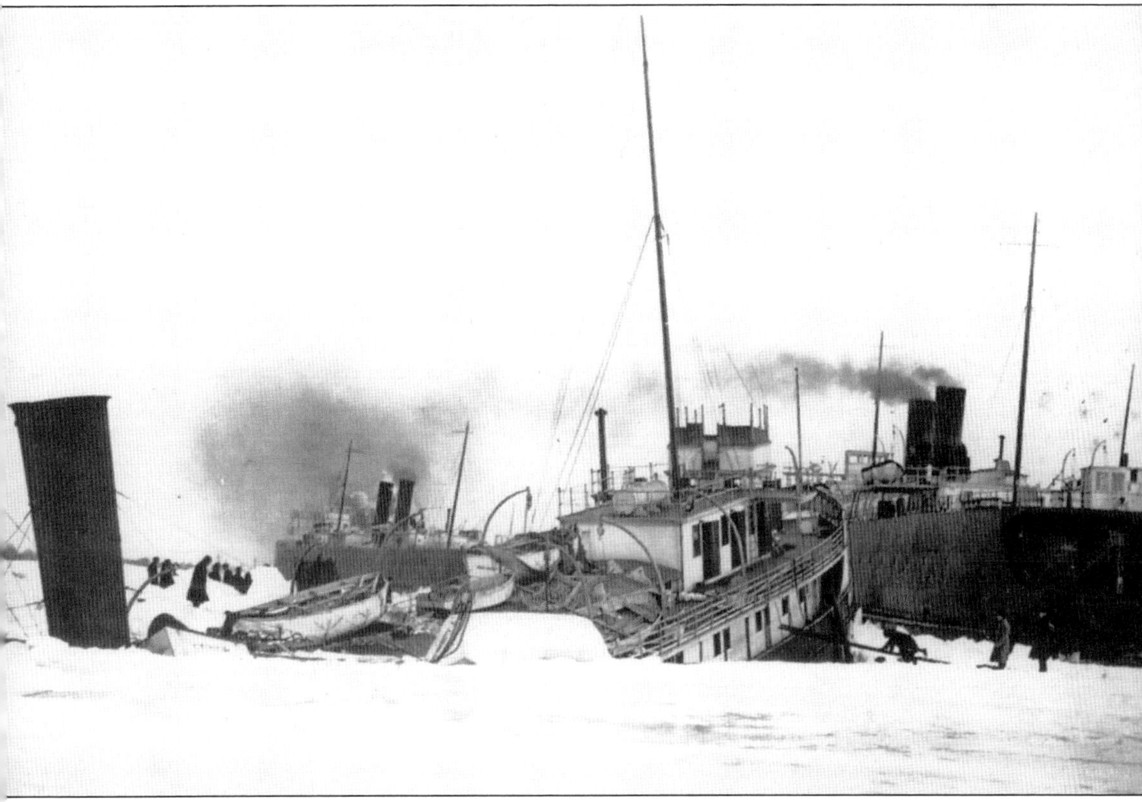

This postcard photograph shows the sinking, and on the back, Hoxie wrote, "Steamer *Pere Marquette 3* crushed in the ice and sank off Ludington Harbor on the night of March 7th 1920 at 10:30 pm and stayed in this position, her bow held up by ice until 10 am Tuesday March 9th 1920 when it sank leaving the top of the pilot house smoke stack and spurs above the water and which was carried away two days later by the moving ice. The car ferry to the right [*PM 18*] was only one hundred feet away and is the one that the crew went aboard that night. The *PM 3* had run across Lake Michigan for 32 years winter and summer." In the postcard, people are out on the ice and milling about the ship as it is being crushed and sinking. The *PM 3* was raised by the tug *Favorite* in July 1920 and towed to Manitowoc, Wisconsin. The ship was declared a total loss. (Author's collection.)

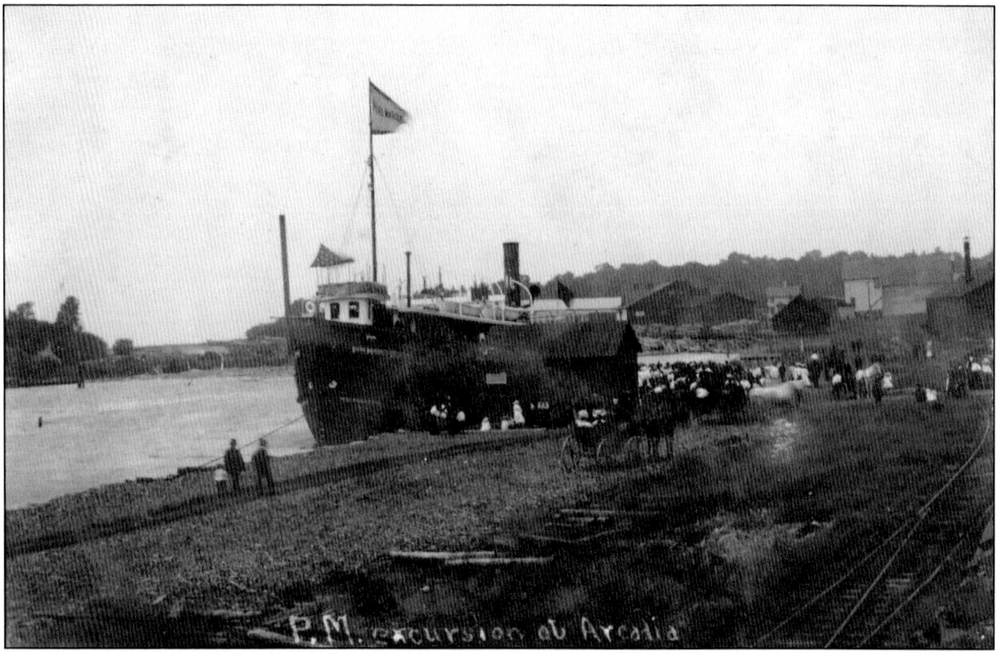

The *Pere Marquette 4* is shown at the docks in Arcadia taking on a group for a Sunday excursion along the lakeshore about 1910. The boat was built in 1888 by the Detroit Dry Dock Company to handle the increasing break-bulk business that was being handled by the railroad. (Author's collection.)

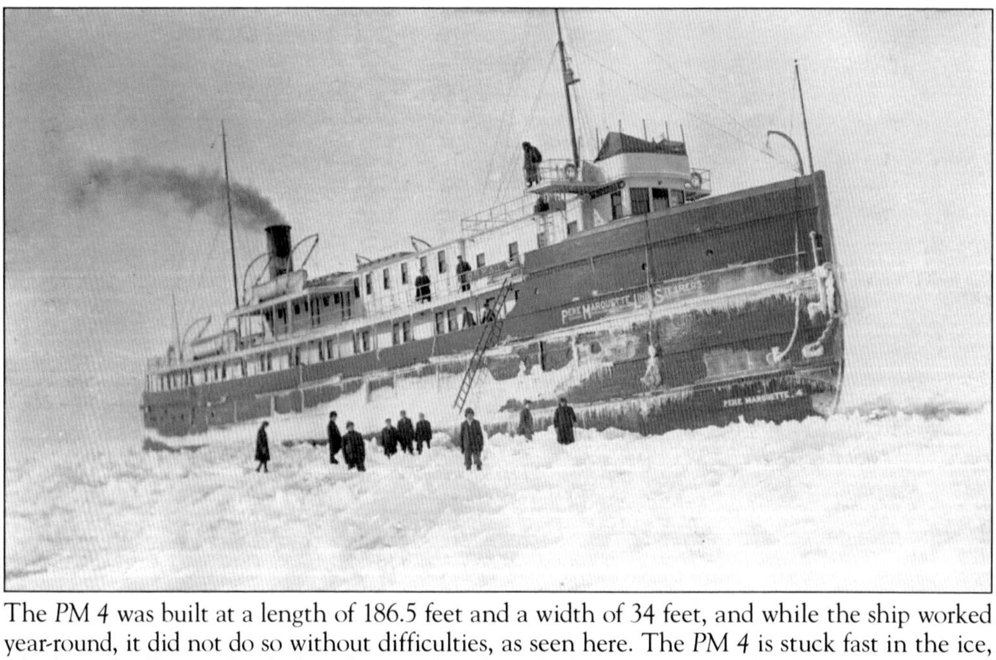

The *PM 4* was built at a length of 186.5 feet and a width of 34 feet, and while the ship worked year-round, it did not do so without difficulties, as seen here. The *PM 4* is stuck fast in the ice, which is of sufficient depth that the crew has disembarked onto the ice for the photographer to set up and take a photograph. (Courtesy of James F. Fay.)

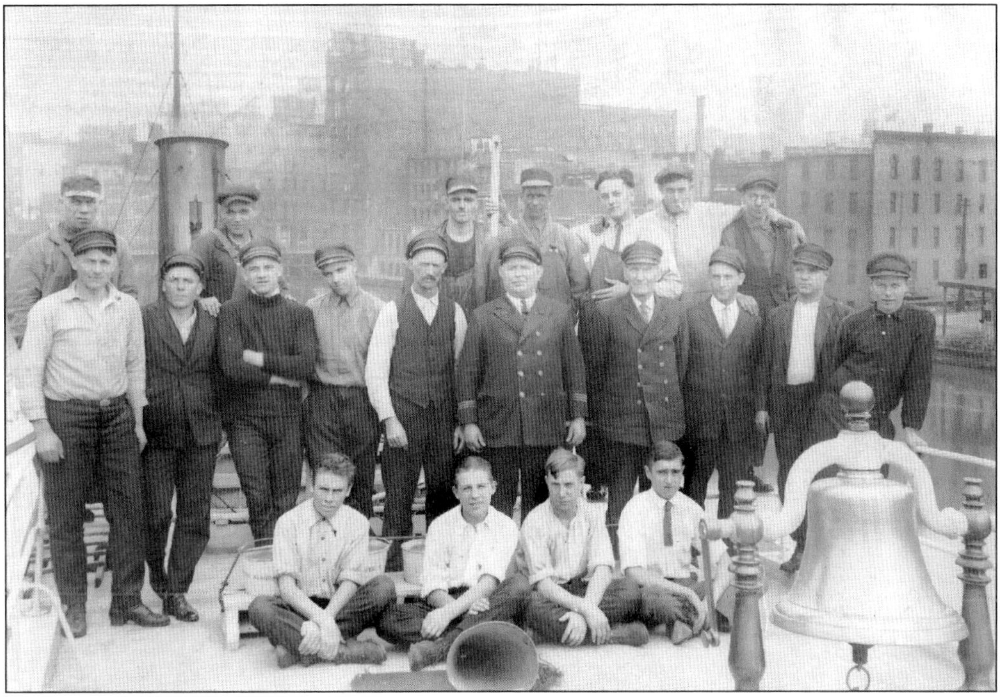

The captain and crew pose for a rare glimpse into the past in this *c.* 1905 photograph taken in Chicago. The *PM 4* was purchased by the Columbia Yacht Club and used as a floating clubhouse in 1924 after a collision with *Pere Marquette 17*, thus ending the boat's commercial career. (Courtesy of Steve Elve.)

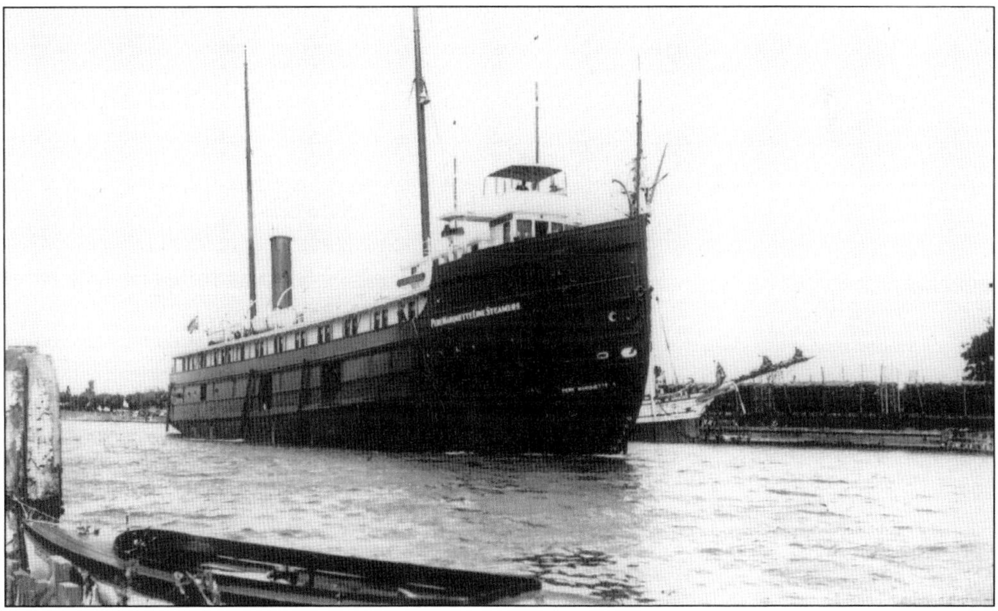

The *PM 4* provided a unique clubhouse for the yacht club, which held an annual regatta. The club repaired the damage to the sliced bow on the boat and used it for 12 years before dry rot became excessive, and the club opted to purchase the steamer *Florida* as a replacement. (Courtesy of Steve Elve.)

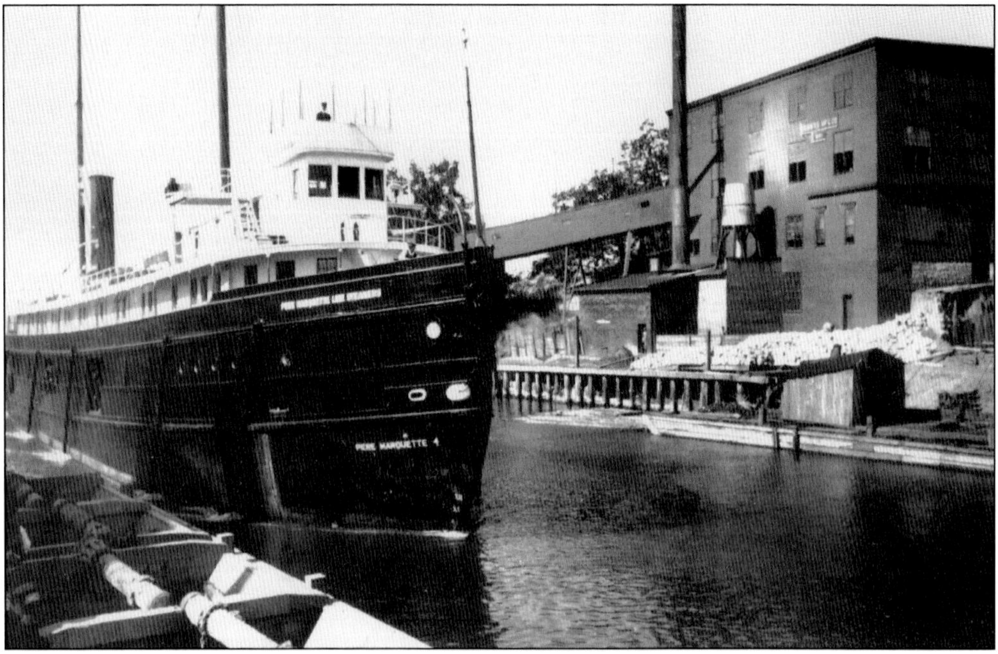

The *PM 4* is coming down the channel at Manistee to unload and take on passengers at the Pere Marquette Line's dock. Manistee was the home of Gus Kitzinger, the owner of the PM line, and the boats were frequent visitors as they completed their daily runs. (Courtesy of Steve Elve.)

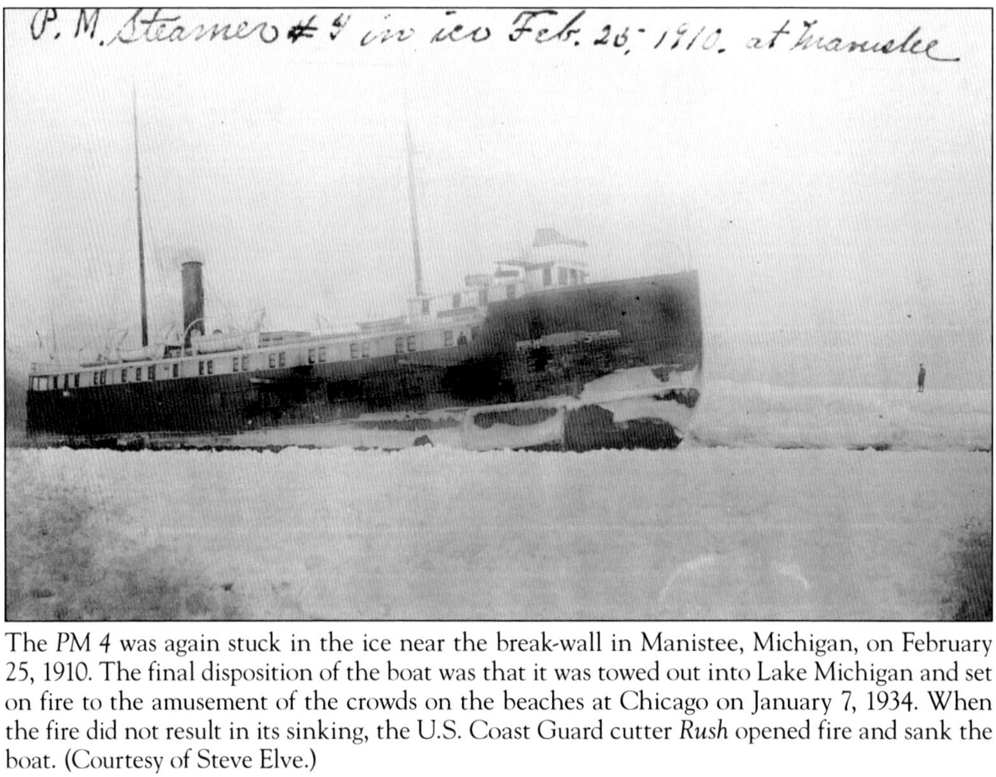

The *PM 4* was again stuck in the ice near the break-wall in Manistee, Michigan, on February 25, 1910. The final disposition of the boat was that it was towed out into Lake Michigan and set on fire to the amusement of the crowds on the beaches at Chicago on January 7, 1934. When the fire did not result in its sinking, the U.S. Coast Guard cutter *Rush* opened fire and sank the boat. (Courtesy of Steve Elve.)

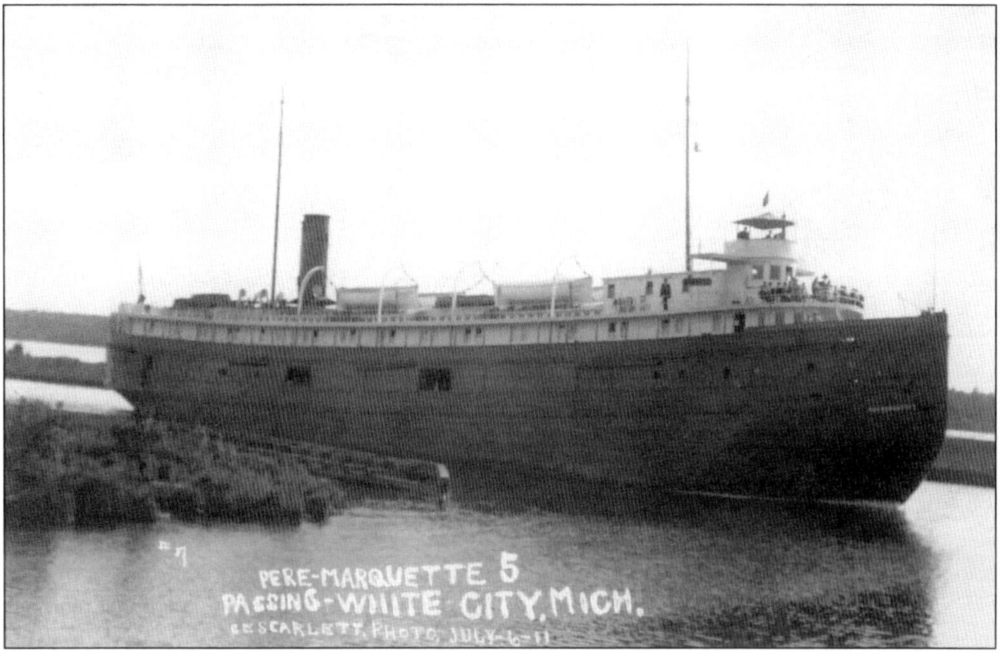

The *Flint and Pere Marquette No. 5* was built by the F. W. Wheeler Company in West Bay City, Michigan, in 1890. At 226 feet in length, the boat was 20 percent larger then its predecessor. As the *Pere Marquette 5*, it is shown here passing White City, Michigan, in 1911. (Courtesy of Steve Elve.)

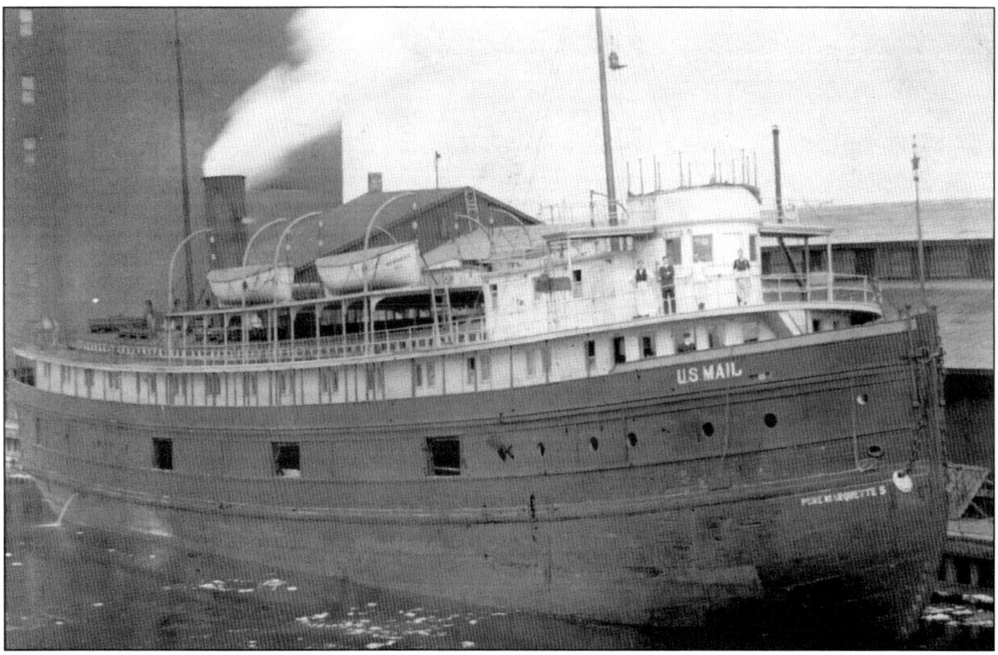

Around 1900, boats were being built increasingly larger, but there was only so much that could be done with a wooden hull. Boats of that construction were on the verge of becoming obsolete, as steel-hulled boats would soon be taking over the work on the Great Lakes. (Courtesy of Steve Elve.)

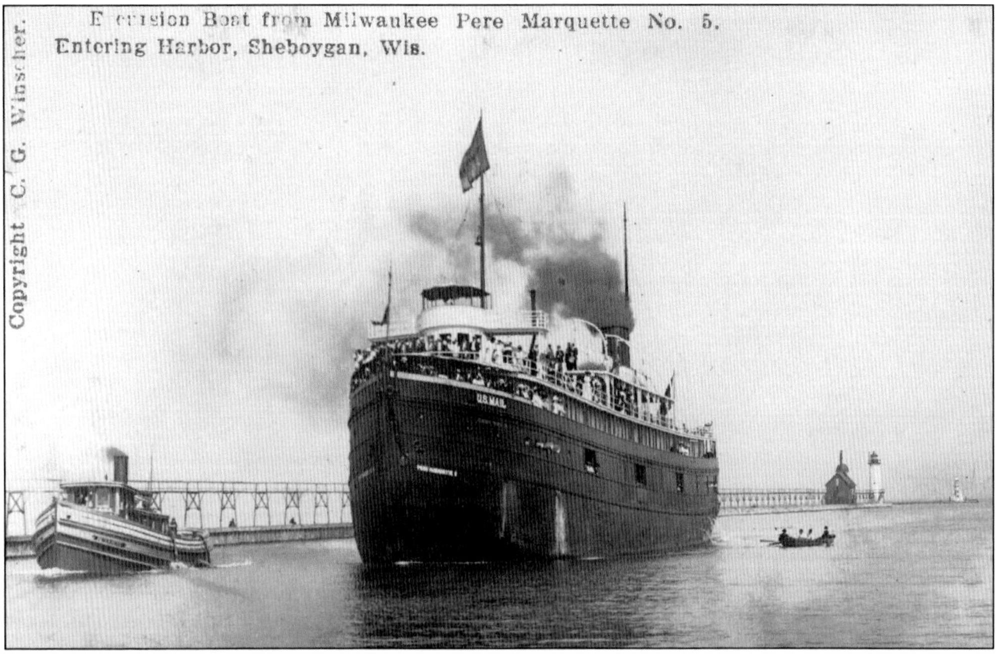

This early postcard view of the *Pere Marquette 5* shows a busy Sheboygan Channel. The tugboat *Peter Reiss* is racing along the side of the *PM 5*, and some pleasure boaters to the right are getting dangerously close to the boat as they welcome the passengers aboard ship. (Courtesy of Steve Elve.)

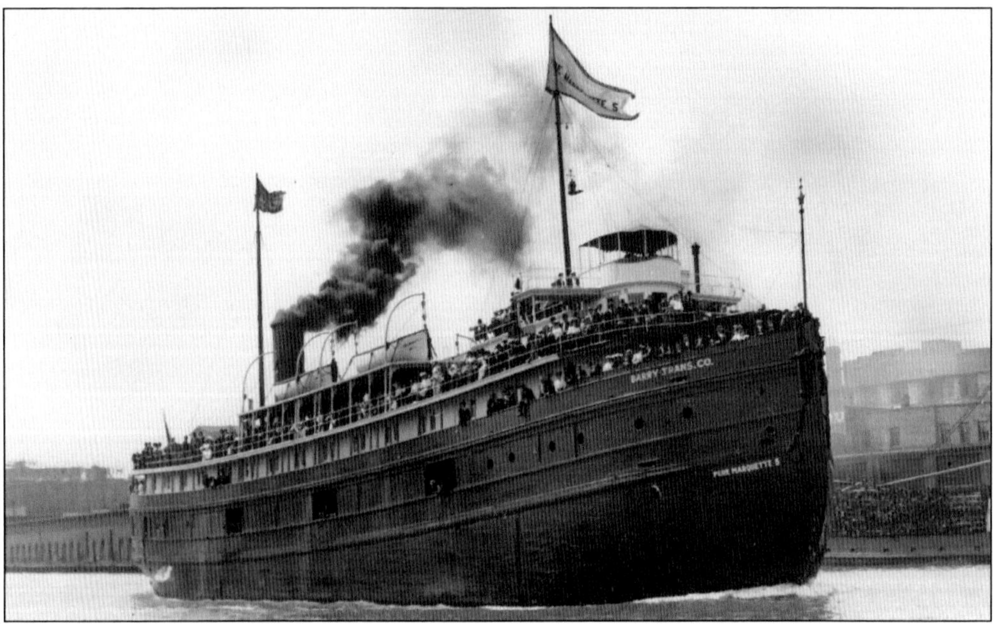

The *PM 5* was built without staterooms but was remodeled in 1901. The boat is shown here with an excursion group in 1907 after being purchased by the Barry Transportation Company. The *PM 5* did come back to Ludington in 1909, when it was purchased by the Pere Marquette Line. The boat was sold in 1916, sent to the Atlantic seaboard, and renamed the *Anzac*. On February 23, 1917, the ship was lost while carrying a load of pulpwood. (Courtesy of Steve Elve.)

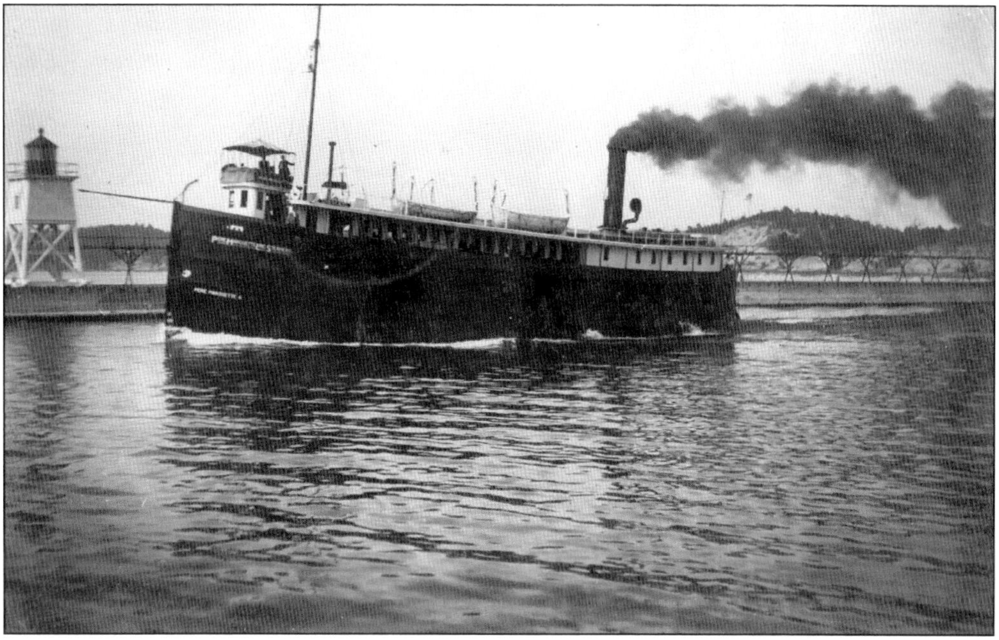

The *Mark B. Covell* was built in 1888 by Burger and Burger in Manitowoc, Wisconsin, as a steam barge. Similar in design to the *Marshall F. Butters*, the *Covell* moved lumber and other freight for its owners until 1905, when it was purchased by Gus Kitzinger. (Courtesy of Steve Elve.)

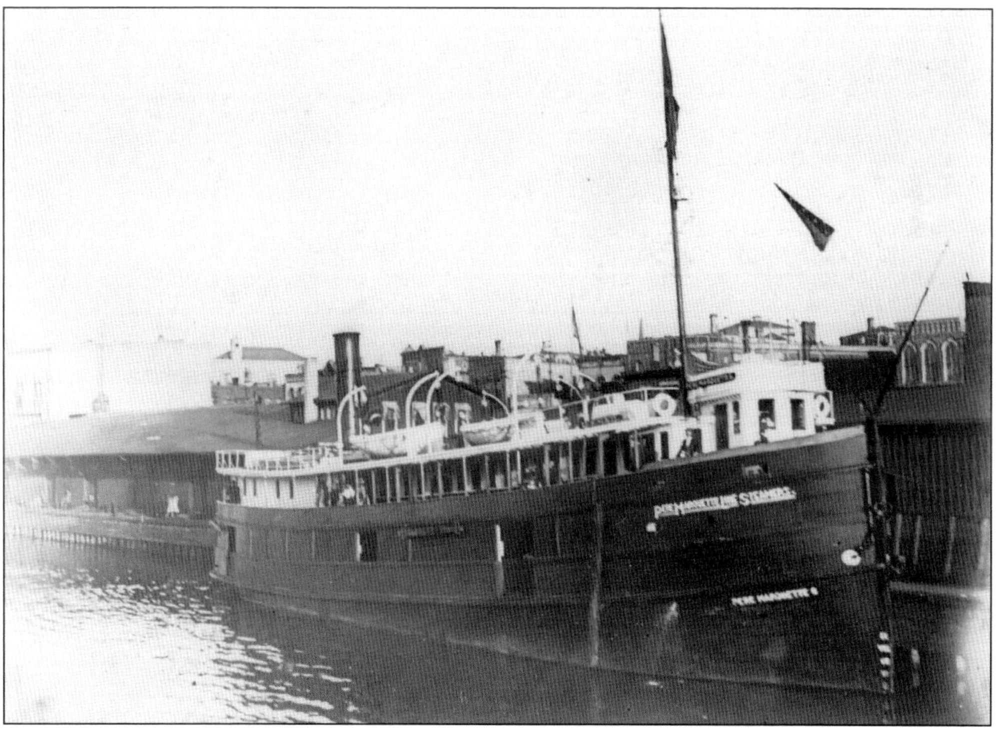

The *PM 6* is docked in the Manistee River about 1910. The break-bulk freighters of the Pere Marquette Line would travel up and down the lakeshore stopping at any port along the way to pick up freight and passengers. (Courtesy of Steve Elve.)

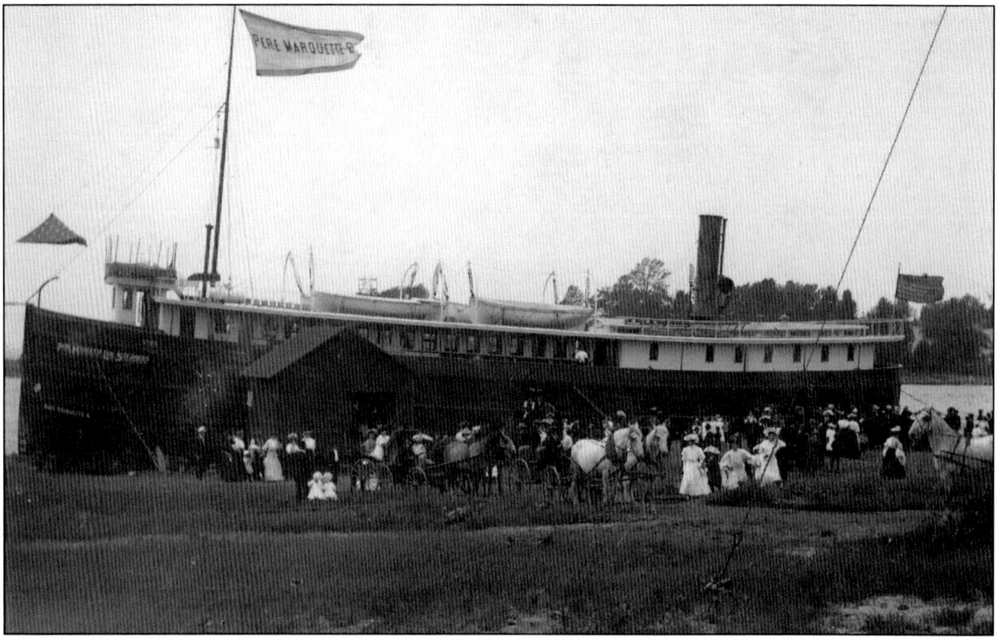

The *PM* 6 is taking on passengers for an excursion at Frankfort, Michigan, about 1910. After Kitzinger purchased the *Mark B. Covell*, he had passenger accommodations added and refitted the boat to be able to handle freight. (Courtesy of Steve Elve.)

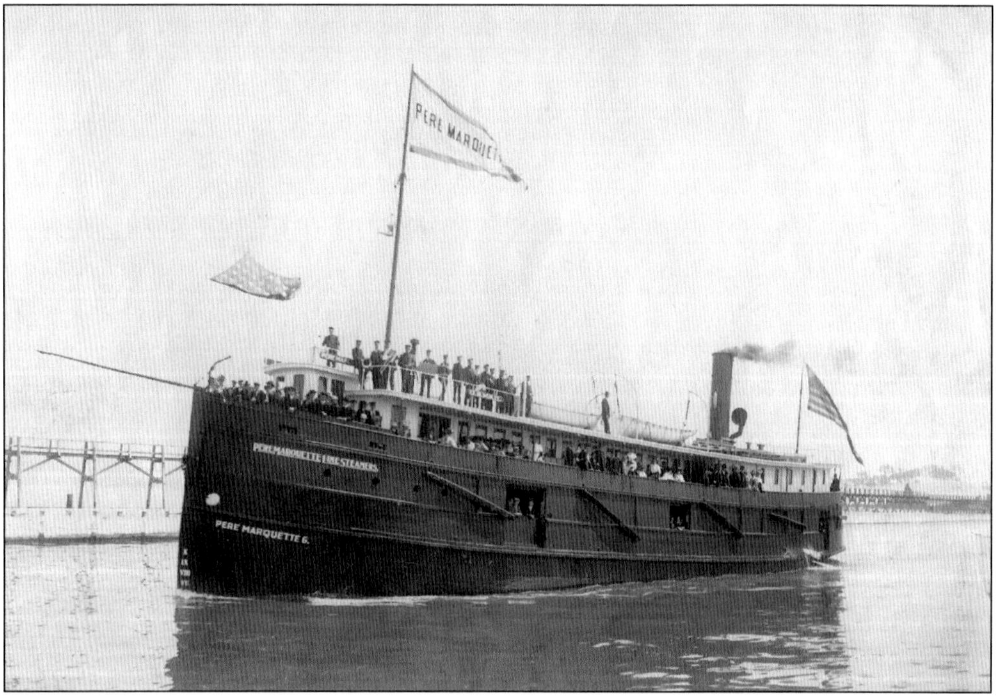

The *PM* 6 is heading out from the port of Manistee with a ship full of residents for a day trip on the big Lake Michigan. The boat was eventually sold and cut back down to the steam barge it was originally constructed as. In 1936, the boat was burned on the lake by the City of Manitowoc as part of their centennial celebration. (Courtesy of Steve Elve.)

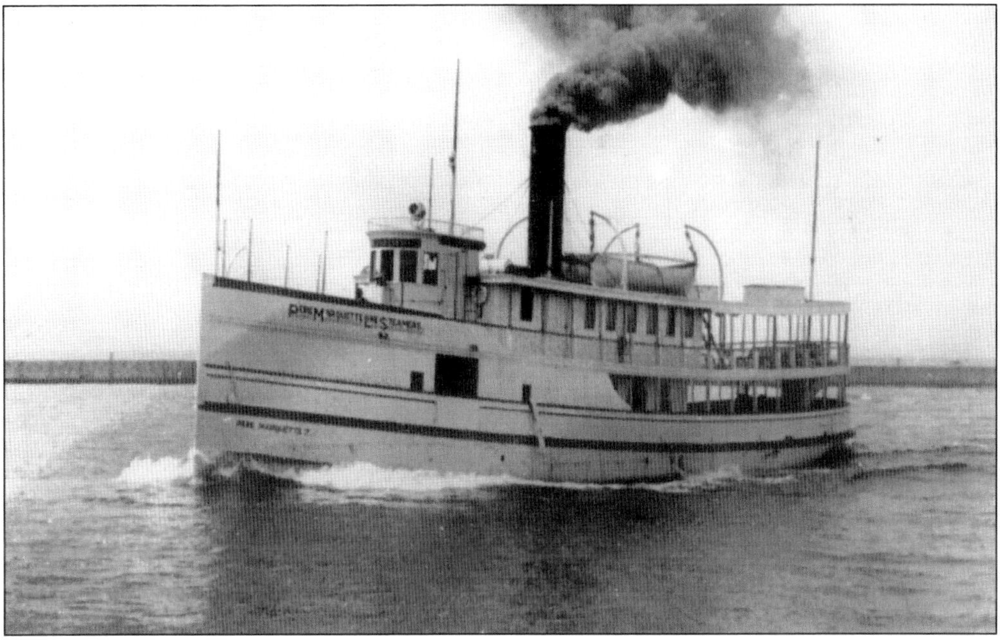

The *Chequamegon*, with a 430-person capacity, was originally built in 1903 by the Manitowoc Dry Dock Company for Louis Cartier at a cost of $25,000. The ship was built with a triple expansion engine that could achieve 16 miles per hour and had electric lights. Originally designed for passenger service and excursions between ports, it was operated by the Pabst Brewing Company from 1905 to 1908. (Author's collection.)

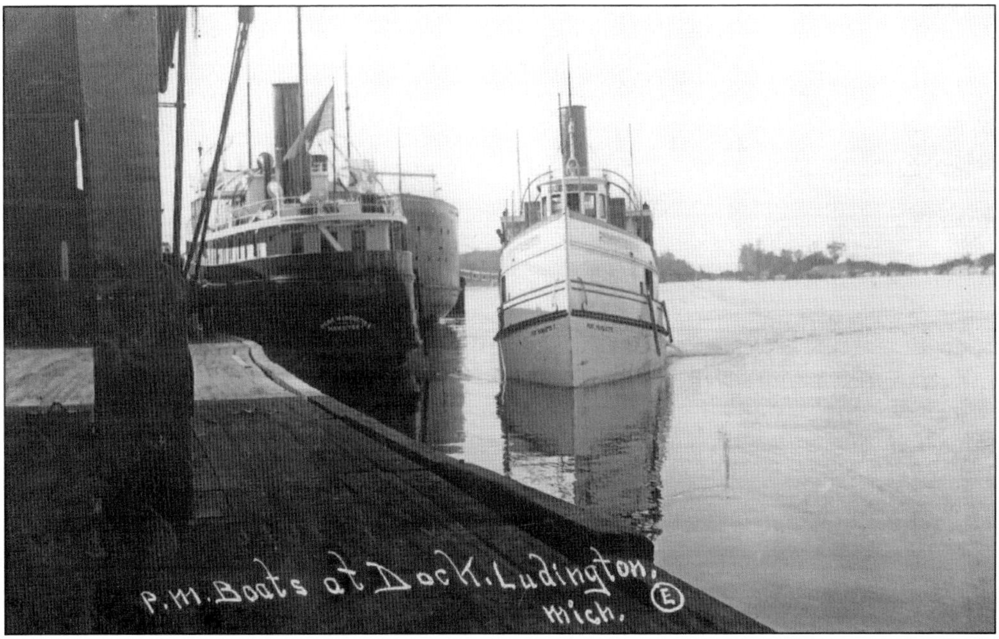

The captain of the *Chequamegon* was so tall that Lunde Boat Works had to renovate the cabin and build a lifeboat to accommodate his size. Louis Cartier sold the boat in 1907 to a buyer in Traverse City. The boat was used to make trips from Traverse City to Bassett's Island, where a dance pavilion was built. (Courtesy of James F. Fay.)

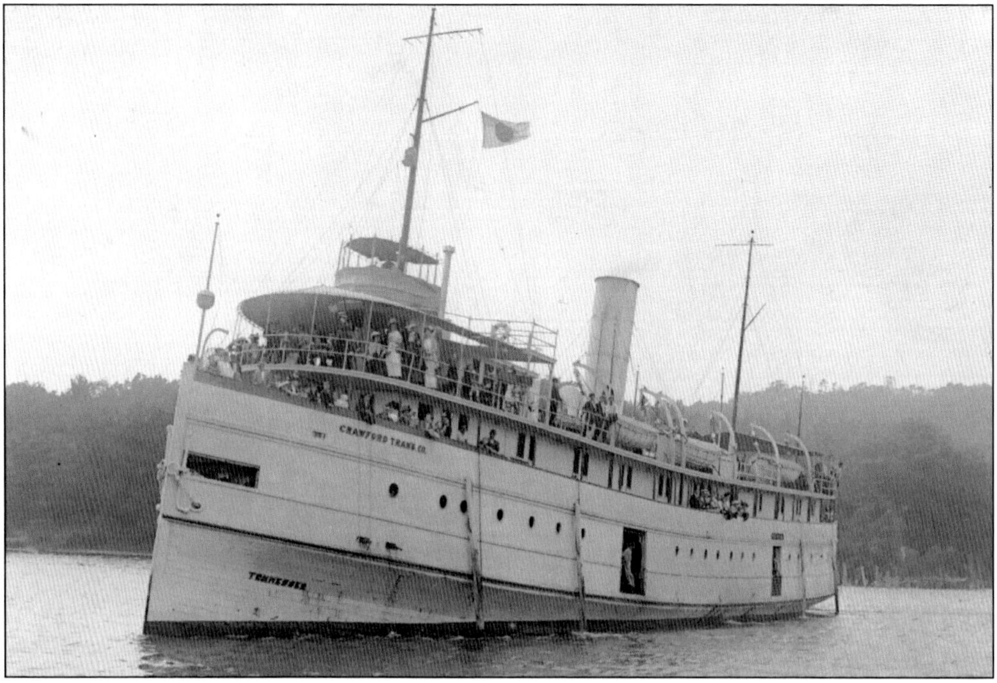

The *Chequamegon* was purchased by Gus Kitzinger for the Pere Marquette Line in 1911, operated on local excursions, and provided passenger service until 1918, when the *Pere Marquette 7* was sold to the Pringle Line. It was rebuilt as the tugboat *Robert C. Pringle*. On June 19, 1922, while towing the *Venezuela* to Sandusky, Ohio, the boat foundered and sank off Sheboygan, Wisconsin. The wreck was discovered in 2008 by divers. (Courtesy of Steve Elve.)

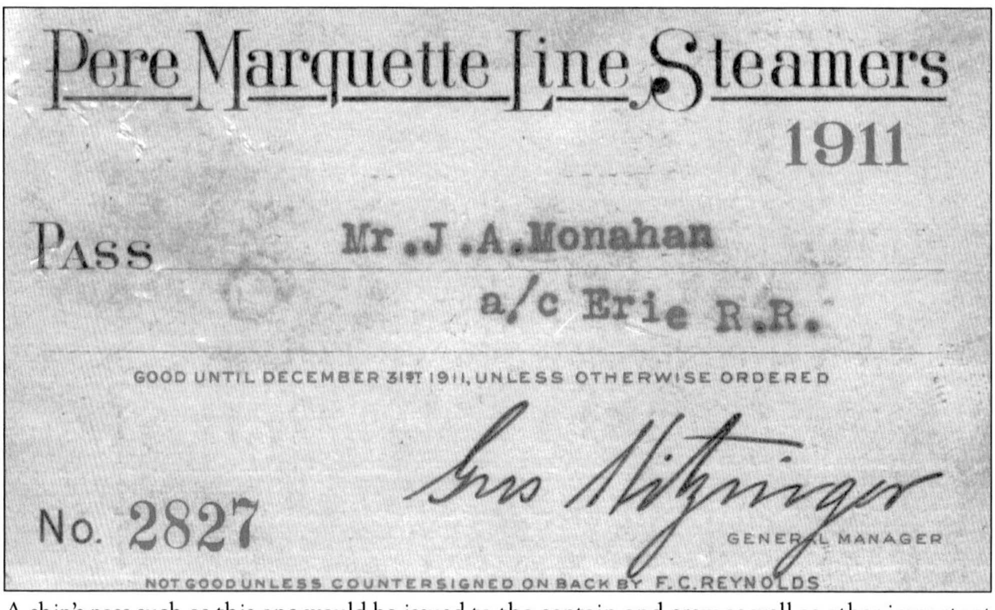

A ship's pass such as this one would be issued to the captain and crew as well as other important guests and family members to provide free passage on ships of the line. In the days before radio and television, it was not uncommon for family members to take trips and spend the day on the lake as though they were on a Sunday excursion. (Courtesy of Steve Elve.)

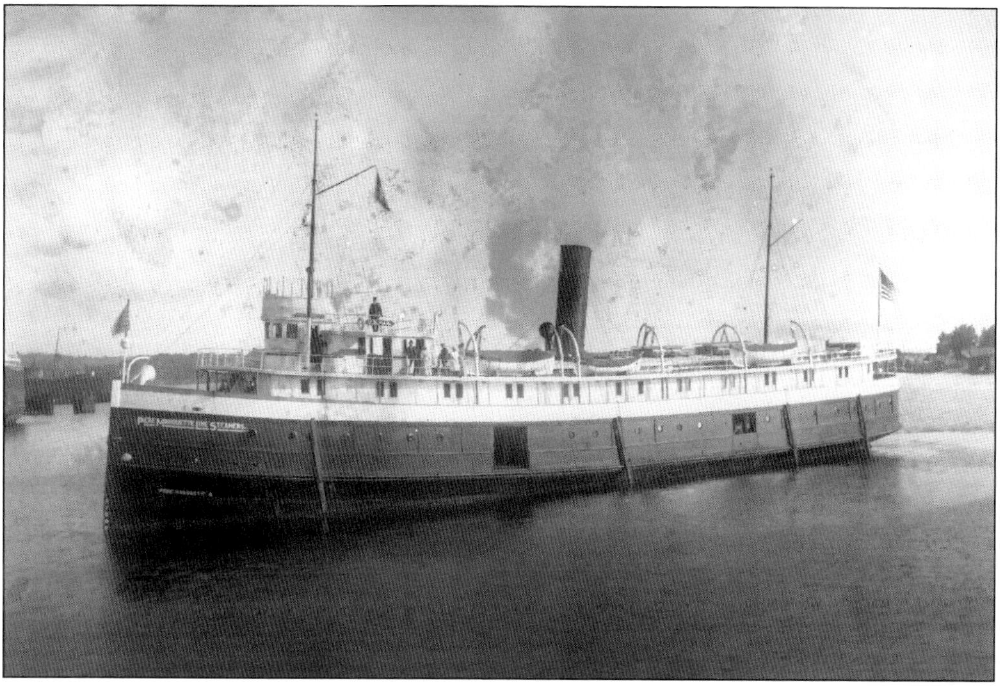

The *Tennessee* was originally built as the *H. W. Williams* in 1888 by John Martel for the H. W. Williams Line. The boat was 140 feet in length and 28 feet wide. In 1902, after the death of H. W. Williams, the Dunkley Transportation Company bought the three existing steamers of the line for $125,000. (Courtesy of Steve Elve.)

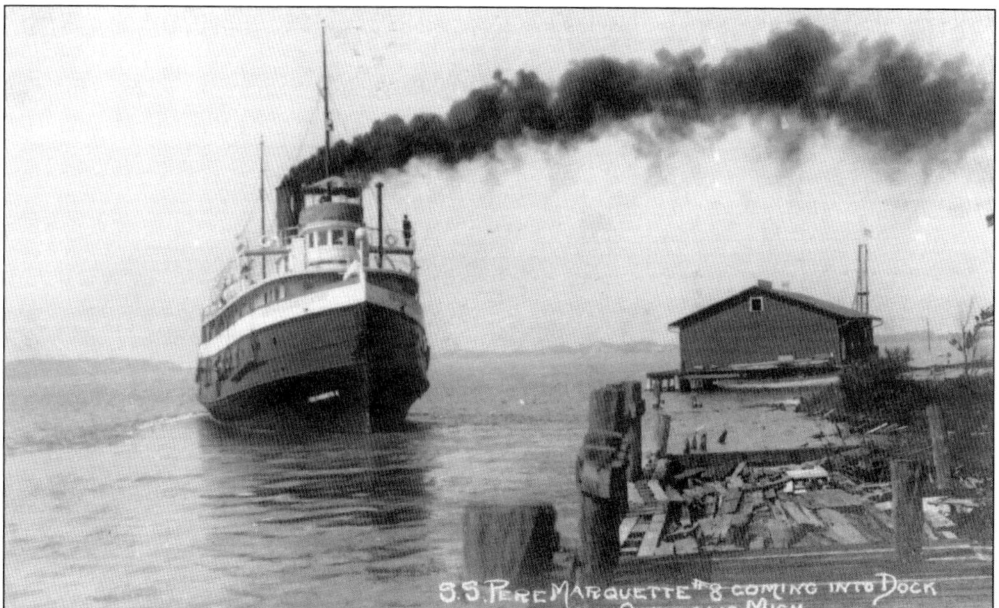

In 1910, the Dunkley-Williams Line sold the H. W. Williams to the Crawford Line, which operated the steamer until 1913, when it was in turn sold to the Pere Marquette Line and renamed the *Pere Marquette* 8. The boat is shown in this c. 1915 view coming into the dock at Onekama. (Courtesy of Steve Elve.)

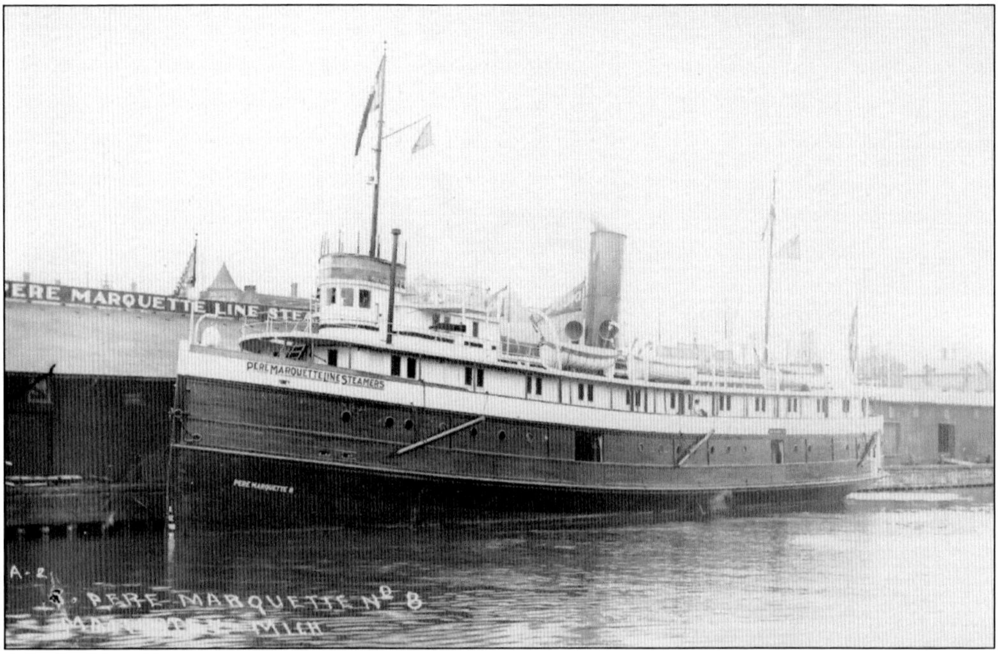

The *PM 8* is tied up to the freight docks at Manistee. The Pere Marquette Line was organized in 1903 with Gus Kitzinger as general manager. Kitzinger eventually was named president, and he remained in control until his death in 1929. (Courtesy of Steve Elve.)

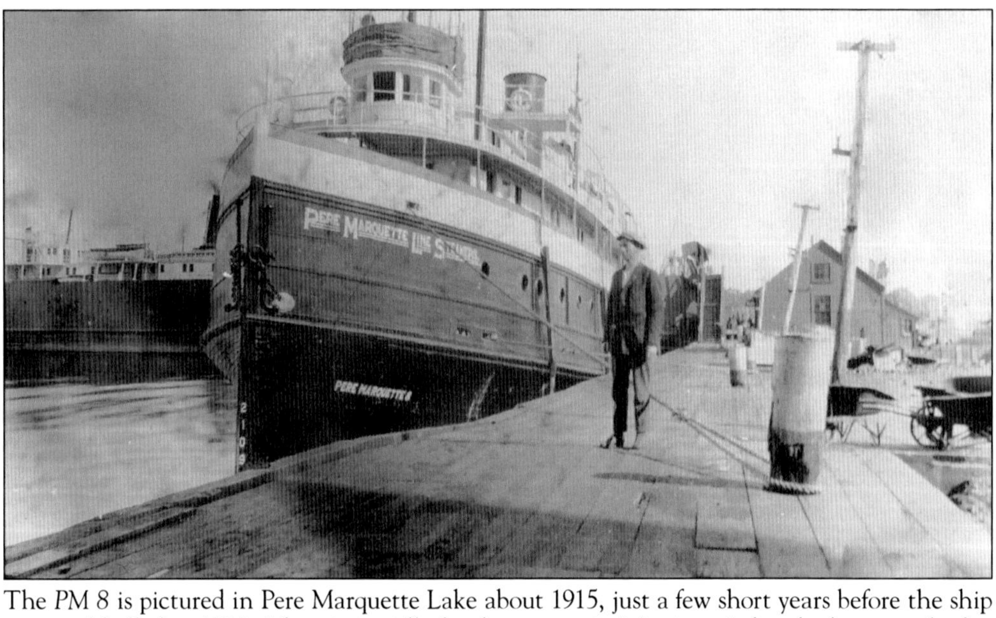

The *PM 8* is pictured in Pere Marquette Lake about 1915, just a few short years before the ship was mothballed in 1924. After sitting idle for three years in Manistee Lake, the boat caught fire and was burned in a total loss in October 1927. (Courtesy of Steve Elve.)

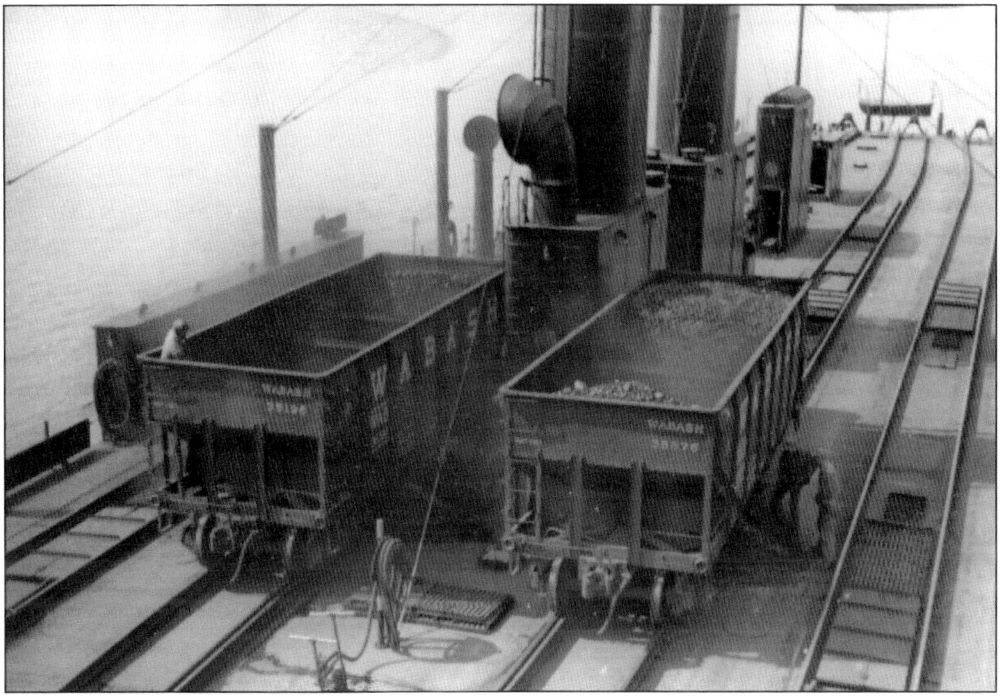

The railroad acquired its first river ferry, the *International*, in a merger in 1903, and while the river ferries did not operate out of Ludington, they were still part of the fleet and are mentioned here for that reason. The *Pere Marquette No. 10* was the last, having been built by the Manitowoc Shipbuilding Company and launched in 1945. (Author's collection.)

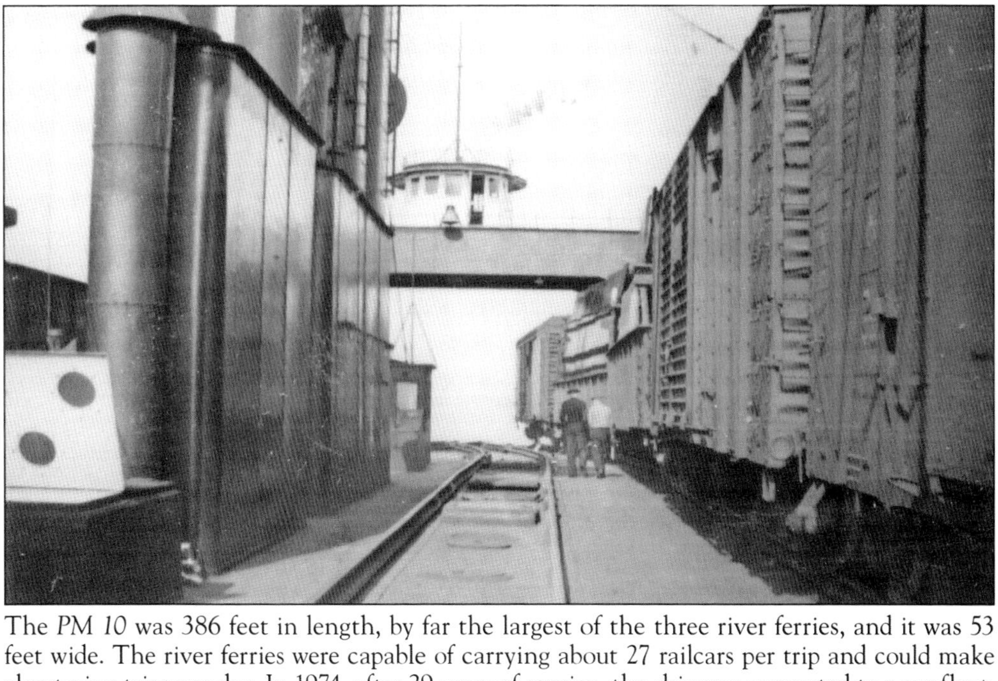

The *PM 10* was 386 feet in length, by far the largest of the three river ferries, and it was 53 feet wide. The river ferries were capable of carrying about 27 railcars per trip and could make about nine trips per day. In 1974, after 29 years of service, the ship was converted to a car float. (Author's collection.)

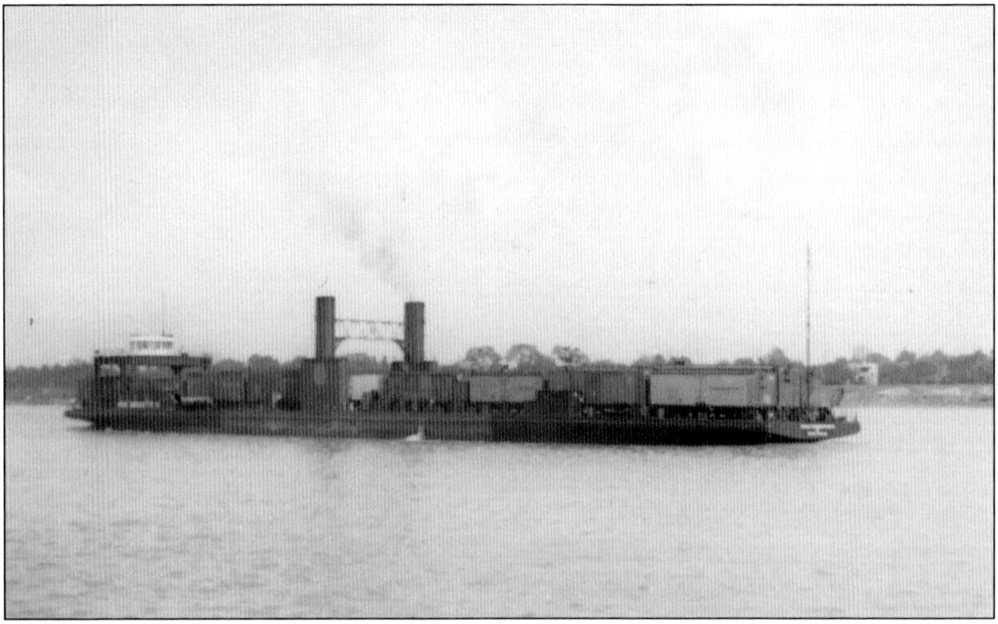

The *Pere Marquette 12* was also built by the Manitowoc Shipbuilding Company and launched in 1927. The river ferries had three tracks and could make the crossing in a matter of minutes. They could operate 24 hours a day with continuous shifts and did not carry passengers, only railway cars. (Author's collection.)

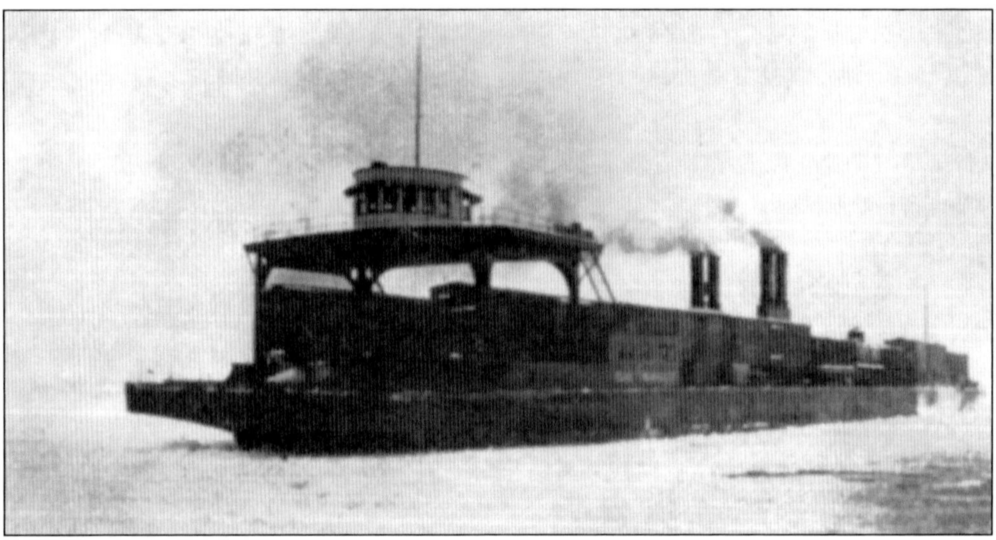

The *Pere Marquette 14* was built by the Detroit Ship Building Company in Detroit, Michigan, in 1904. The *PM 14* was of steel construction, 327 feet in length, and 52 feet wide. This boat was built to cross the Detroit River and provided service under the Pere Marquette Railway and then the Chesapeake and Ohio until 1957, when it was scrapped. (Author's collection.)

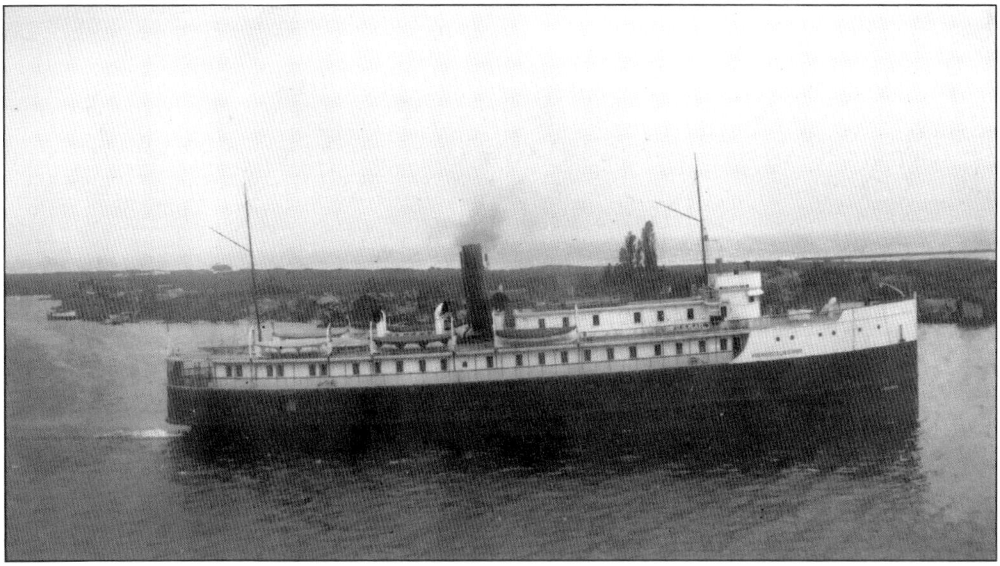

The *Virginia* is shown here steaming out of Pere Marquette Lake around 1930. It was built in 1902 by the William R. Trigg Company and launched as the *Berkeley*, a part of the old Dominion Line. Renamed in 1923, the *Virginia* became a part of the Pere Marquette Line of steamers until 1935, when the company merged into Muskegon Dock and Fuel Company. (Photograph by Erhardt Peters, author's collection.)

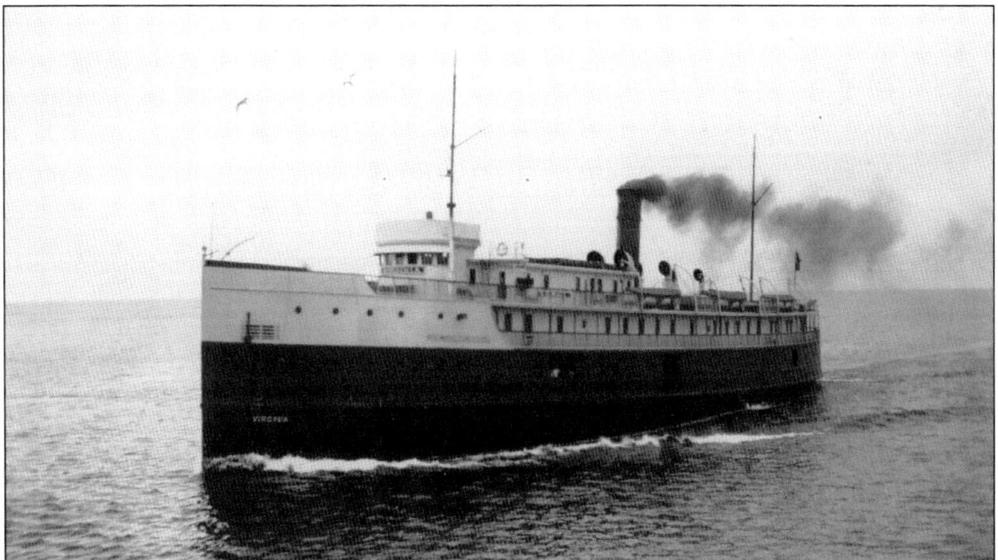

The *Virginia*, at 201 feet in length and 39 feet wide, provided service on the Great Lakes until 1952. The U.S. government owned the *Virginia* from 1942 to 1952, and it was last known to have been sold to shipping interests in China. Its final disposition is unknown. (Photograph by Erhardt Peters, author's collection.)

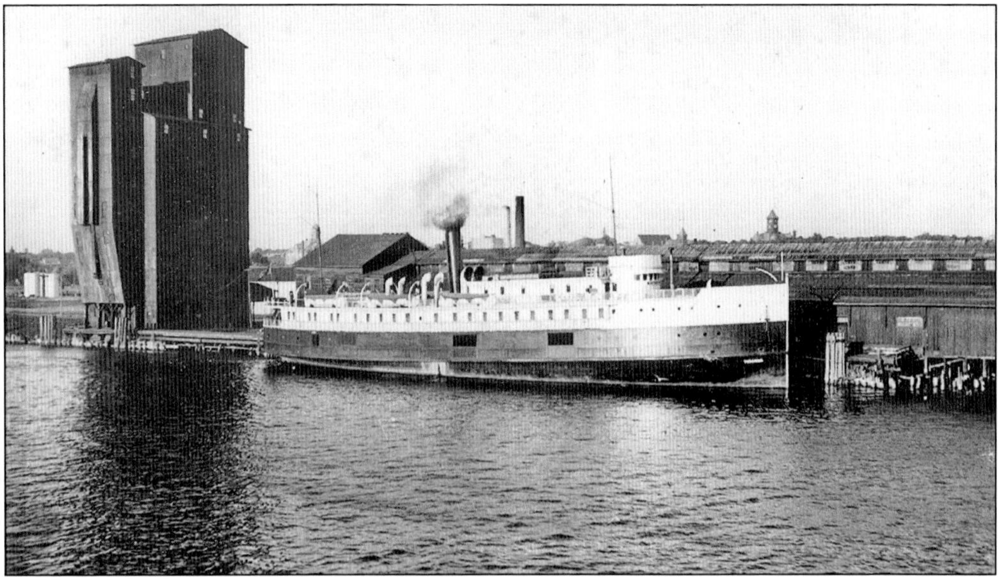

In March 1932, a blizzard caught the steamer *Virginia* under the command of Capt. Andrew Coleman in its grips and refused to let go. The steamer was able to back off to a position a half-mile off shore and was being tossed helplessly about in 35-mile-per-hour gale-force winds and waves of 15 feet. (Photograph by Erhardt Peters, author's collection.)

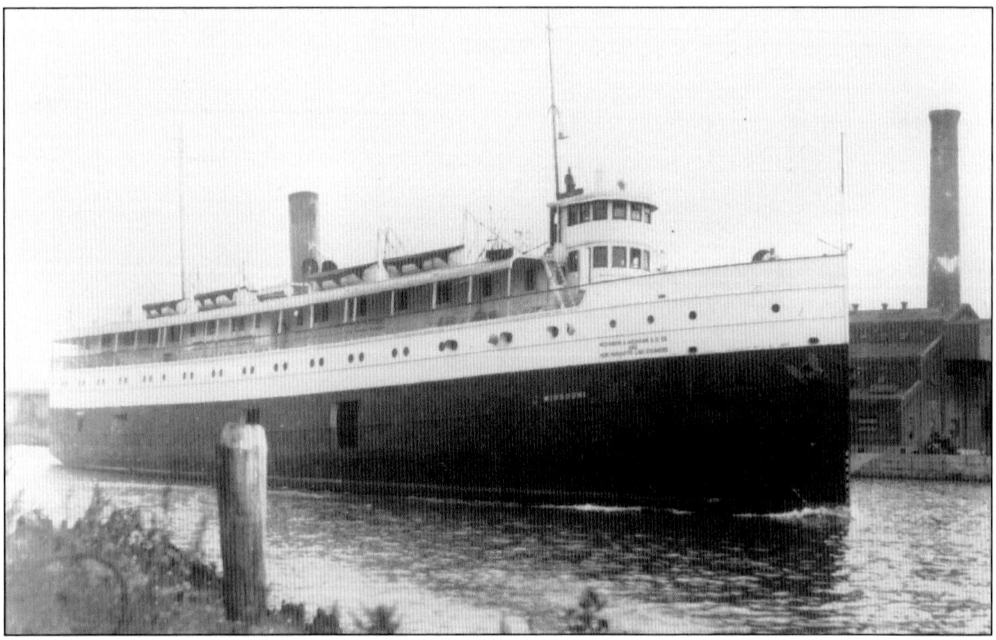

The *Missouri* was built in 1904 for the Northern Michigan Transportation Company at the Chicago Shipbuilding yards in Chicago. Included in the list of owners were Warren Cartier, a Ludington businessman, and the Sand Products Corporation, which operated the remaining ships of the Pere Marquette Line, the *Nevada* and *Illinois*, after the 1935 merger with the Wisconsin Michigan Steamship Company. (Author's collection.)

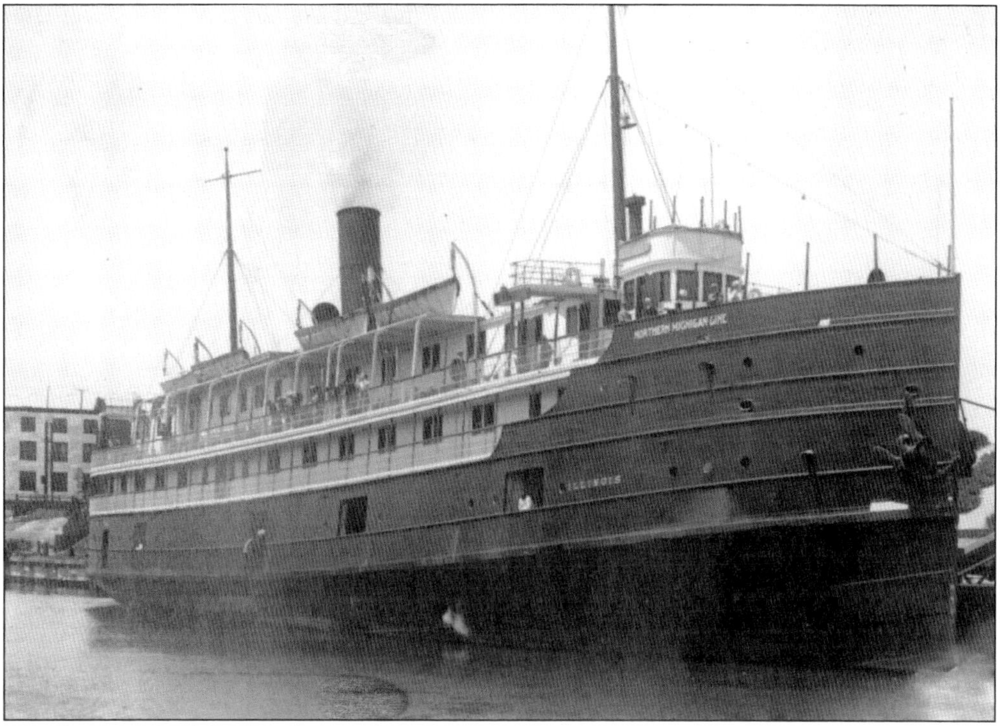

The *Illinois* was built by the Chicago Shipbuilding Company in 1899 for the Northern Transportation Company. At 225 feet in length and 40 feet in width, this steel-hulled ship was an impressive sight as it cruised into ports along the Lake Michigan shoreline to bring mail, freight, and passengers. (Author's collection.)

The *Illinois* came under the ownership of the Goodrich Transit Company in 1922, and in 1933, it was under the ownership of the Wisconsin Michigan Steamship Company, which also became the parent organization of the Pere Marquette Line once it moved to Muskegon from Ludington. Hoxie continued to work for the restructured corporation as captain of the Illinois until the new *Milwaukee Clipper* was launched. (Author's collection.)

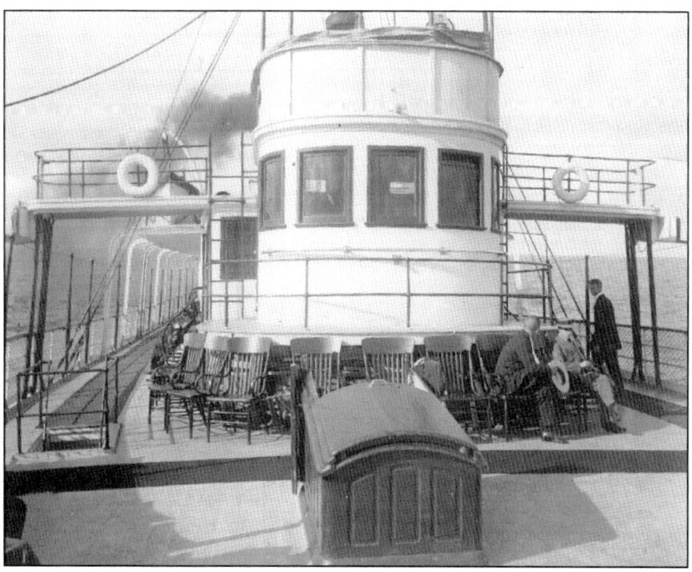

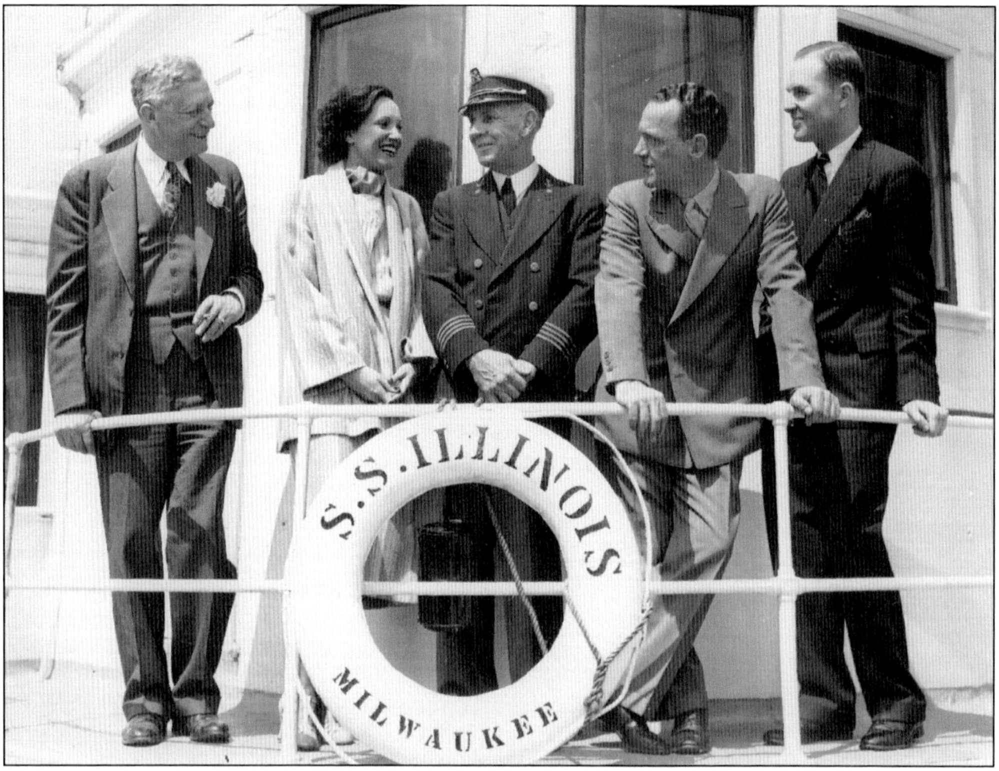

Captain Hoxie is entertaining guests aboard the steamer *Illinois*. He was called the "dean of the Great Lakes" due to his many years of service. The woman is rumored to be a movie star of the time and certainly has the captain's attention, as this is the only known photograph where he is smiling. (Author's collection.)

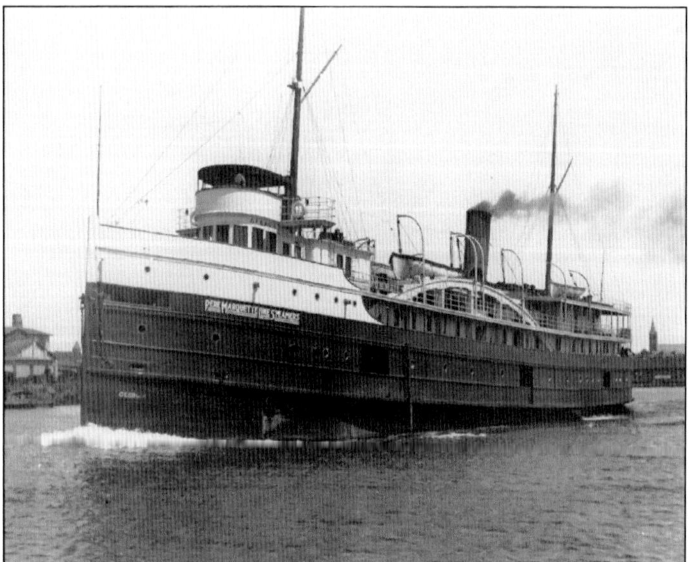

This boat was originally launched as the *City of Ludington* in 1880 and was built by the Goodrich Line to run freight for the Flint and Pere Marquette Railroad until 1883. The boat was rebuilt and renamed the *Georgia* in 1898 and eventually came under the ownership of the Pere Marquette Line in the 1920s. In 1933, the hull was purchased by Capt. John Roen, who sunk the boat for use as a break-wall. (Author's collection.)

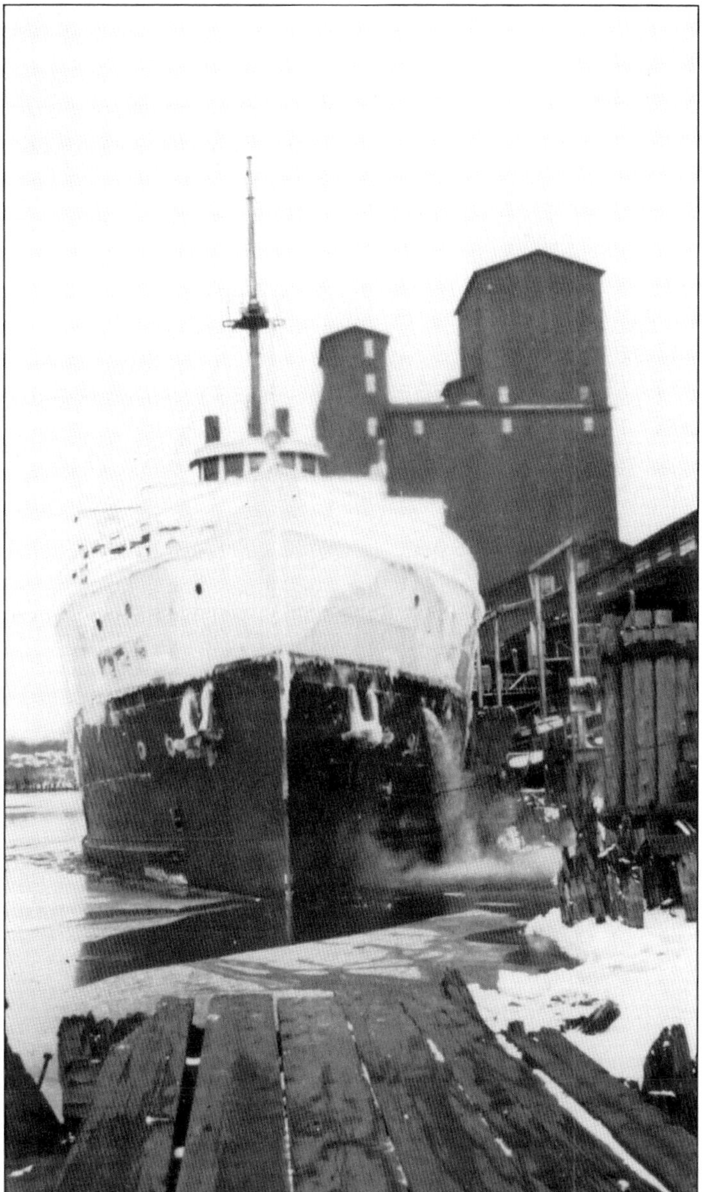

The steamer *Nevada* is docked at the freight shed in Ludington during an exceptionally hard winter in the 1930s. The *Nevada* was built in 1915 by the Manitowoc Shipbuilding Company for the Goodrich Transit Company with icebreaking capabilities. It was sold two years later to the Russian government. The *Nevada* was then renamed the *Rogday*, but before it could be delivered, the Russian Revolution had begun, and the ship was held, moored, and eventually transferred to the U.S. Navy in November 1918 with plans to use the *Rogday* for its icebreaking capabilities. The *Rogday* was moved once and then remained moored in Boston until June 1921, when it was activated and was called out to assist a cargo ship at sea. Once that mission was completed, the *Rogday* returned to dock and remained idle until September 1921, when the boat was returned to the new Russian government. It was purchased from the Russian government by the Pere Marquette Steamers Line on that same day for service on the Great Lakes. (Author's collection.)

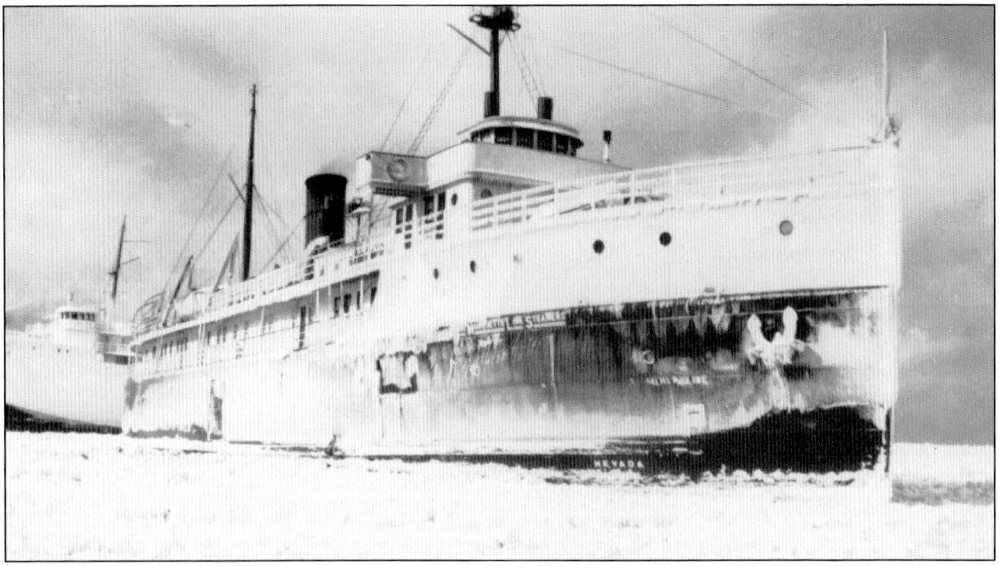

The *Nevada* is stuck fast in the ice in the Ludington Harbor. When the *Nevada* was refitted for ocean service, the ship's wheel was replaced with a smaller wheel, which was better for service on the Atlantic. Captain Hoxie hung the original wheel on his cabin along with the name plate and installed the ships whistle on the *Milwaukee Clipper*. (Author's collection.)

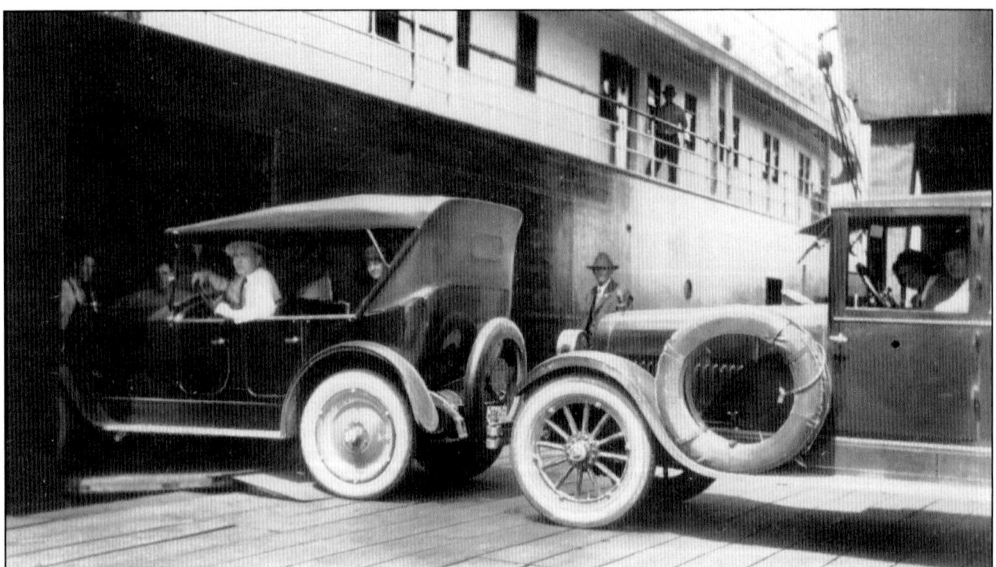

The doors on the *Nevada* could be opened to take on automobiles in the cargo bays. While not necessarily designed to be able to move cars, the tin lizzy of the 1920s could be easily loaded and unloaded at the docks, as is being done in this 1925 photograph taken in Ludington next to the freight shed. (Photograph by Alan Hoxie, author's collection.)

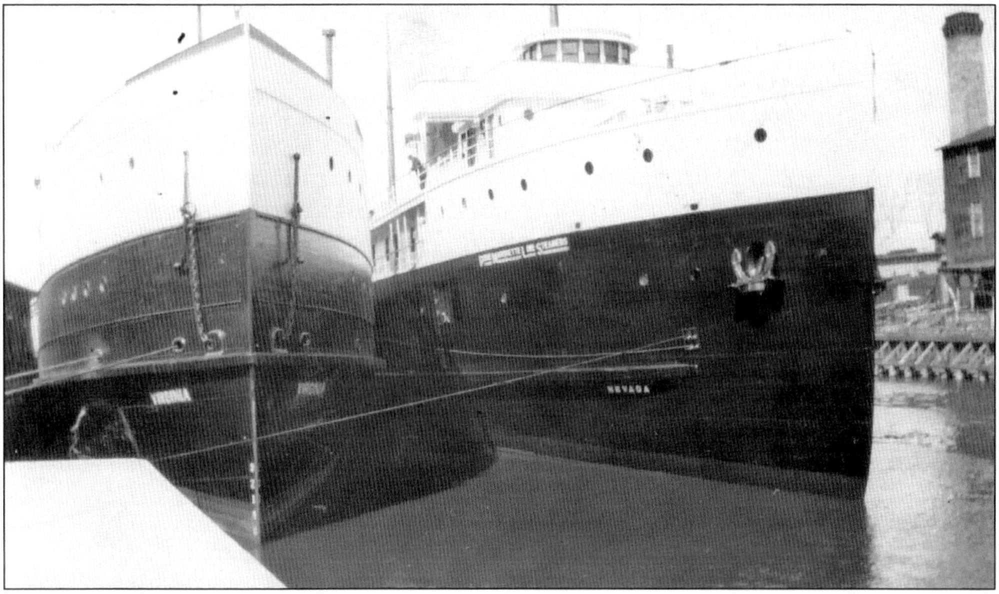

In 1942, the *Nevada* was sold to the war department. In December 1943, the storm-crippled ship foundered in the North Atlantic Ocean. The U.S. Coast Guard ship *Comanche* was able to save 29 people in a dramatic high seas rescue, but 34 were lost. Interestingly enough, *Rogday* is the name of a knight in a Russian fairy tale who met his death attempting to save a princess when he fell into the raging waters of the Dnieper River. (Photograph by Alan Hoxie, author's collection.)

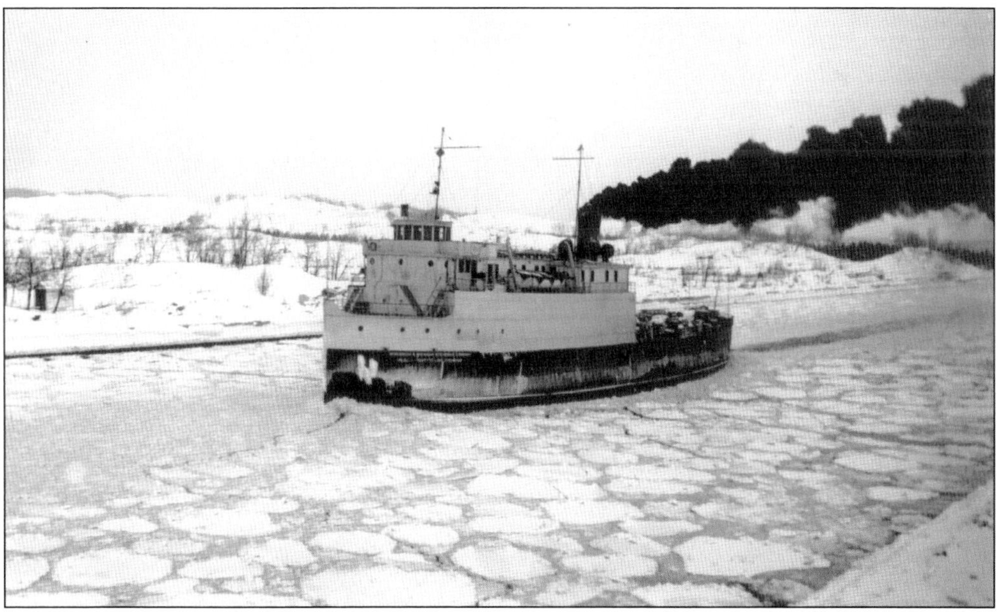

The Wisconsin Michigan Steamship Company cut the *Nevada* down in order to transport more automobiles on its deck; it is shown here coming out of the channel at Muskegon with a full load of cars destined for Wisconsin about 1936. (Author's collection.)

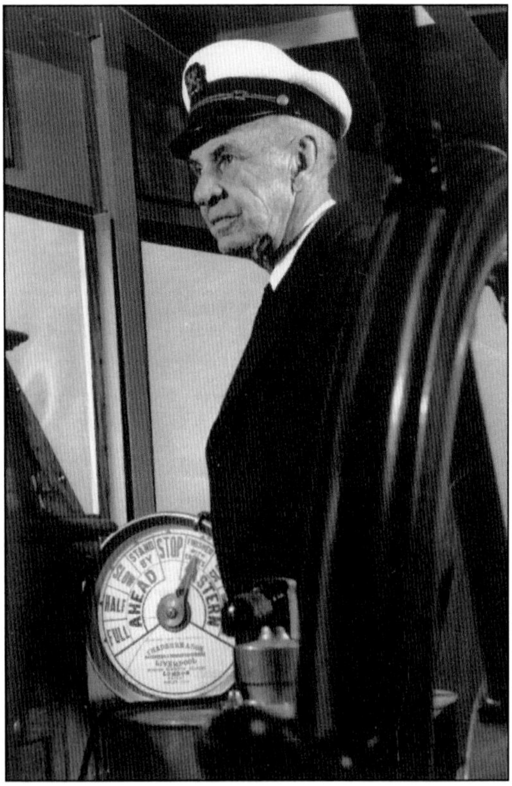

Captain Hoxie is at the wheel on the *Milwaukee Clipper* after leaving with the company and relocating in Muskegon. Hoxie had started working on the lakes after an incident where a coworker hit him on the back when he had a mouth full of tacks. Without his parents' knowledge, he signed on to work on the lakes and shipped out as a deckhand. (Author's collection.)

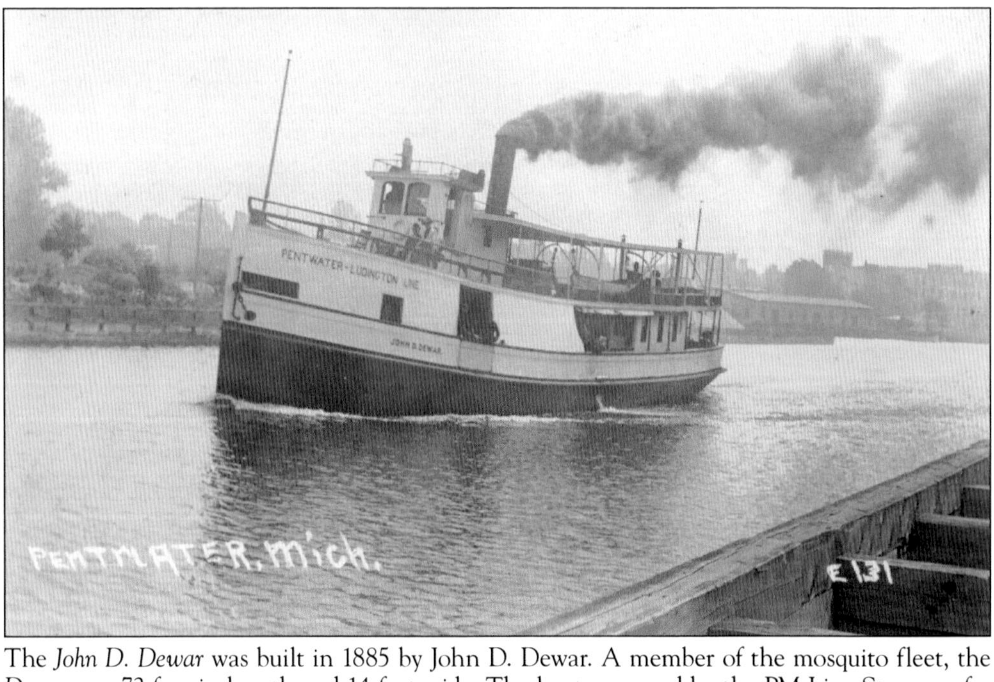

The *John D. Dewar* was built in 1885 by John D. Dewar. A member of the mosquito fleet, the *Dewar* was 72 feet in length and 14 feet wide. The boat was used by the PM Line Steamers for the Pentwater run and is shown here coming into Pentwater, Michigan, about 1910. (Courtesy of James F. Fay.)

Two

THE CAR FERRIES

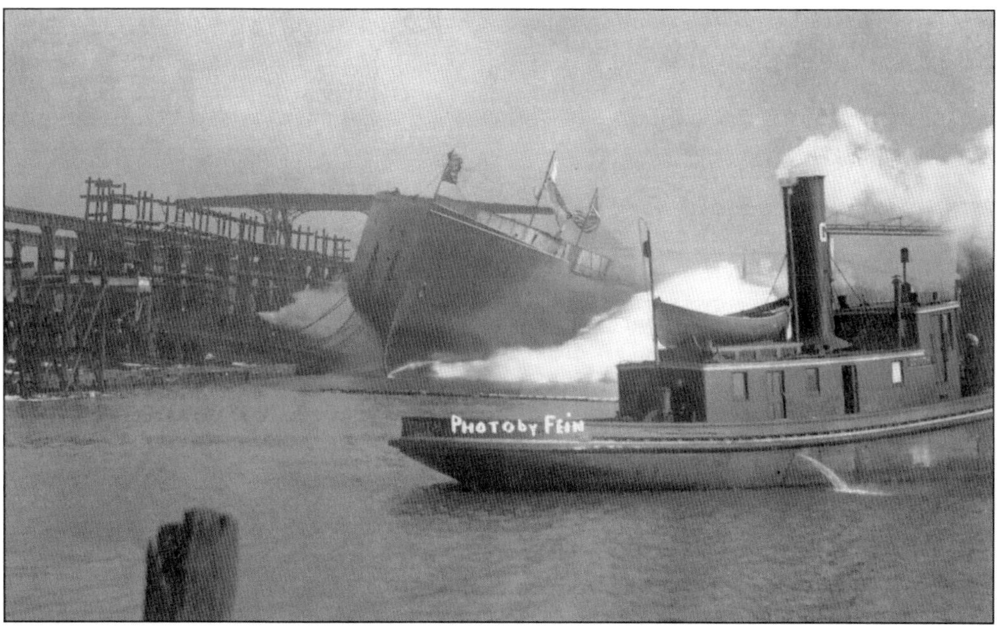

The *Pere Marquette* is being launched at Bay City, Michigan. This great ship was designed by Robert Logan and built by F. W. Wheeler of Bay City. The ship was reinforced with double plating and heavy bracing to help it withstand the rigors of continuous operation year-round in Lake Michigan. (Courtesy of James F. Fay.)

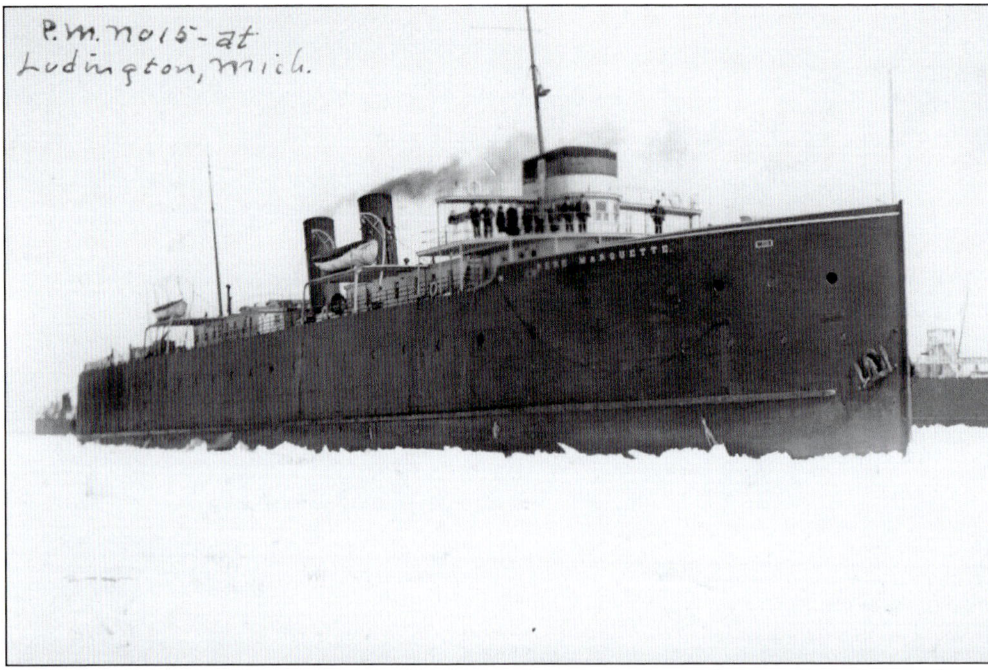

W. L. Mercereau, car ferry superintendent in a 1914, wrote an article regarding the car ferries and was quoted as saying "The car-ferry is no respecter of weather—it must run summer and winter, for freight must move and passengers must travel during all seasons." In 1924, this boat was renamed the *Pere Marquette 15*. It remained in service until 1930 and was scrapped in 1935. (Author's collection.)

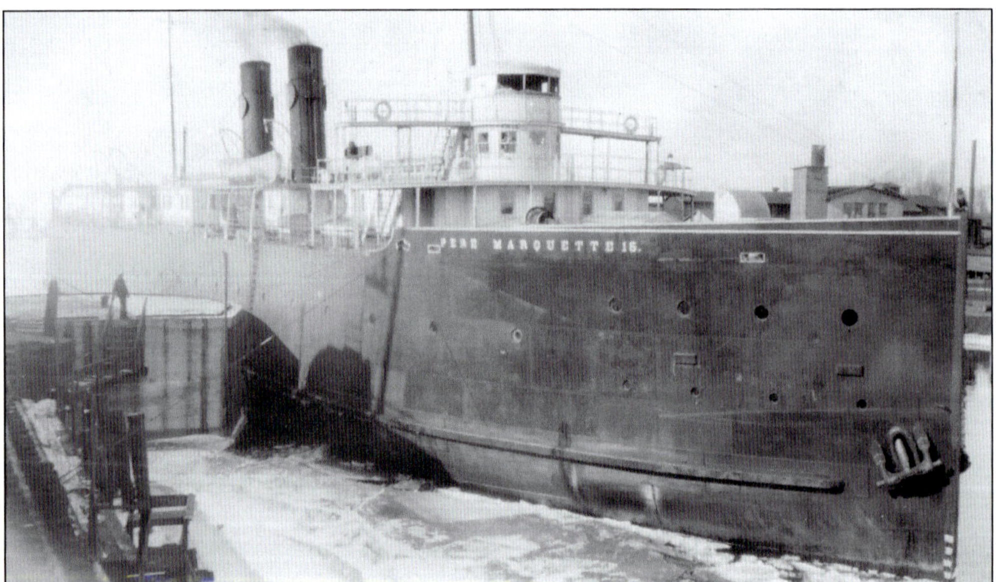

The movement of the freight from railroad car to boat and back off again provided more opportunities for damage to goods, and there was a desire to find a way to move more freight across the lake more easily, quickly, and year-round. This challenge was met by the new *Pere Marquette* car ferry in 1897. (Author's collection.)

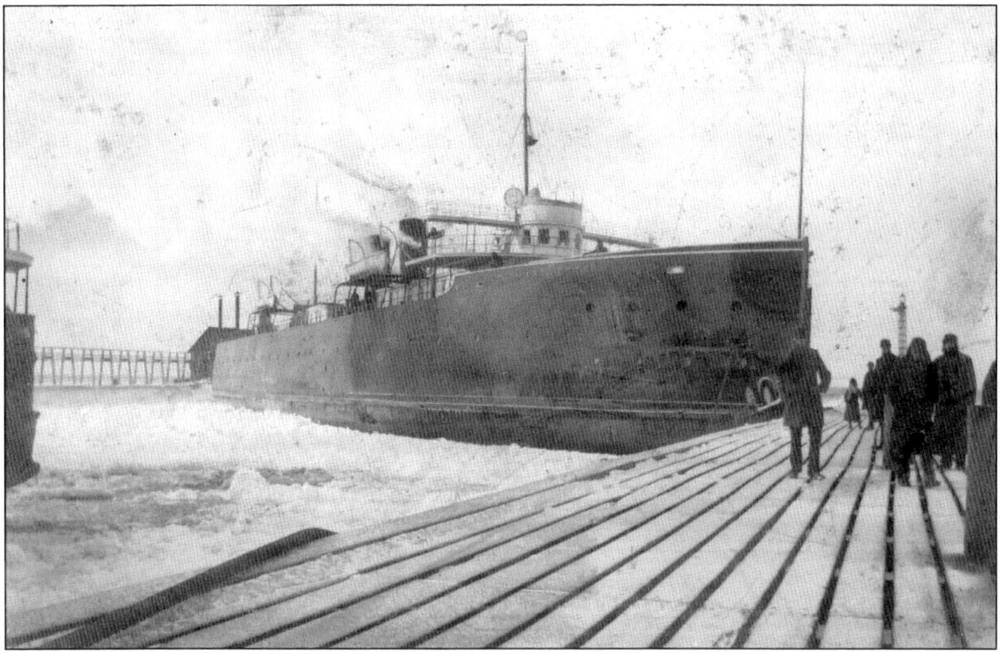

Although there were ships carrying loaded train cars, *Leslie's Weekly* stated in 1897 that "no car ferry was ever before built on such a mammoth scale." The *Pere Marquette* had four tracks and was capable of transporting 30 loaded railway cars. It was 56 feet wide, 350 feet long, had twin screws, and could attain a top speed of 16 miles per hour. (Author's collection.)

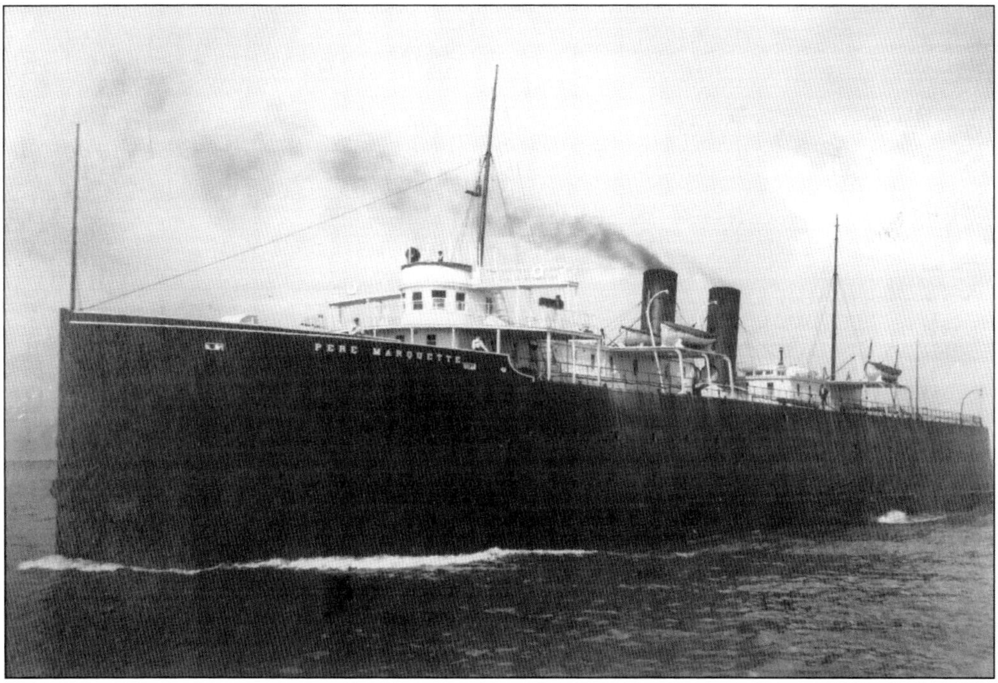

The *Pere Marquette* was to have its designation changed after the 1900 merger, but the change was not made officially until 1924. The boat was known and referred to as the *15* for close to 20 years before the redesignation as *Pere Marquette 15* was official. (Author's collection.)

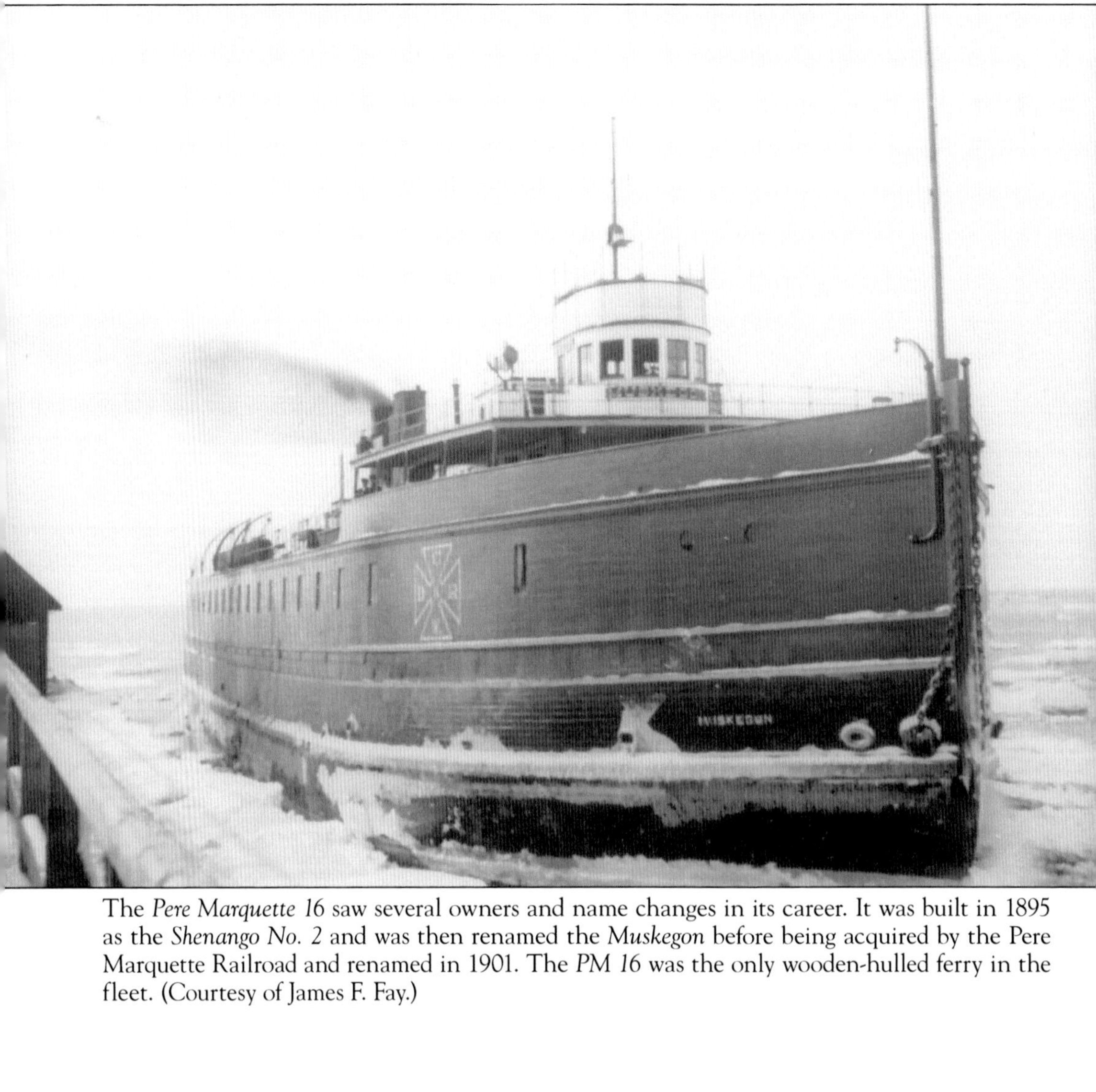

The *Pere Marquette 16* saw several owners and name changes in its career. It was built in 1895 as the *Shenango No. 2* and was then renamed the *Muskegon* before being acquired by the Pere Marquette Railroad and renamed in 1901. The *PM 16* was the only wooden-hulled ferry in the fleet. (Courtesy of James F. Fay.)

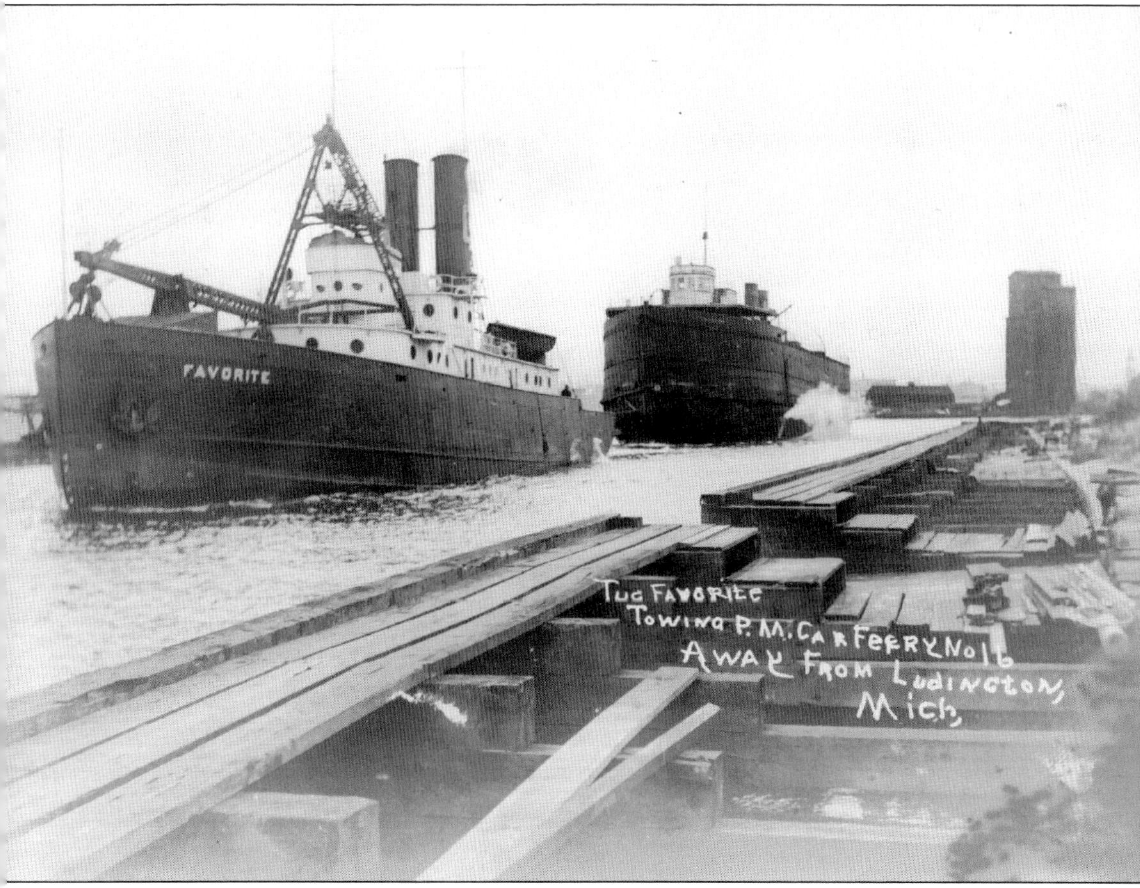

There were a series of mergers, and the Port Huron and Northwestern from Saginaw to Port Huron was added. In 1900, the Flint and Pere Marquette merged with the Detroit, Grand Rapids, and Western; and the Chicago, West Michigan, and Detroit railroads to form the Pere Marquette Railway Company. At the time of this merger, the railroad acquired the *Muskegon*. The *Muskegon*, as the *Pere Marquette 16*, had several mishaps over the years the boat was in operation and one incident in which a car ferry employee was killed by steam escaping from a ruptured pipe in the engine room. Eventually laid up and sold to carry pulpwood, the *PM 16* was renamed again as the *Harriet B*, was converted to a barge in 1921, and sank in Lake Superior in 1922. (Author's collection.)

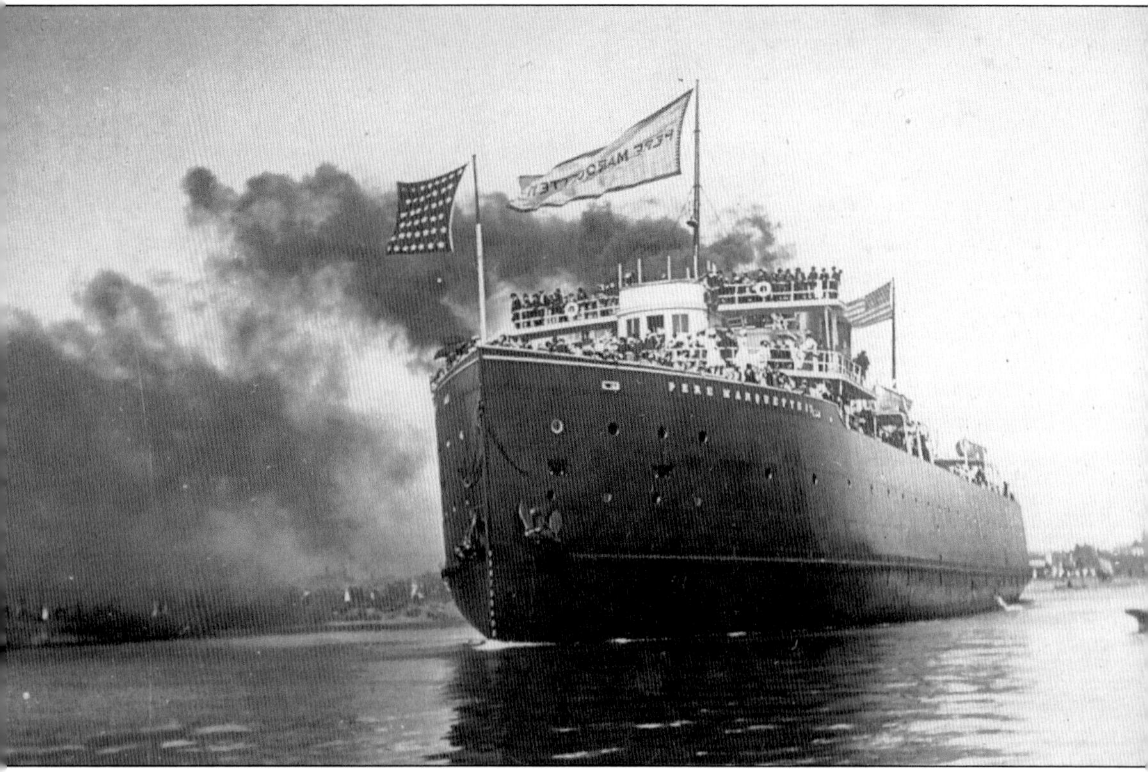

The *Pere Marquette 17*, shown here steaming into the Ludington Harbor, was built in 1901, laid up in the 1930s, and eventually sold to the State of Michigan, where it was converted, renamed the *City of Petoskey*, and repainted white for use in the Straits of Mackinaw as an auto ferry until 1959. It was scrapped in 1961. (Author's collection.)

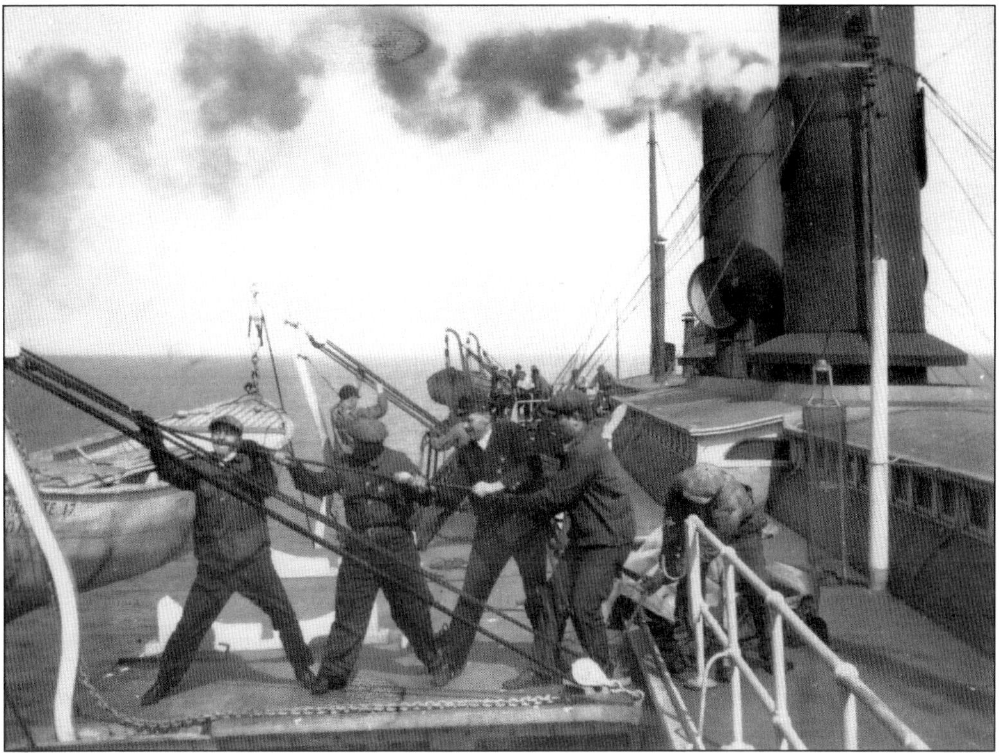

The men of the *Pere Marquette 17* are practicing their weekly lifeboat drill as required by regulations. It was not until after the sinking of the *Titanic* that an adequate number of lifeboats were required for the passengers on board ships. (Photograph by Erhardt Peters, author's collection.)

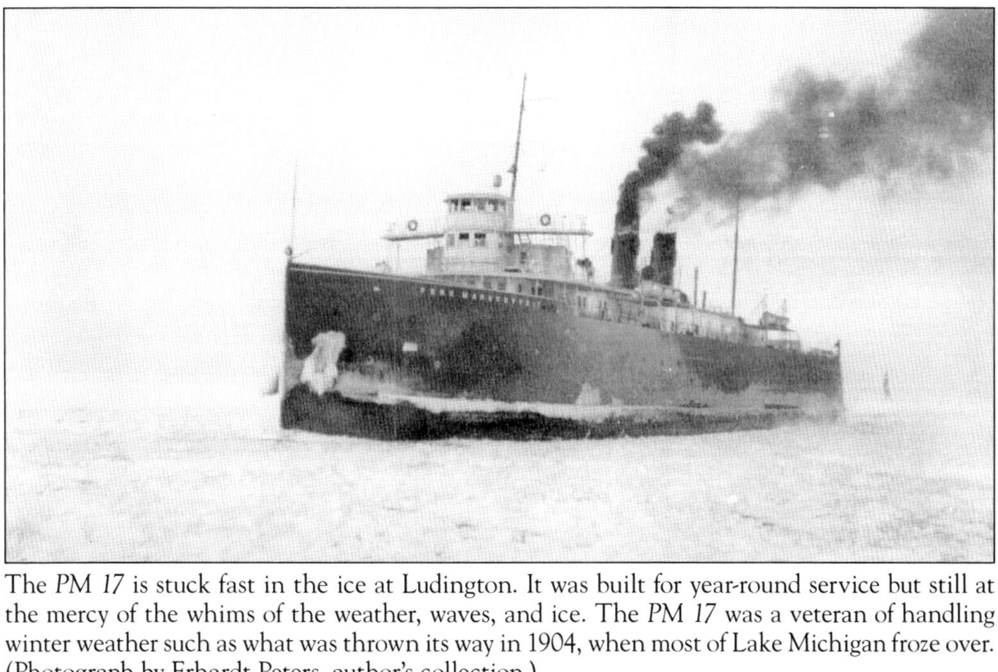

The *PM 17* is stuck fast in the ice at Ludington. It was built for year-round service but still at the mercy of the whims of the weather, waves, and ice. The *PM 17* was a veteran of handling winter weather such as what was thrown its way in 1904, when most of Lake Michigan froze over. (Photograph by Erhardt Peters, author's collection.)

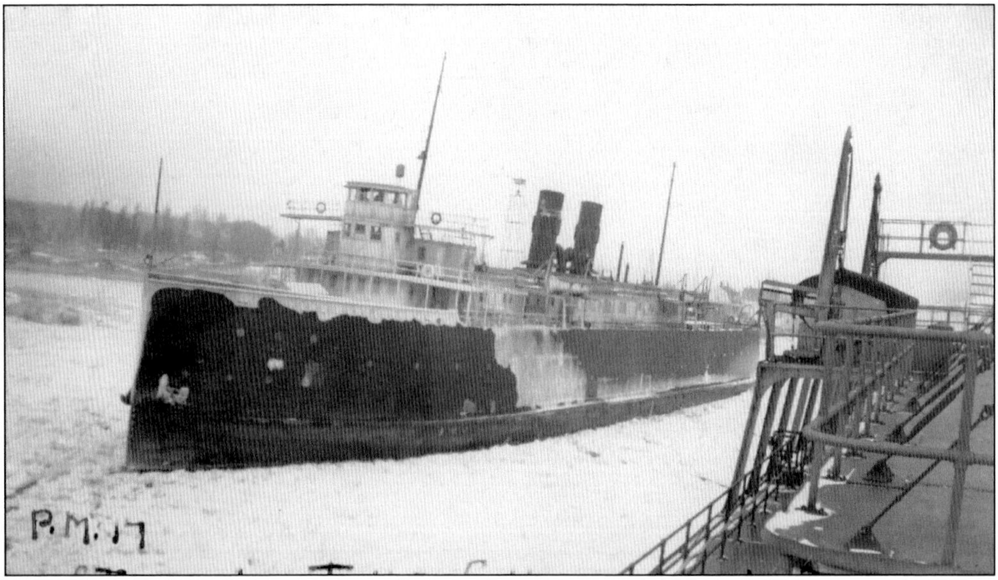

The *PM 17* is locked in the ice again during one of the winters during the Great Depression. At various times, the railroad contracted icebreaking tugs to assist the car ferries. The winters between 1933 and 1936 were severe, but the car ferries endured and managed to maintain fairly regular service. (Photograph by Erhardt Peters, author's collection.)

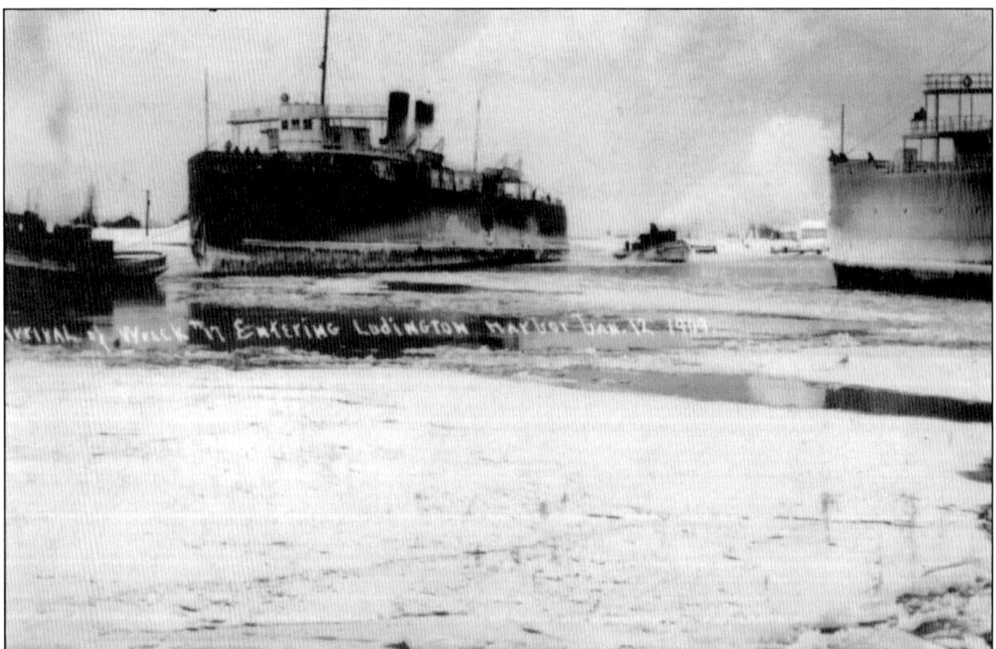

In January 1909, the *PM 17* was driven aground in a storm and was not freed until *Knights Templar* and *Welcome* arrived. The *PM 17* was towed into the port of Ludington on January 12, 1909, and then taken to Milwaukee for repairs. (Courtesy of James F. Fay.)

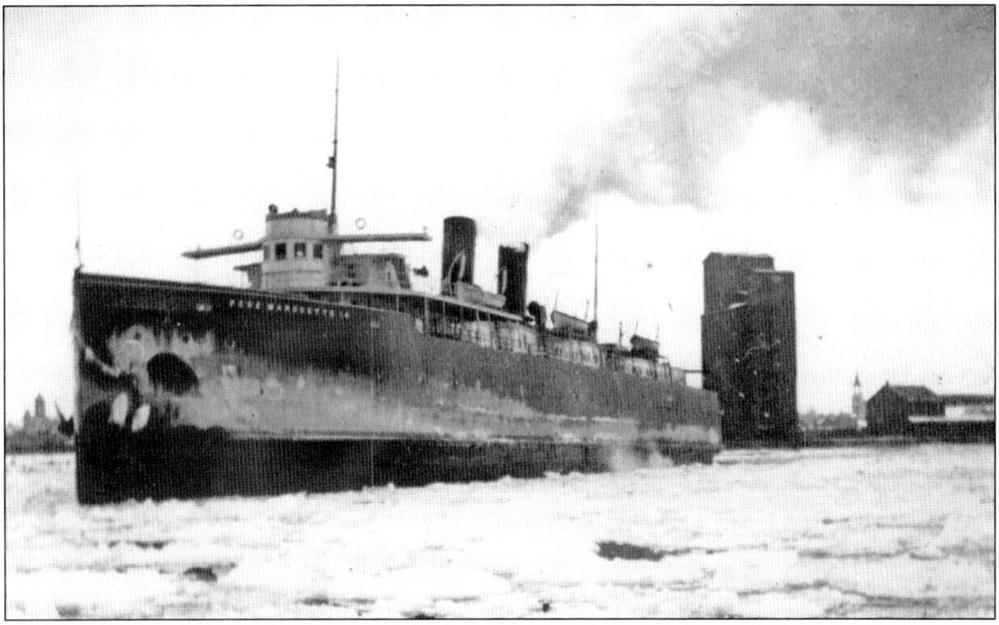

The *PM 18* was built in 1902 by the American Shipbuilding Company in Cleveland, Ohio. The *PM 18* was a steel-hulled 338-foot-long ship made for hauling freight and passengers. For several years, the ship was chartered out in Chicago, a dance floor was built, and it was used for excursions on Lake Michigan. (Author's collection.)

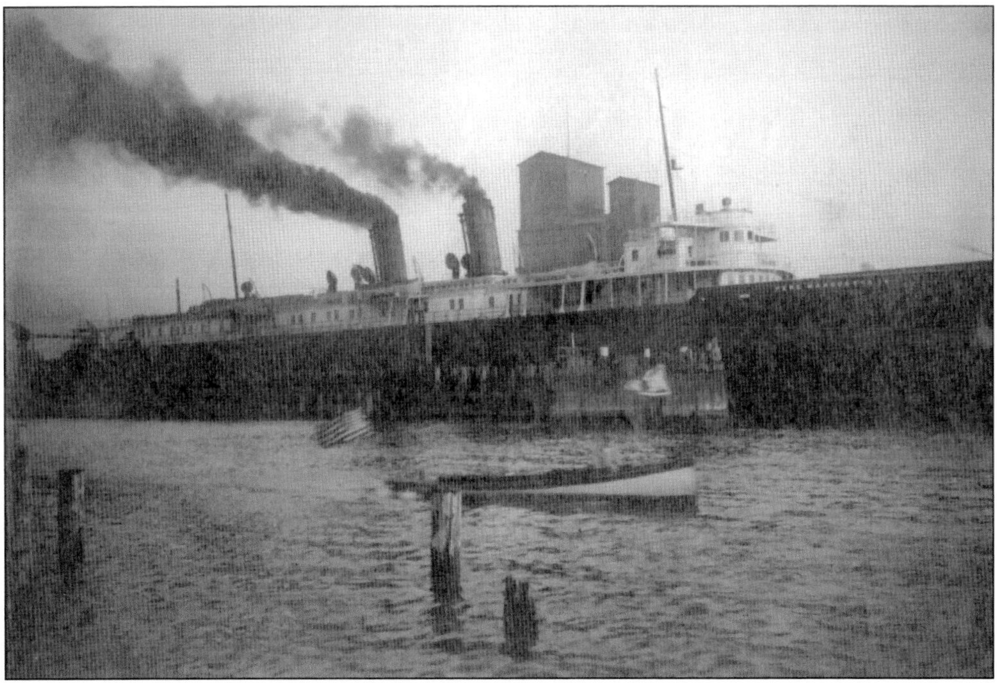

The *PM 18* had been used during its last summer as an excursion vessel and was on its first run of the freight season late on the night of September 9, 1910, when it sank. Afterwards a hearing was held to try and determine the cause of the sinking, but with the loss of all of the officers, the cause could not be determined. (Author's collection.)

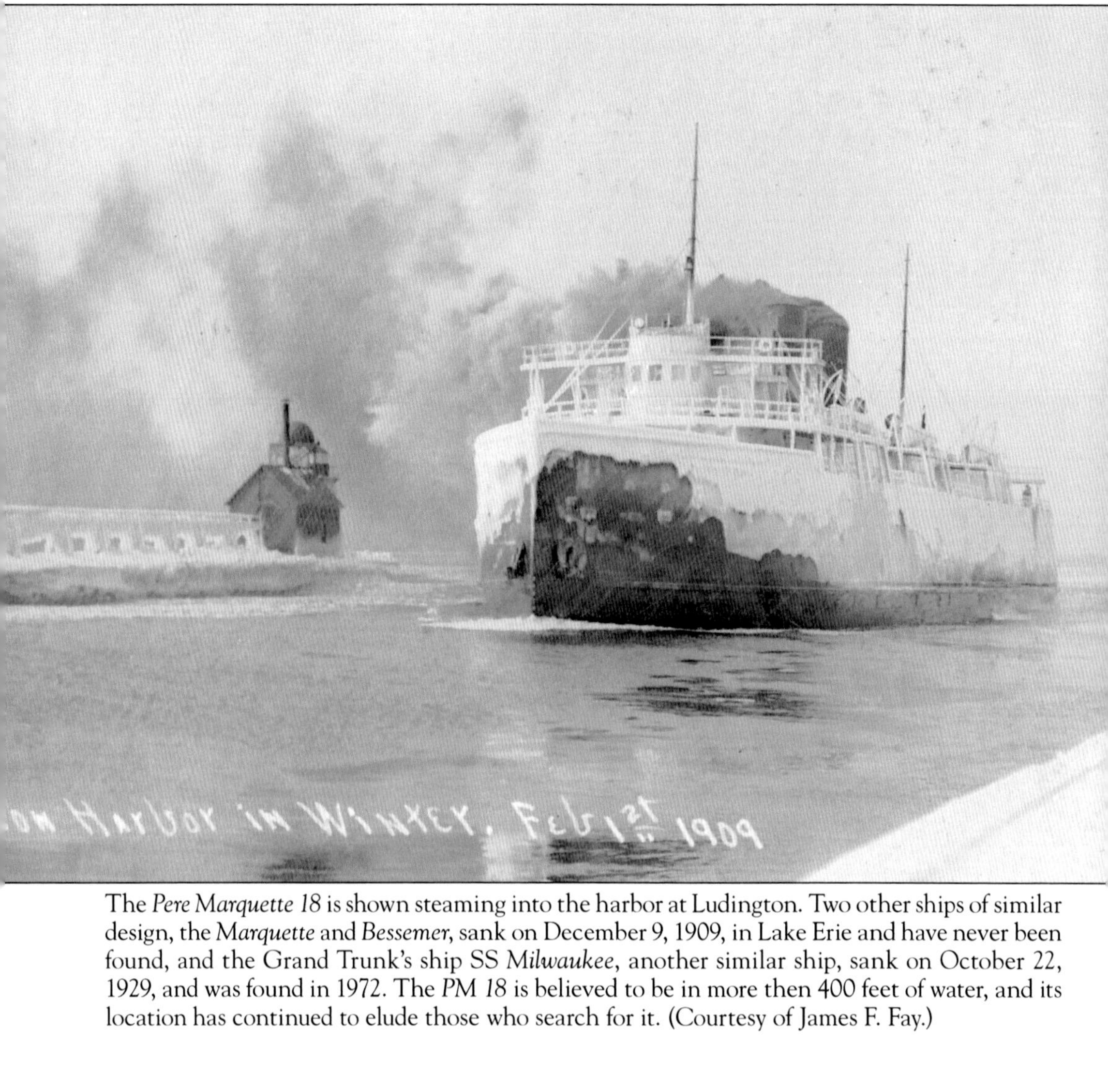

The *Pere Marquette 18* is shown steaming into the harbor at Ludington. Two other ships of similar design, the *Marquette* and *Bessemer*, sank on December 9, 1909, in Lake Erie and have never been found, and the Grand Trunk's ship SS *Milwaukee*, another similar ship, sank on October 22, 1929, and was found in 1972. The *PM 18* is believed to be in more then 400 feet of water, and its location has continued to elude those who search for it. (Courtesy of James F. Fay.)

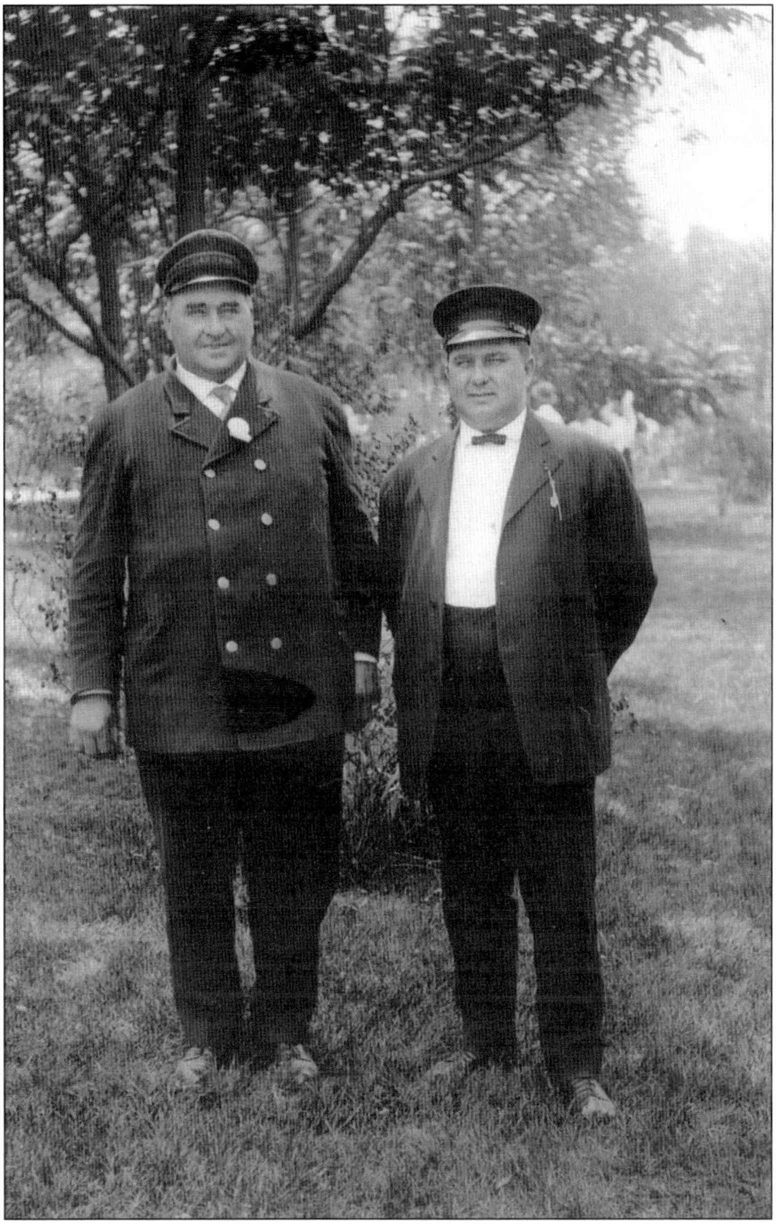

The most well-known officers of the ill-fated *18* are Capt. Peter Kilty (left) and E. Ross Leedham, the chief engineer. Leedham and his crew locked themselves in the engine room and stayed at their post in a heroic attempt to keep the steam up and the engines going as the captain had hoped to turn and make port in Sheboygan, which was closer for them then trying to make port at Milwaukee. Fate had other ideas, and the ship was claimed by the lake early on September 10, 1910, along with 28 souls. The ship had begun to take on water in the early morning from an unknown source; Captain Kilty ordered railcars to be pushed off into the lake in order to lighten the ship and wireless operator Stephen Sczepanek to send the distress call out for help. "PM *No. 18* sinking mid-lake for GOD's sake help us." The *Pere Marquette 17* responded to the distress call and in the lowering of the first life boat lost two of its own crew. Thirty-three of the passengers and crew were saved, but none of the officers survived. (Author's collection.)

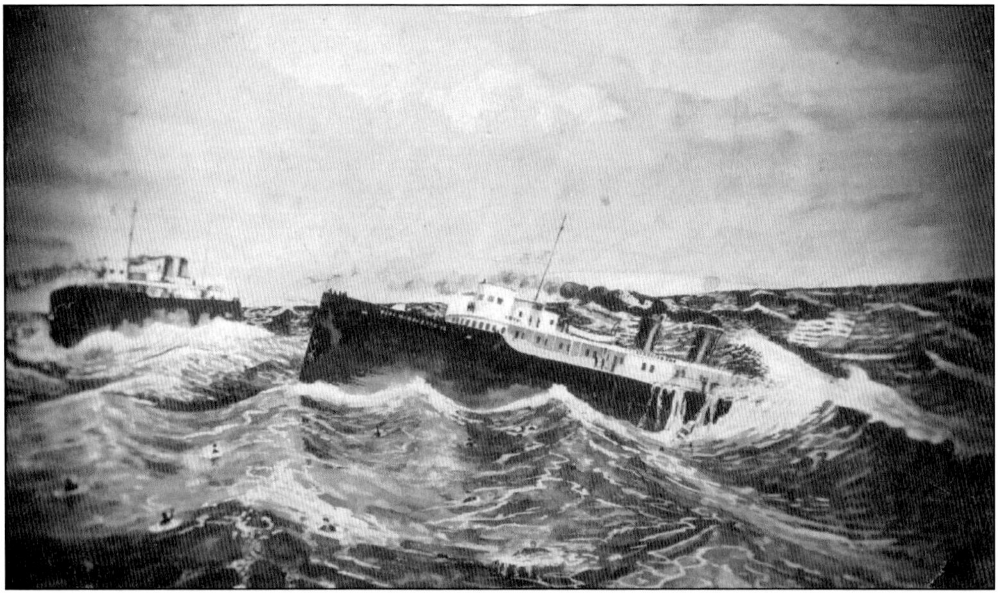

The *PM 18* sank on September 10, 1910, with the loss of 28 lives. The cause of the sinking has been subject to speculation for the past 95 years. Still undiscovered, the location of the vessel when found may yield the clues to put this mystery to rest. A young crewman by the name of Jacob Lunde was on the *PM 17* and witnessed the sinking. He later made several folk paintings of the sinking, and Jacob also became a well-known local historian and created a panorama that he used to illustrate the history of Ludington. (Courtesy of James F. Fay.)

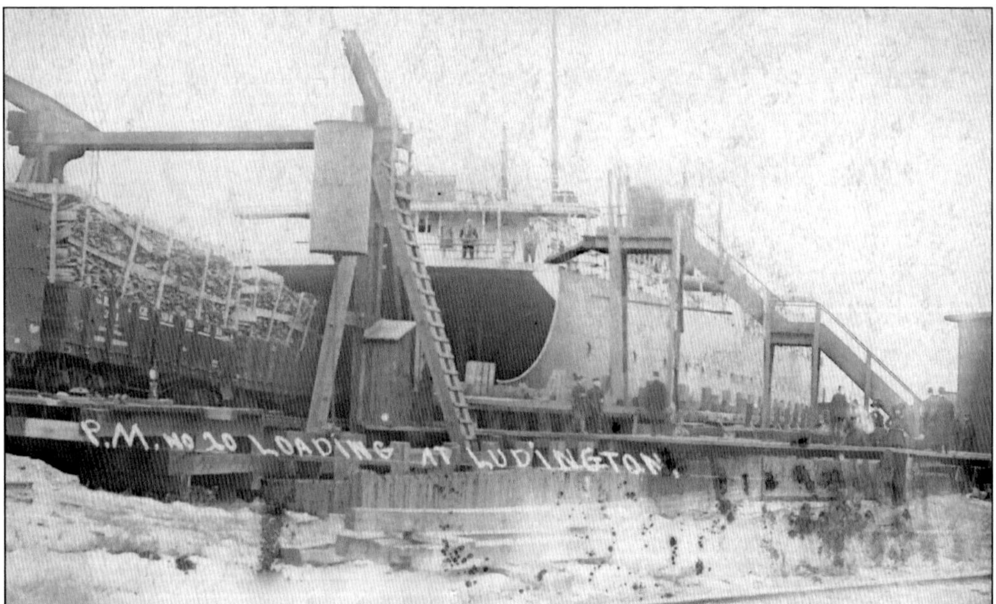

This 1909 view is actually of the *PM 18* in Ludington. One good thing that came out of the investigation was that car ferries had to have seagates installed to help keep the waters of the lake out. It may not have helped the *PM 18*, as the weather was fair on the day of its sinking. (Author's collection.)

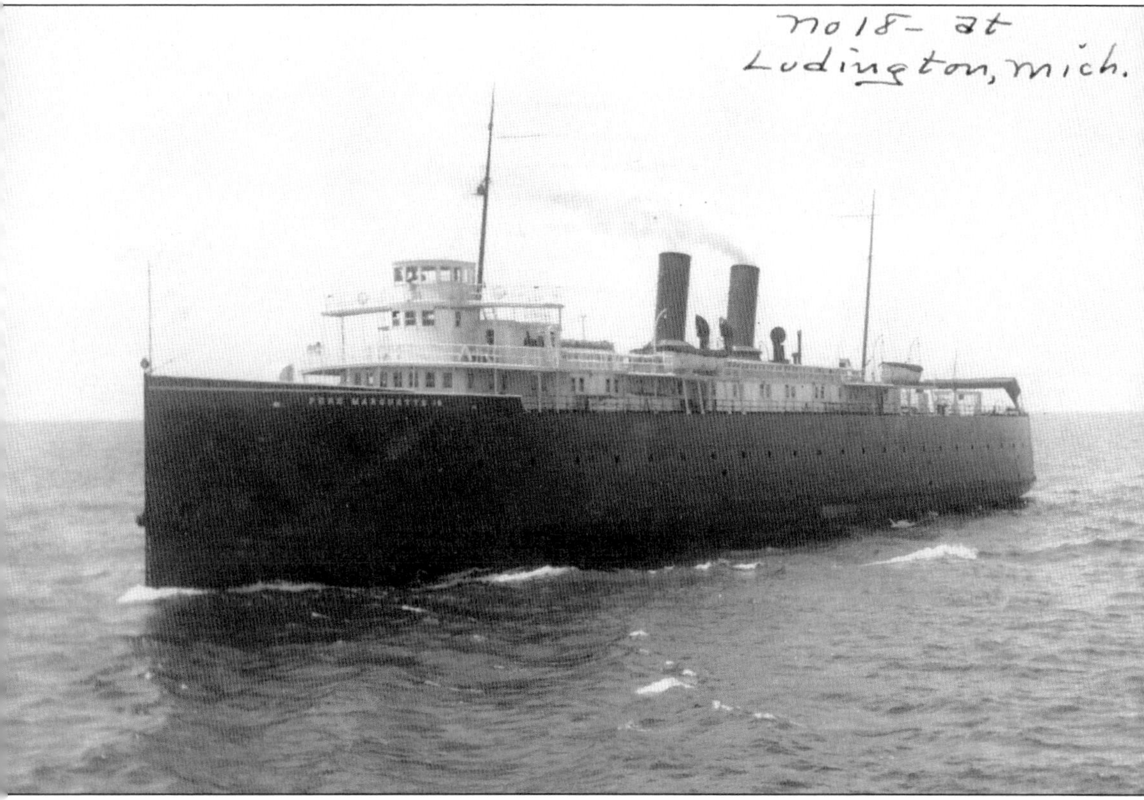

Ignoring all tradition (and superstition), the ship that replaced the *PM 18*, lost in 1910, was also named the *Pere Marquette 18* and was put into service in 1911. It fared much better, having a career on the lakes that spanned four decades before being scrapped. (Author's collection.)

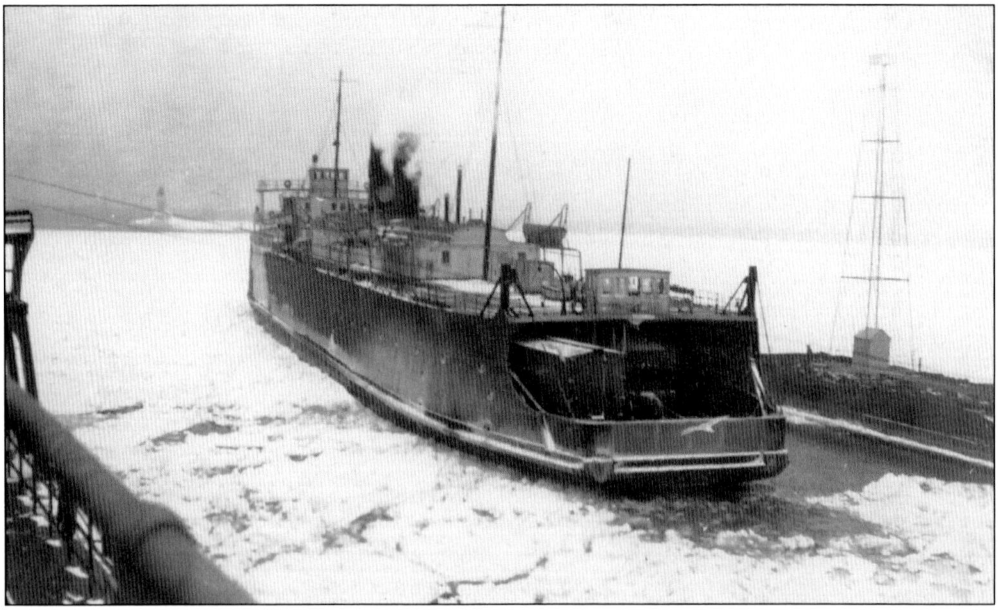

This is a good view of the seagate on the *Pere Marquette 18 II* as it is lodged in the ice in the Ludington Harbor. In August 1926, the car ferries were equipped with new continuous-wave radio systems. These replaced the Quench Gap system of telegraphy that had been used and were similar to the radio equipment used by broadcasters. (Photograph by Erhardt Peters, author's collection.)

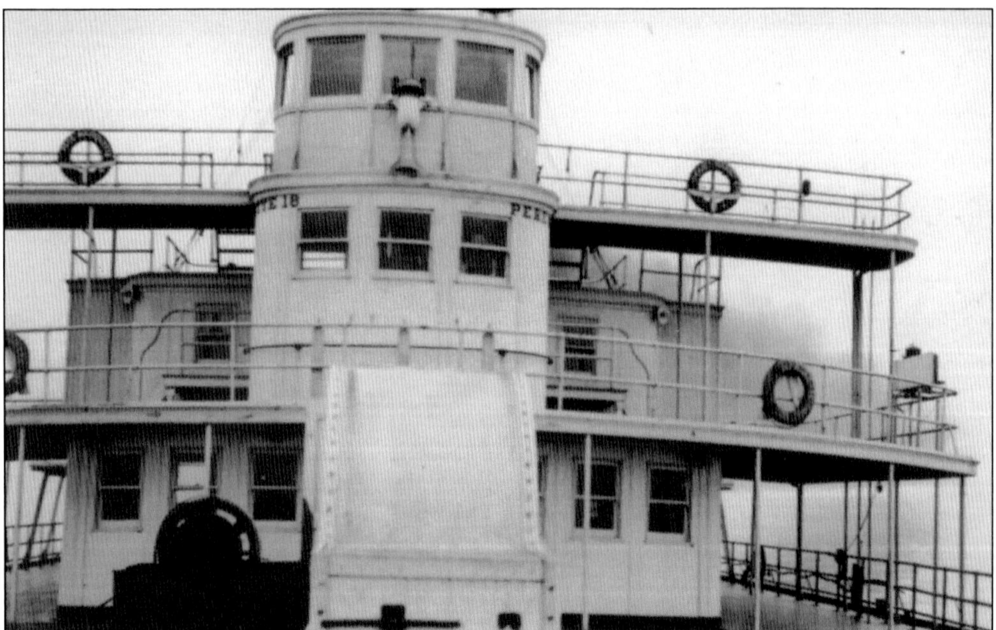

The Pilot House and bridge wings of the *Pere Marquette 18 II* are shown in great detail not usually seen in photographs of the car ferry fleet. Most views commonly available simply show the boats as they enter and leave the harbor. This is a good example of the kind of detail-oriented photographs sought by Peters as he documented the fleet. (Author's collection.)

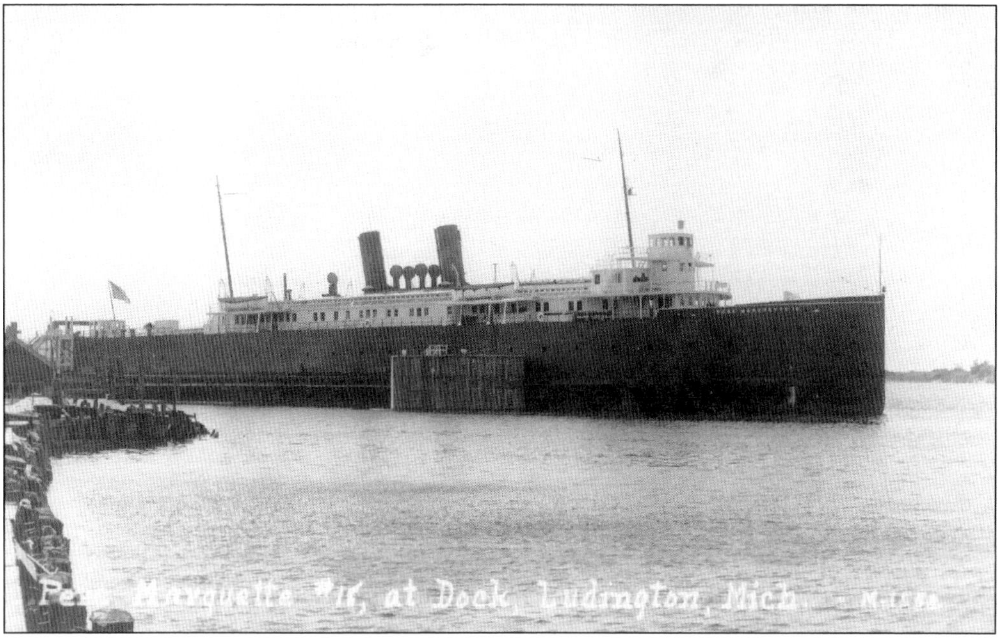

The *Pere Marquette 18 II* is pictured at the dock in Ludington about 1940. In November 1900, one of the ideas for improving communication between ships and the homeport involved the use of carrier pigeons. They had hoped that this method would allow ice-bound ships to send a message for help during winter months. Wireless telegraphy had not sufficiently developed and would not be adopted until 1909 on the Pere Marquette car ferries. The idea of carrier pigeons did not fly. (Author's collection.)

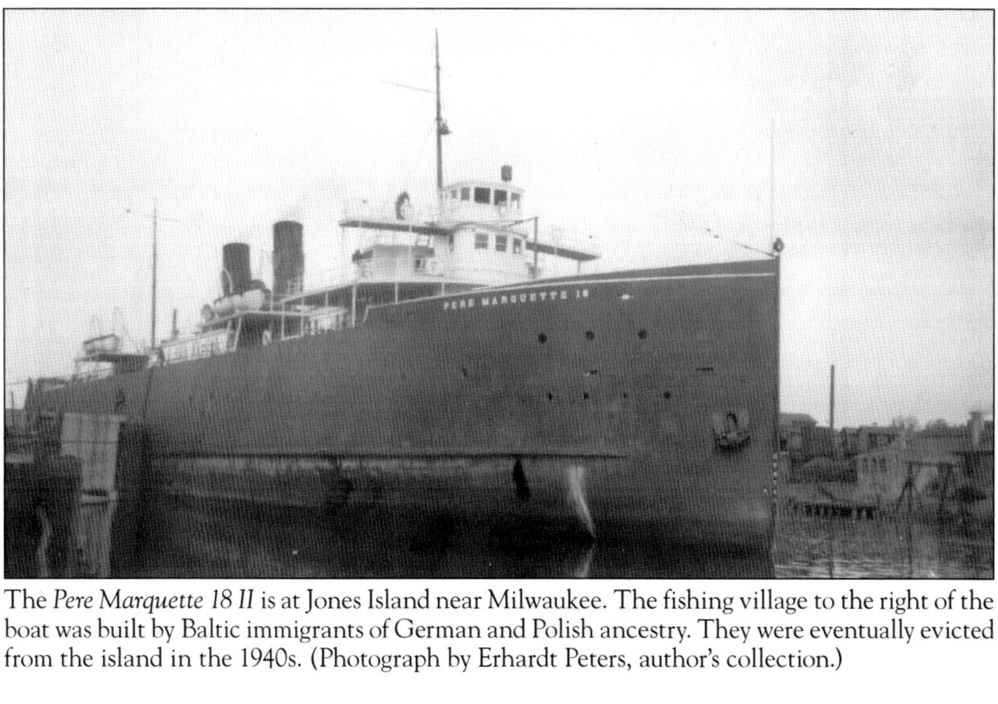

The *Pere Marquette 18 II* is at Jones Island near Milwaukee. The fishing village to the right of the boat was built by Baltic immigrants of German and Polish ancestry. They were eventually evicted from the island in the 1940s. (Photograph by Erhardt Peters, author's collection.)

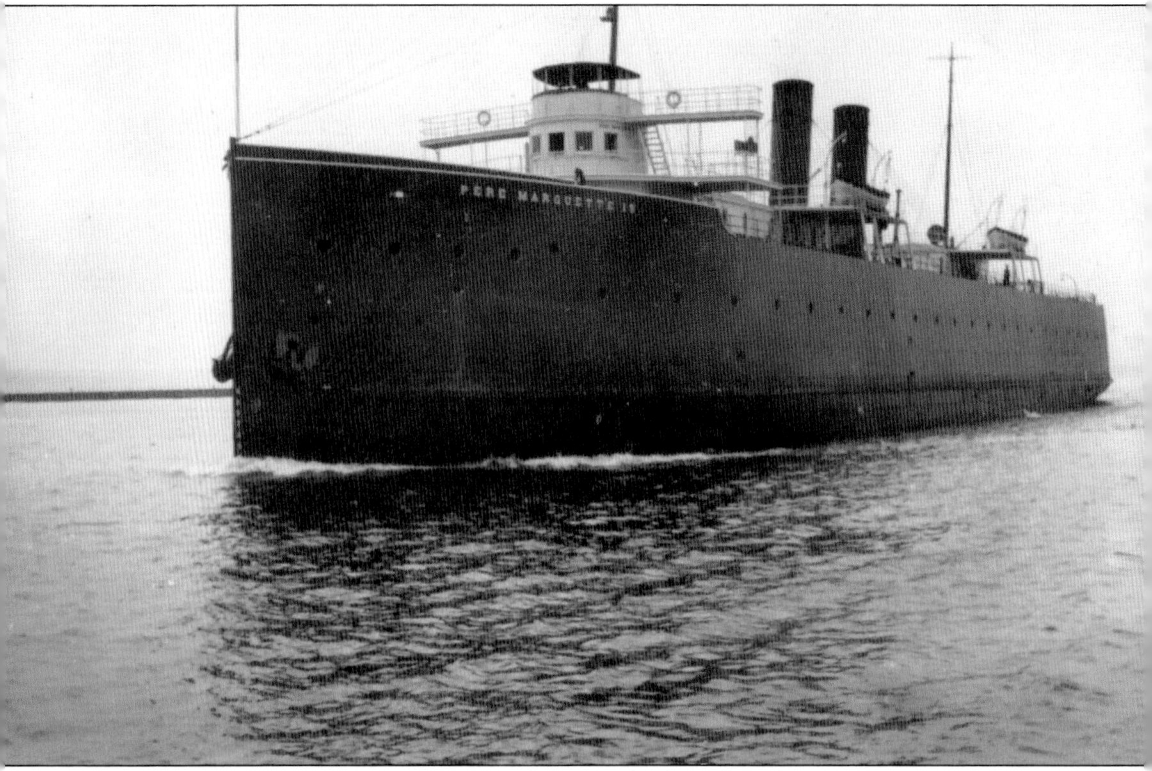

Launched in 1903, *Pere Marquette 19* and *20* were built at the Cleveland yard of the American Shipbuilding Company. Neither ship had been blessed with passenger accommodations, but they were the first sister ships built to the same blueprint. The *PM 19* was sold in 1940, converted to a barge, and renamed *Hilda*. The *PM 20* was sold to the State of Michigan and, like the *17*, was used at the Straits of Mackinaw as an auto ferry. Renamed the *City of Munising*, it also served until completion of the Mackinaw Bridge in 1959. It was finally scrapped in 1973. (Photograph by Erhardt Peters, author's collection.)

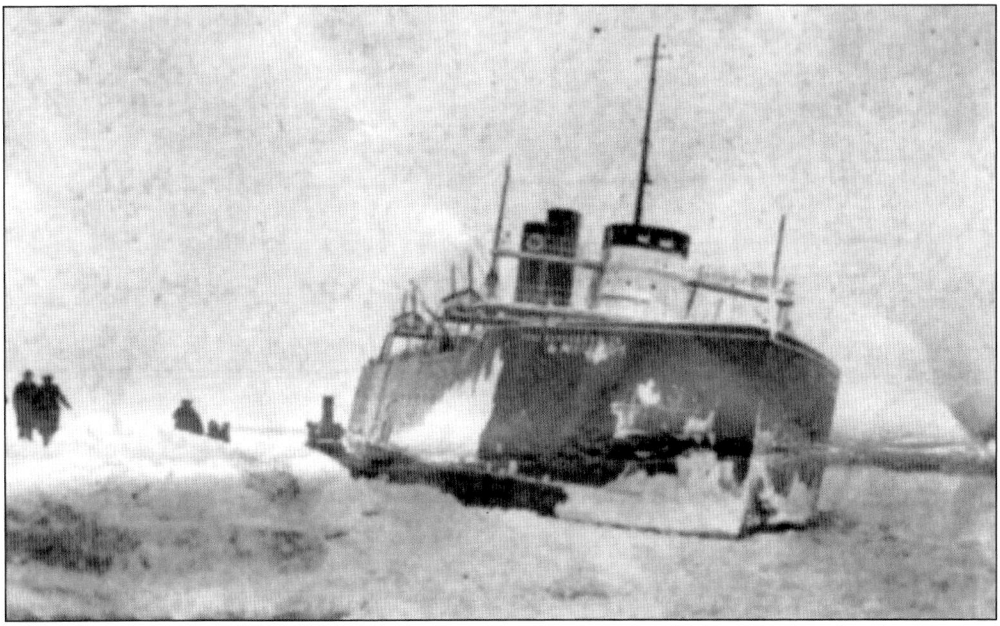

Pere Marquette 19 lies hard aground with its machinery spaces full of water after a hard grounding off Big Sable point in January 1916. Before the advent of modern navigational aids both onboard and ashore, such accidents were commonplace. (Author's collection.)

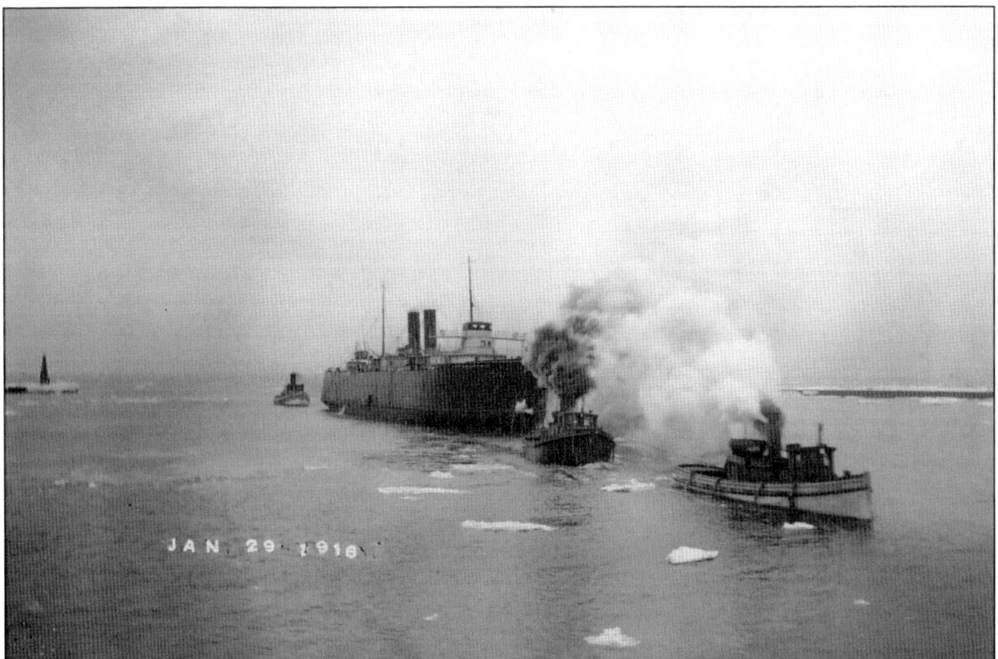

After spending 10 days on the beach, *Pere Marquette 19* gets towed into Ludington Harbor to assess the damage done to its framing and hull plates. From here, it would get towed to the yard of Manitowoc Shipbuilding Company for a complete overhaul and live to see another day. (Author's collection.)

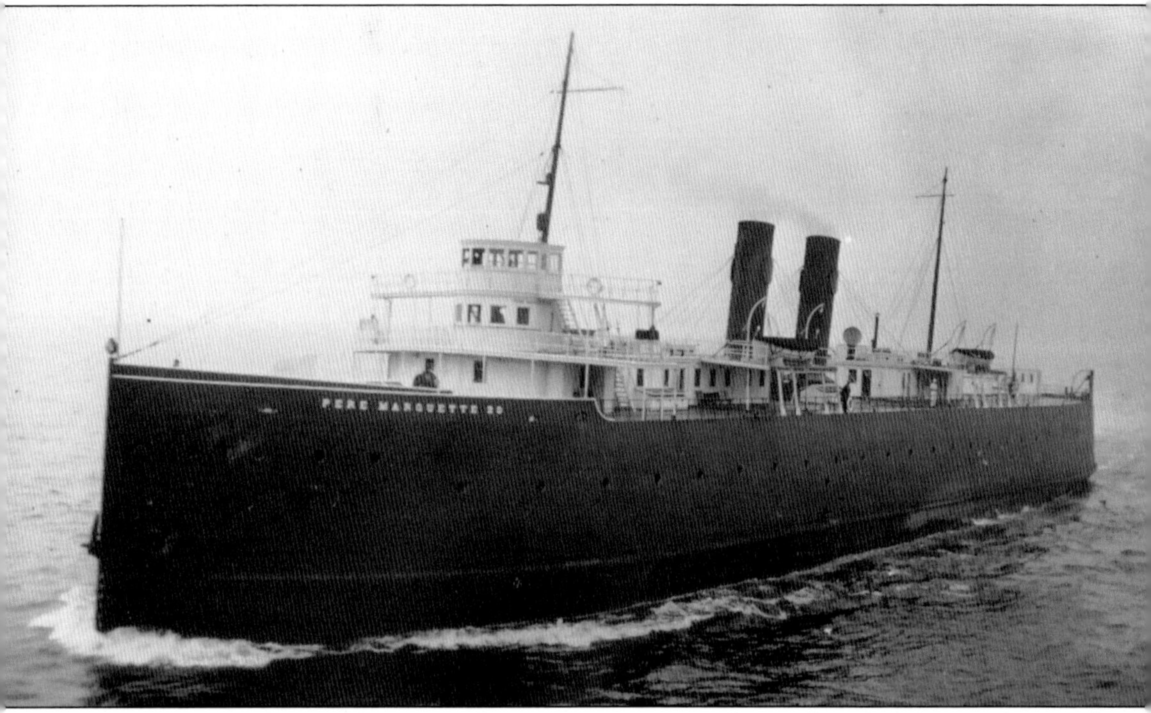

Shown approaching Ludington Harbor, *Pere Marquette 20* shows off its sleek lines and covered upper pilothouse in this view from the late 1920s. As built in the early 1900s, the car ferries typically had an open flying bridge for navigation. Permanent enclosures were added gradually beginning about 1916. (Photograph by Erhardt Peters, author's collection.)

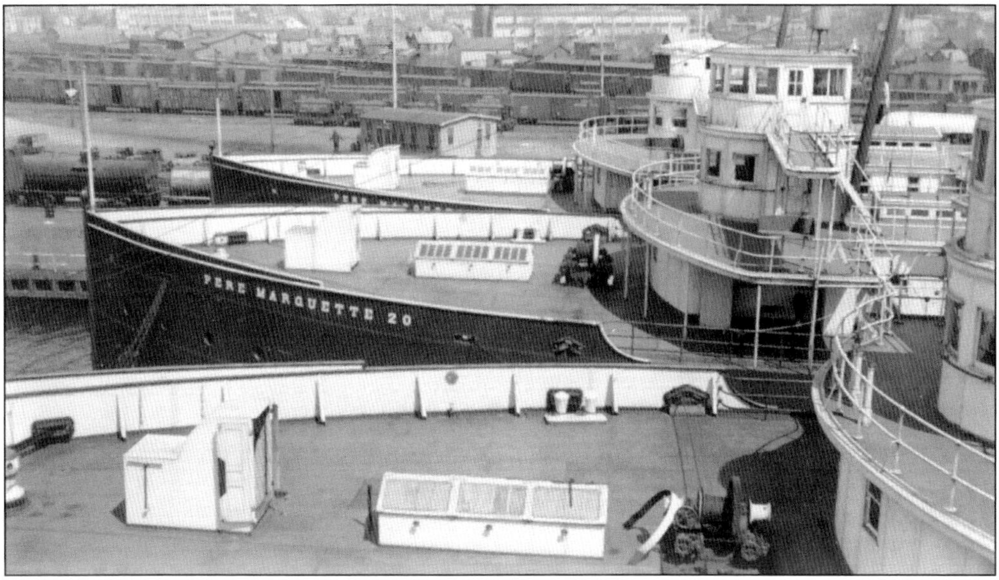

A row of idle Pere Marquette car ferries was a common sight in the area known as "Misery Bay" during the depths of the Depression of the 1930s. Misery Bay was a term used as early as 1926, when six ships were in the docks at one time. The *PM 19* and *21* were receiving new coats of paint, and the *PM 20* was reported in Misery Bay. (Photograph by Erhardt Peters, author's collection.)

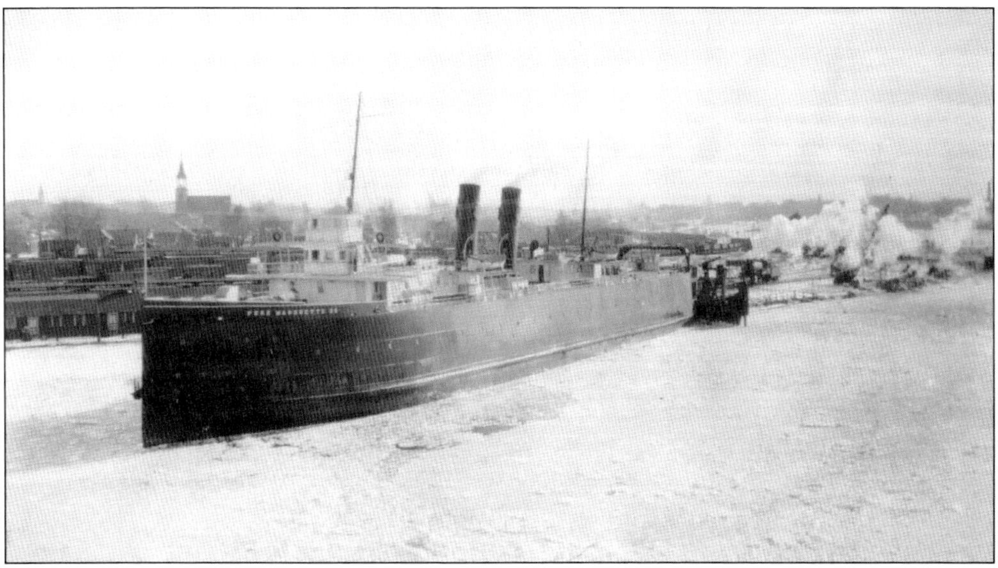

On a frigid winter day during the 1920s, *Pere Marquette 20* takes on a load of freight at the south slip in Ludington. Pere Marquette Lake, which connects to Lake Michigan, often froze heavily during severe winters, requiring the use of tugboats to keep the harbor open while the car ferries were on their way across the lake to Wisconsin. (Photograph by Erhardt Peters, author's collection.)

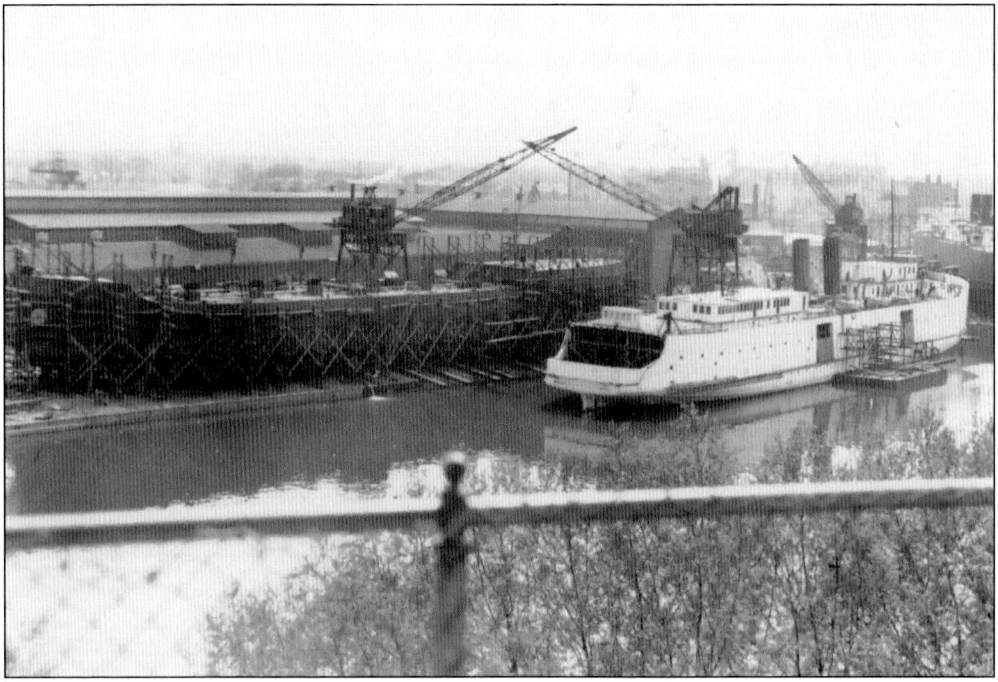

The *Pere Marquette 20* is shown being converted to an automobile ferry for use across the Straits of Mackinaw, connecting the Upper and Lower Peninsulas of Michigan. This work was carried out by Manitowoc Shipbuilding Company in 1938; the contact required new passenger cabins, a revamped main deck, and a new white paint scheme, replacing traditional car ferry black. It was renamed *City of Munising.* (Courtesy of James F. Fay.)

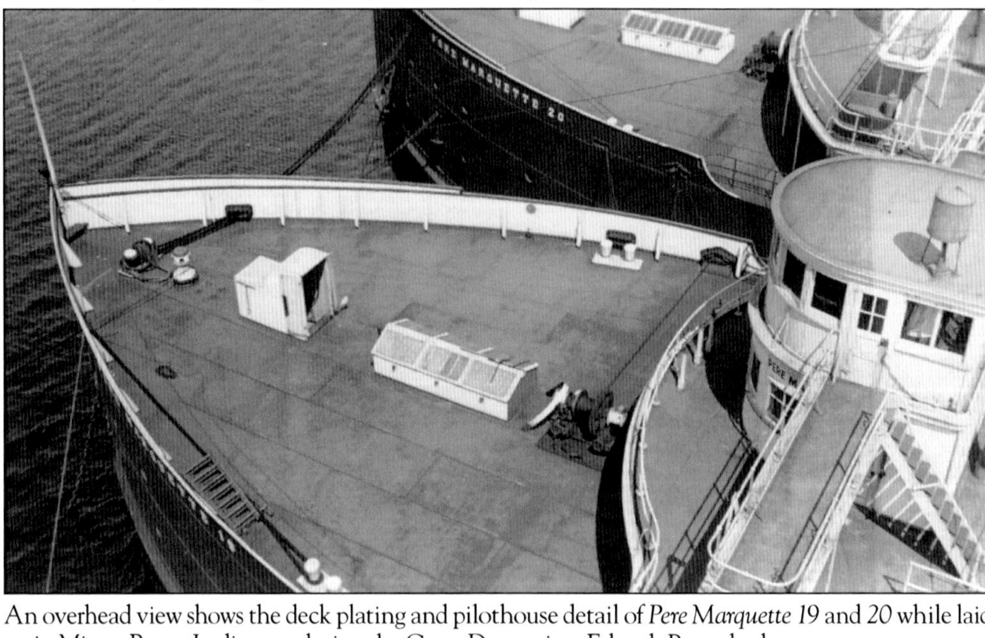

An overhead view shows the deck plating and pilothouse detail of *Pere Marquette 19* and *20* while laid up in Misery Bay at Ludington during the Great Depression. Erhardt Peters had access to many parts of the ships in order to photographically document the ferries. Imagine for a moment the vantage point he had to find to create this photograph. (Photograph by Erhardt Peters, author's collection.)

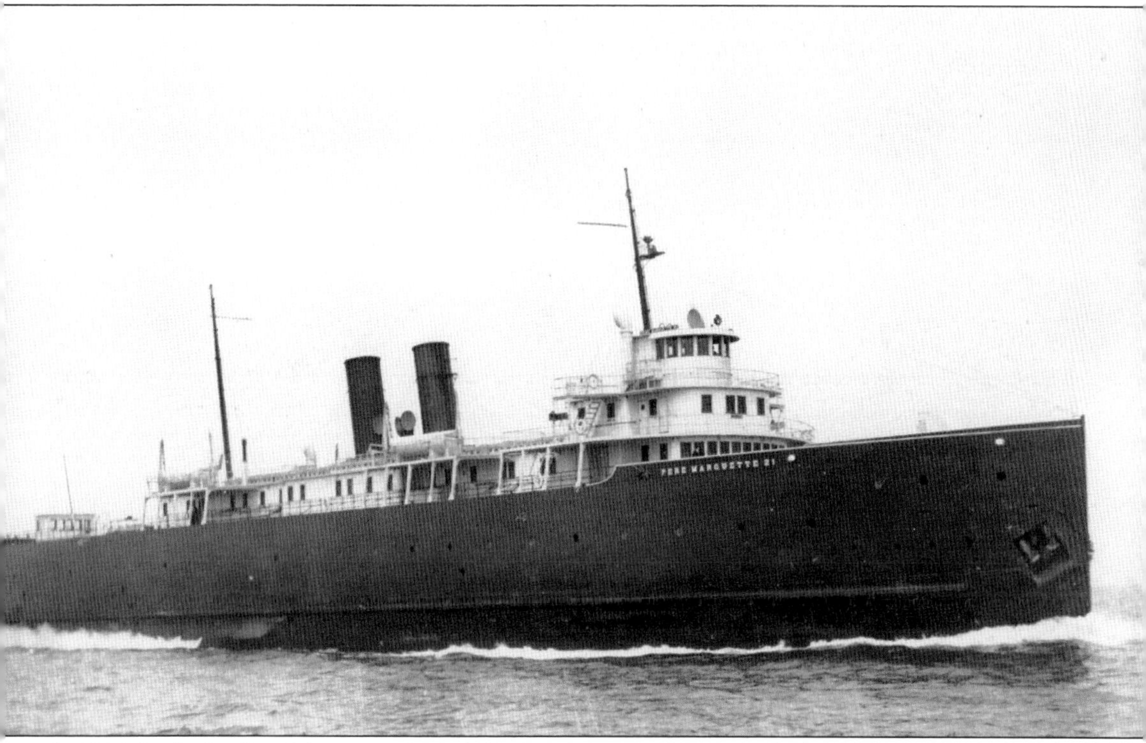

In 1924, both the *Pere Marquette 21* and the *Pere Marquette 22* were built at Manitowoc by the Manitowoc shipbuilding company with limited passenger accommodations. They would however both be refitted and the passenger cabins more than tripled to 40 in 1937. (Photograph by Erhardt Peters, authors collection.)

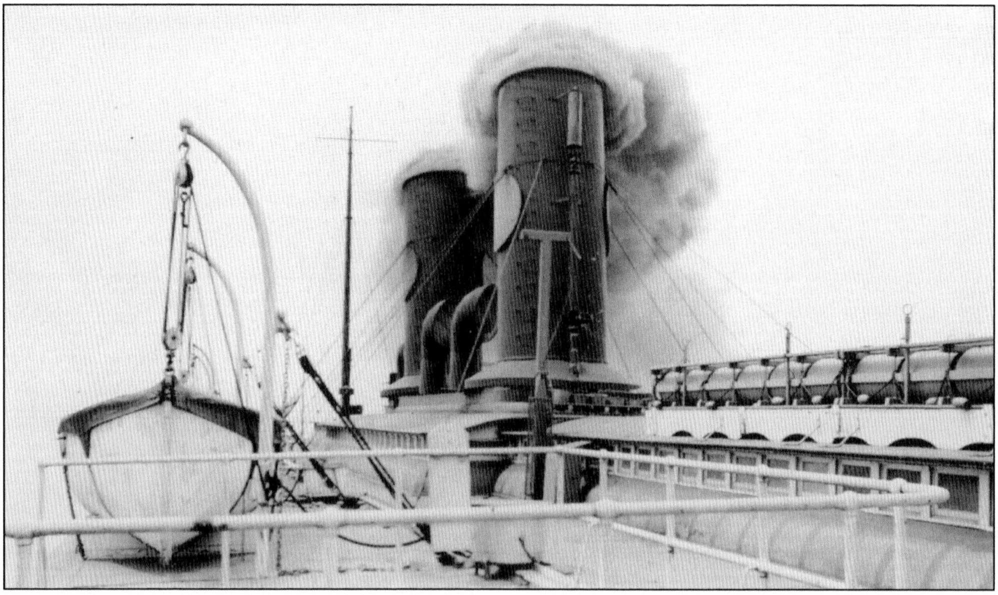

This photograph shows the skylight and smokestack detail of the *Pere Marquette 21*. The *21* and its sister ship, *Pere Marquette 22*, were the first ships in a class of six ferries designed by Manitowoc Shipbuilding Company. They were also the first to attain the operating standard of 14 miles per hour. (Photograph by Erhardt Peters, author's collection.)

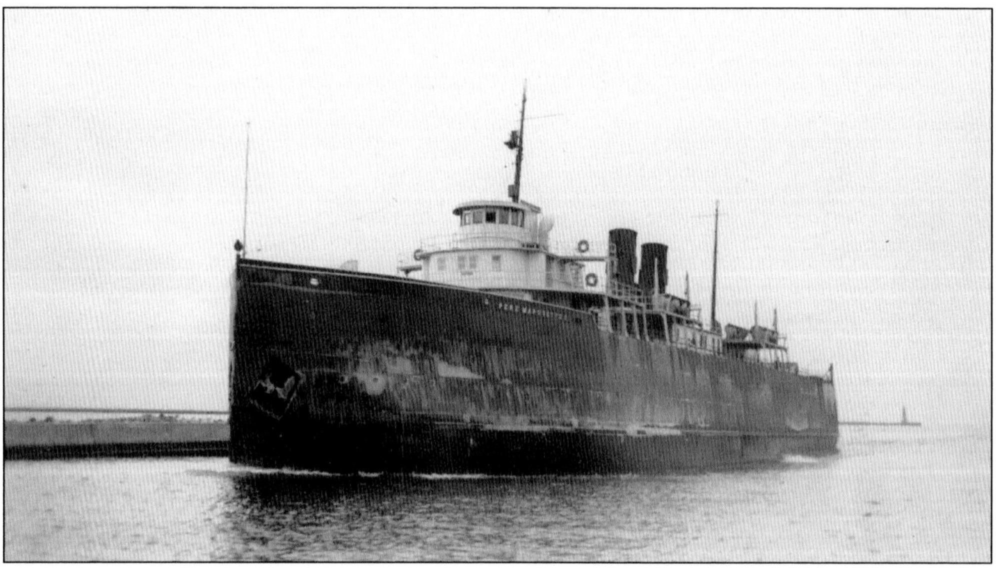

Pere Marquette 21 is shown entering Ludington Harbor after a winter voyage to Wisconsin in the early 1930s. The car ferries and were a major economic force in the city of Ludington and Mason County. During much of the 20th century, there was a constant stream of ships crossing the lakes. The car ferry men like the lumbermen probably never considered that the day would come when it would all change. (Photograph by Erhardt Peters, author's collection.)

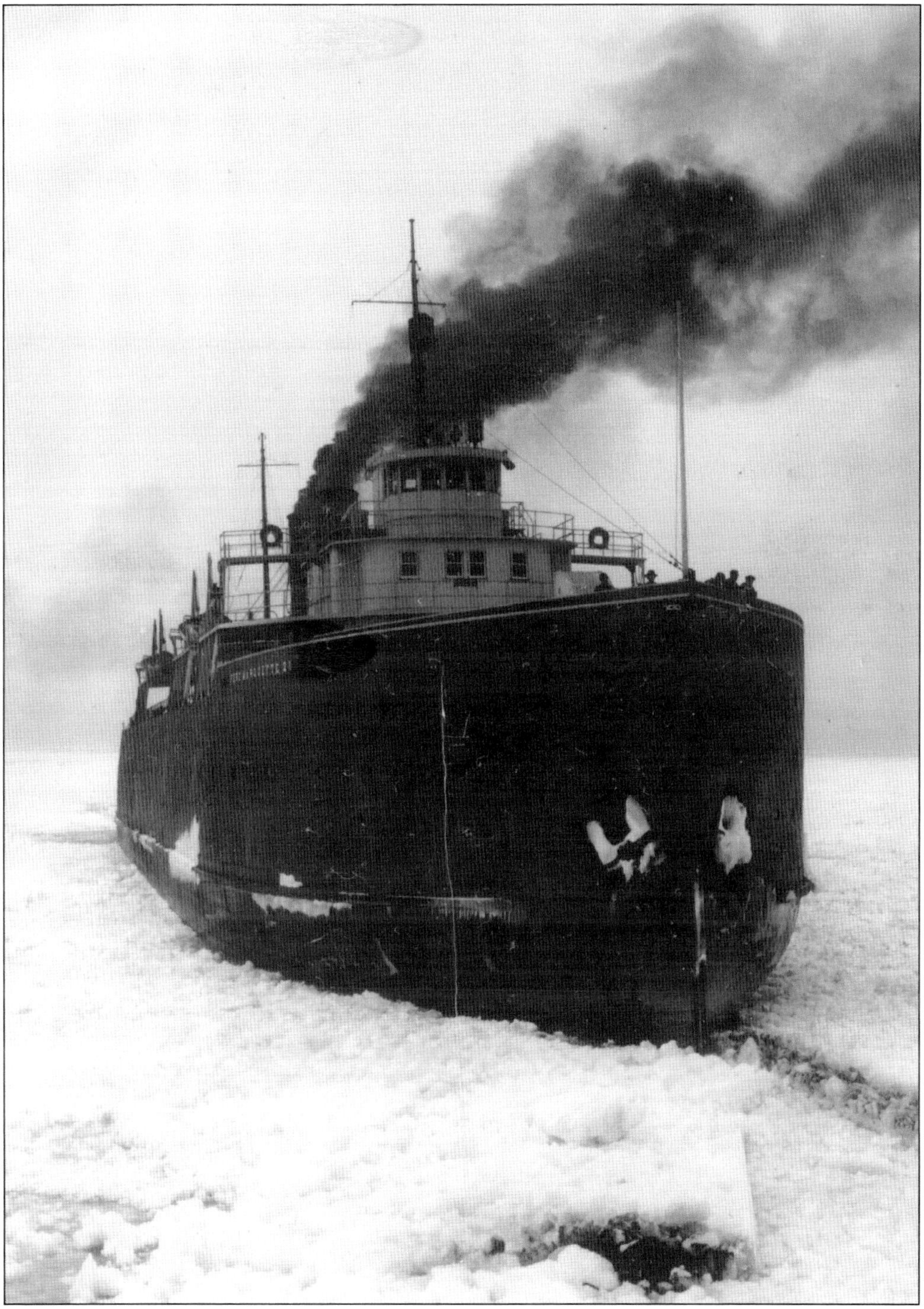

The *Pere Marquette 21*, shown here in a 1930s ice field, was sold in 1973, towed out of Ludington in July 1974, and converted to a barge. The *21* carried the names of *Esgran* and then *Consolidator* before being caught by Hurricane Jean and sunk in 1980 off the Honduras coast. (Photograph by Erhardt Peters, author's collection.)

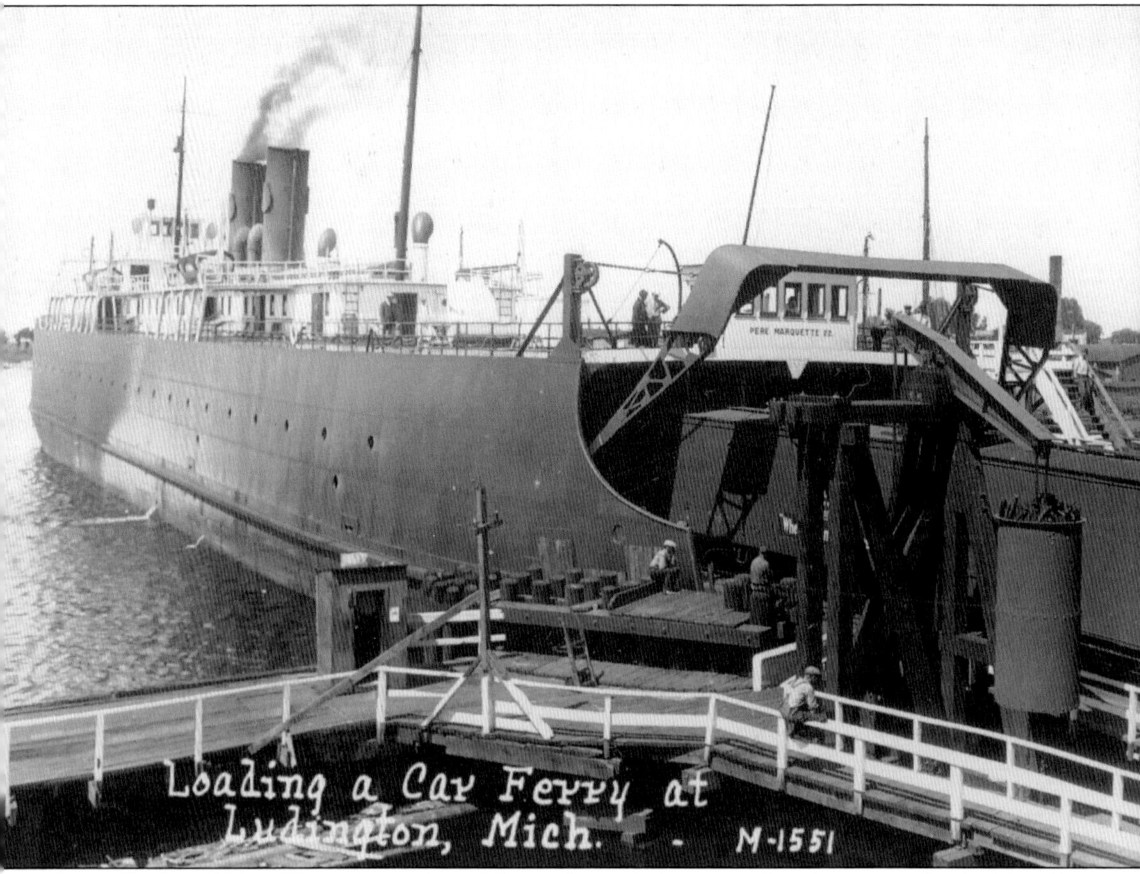

This excellent view is rare in that it shows the *Pere Marquette 22* taking on a load of freight at the North Slip in Ludington during the late 1920s. When a third slip was built in Ludington, this was referred to as Slip No. 1. Many similar views show earlier-generation car ferries from this vantage point. (Author's collection.)

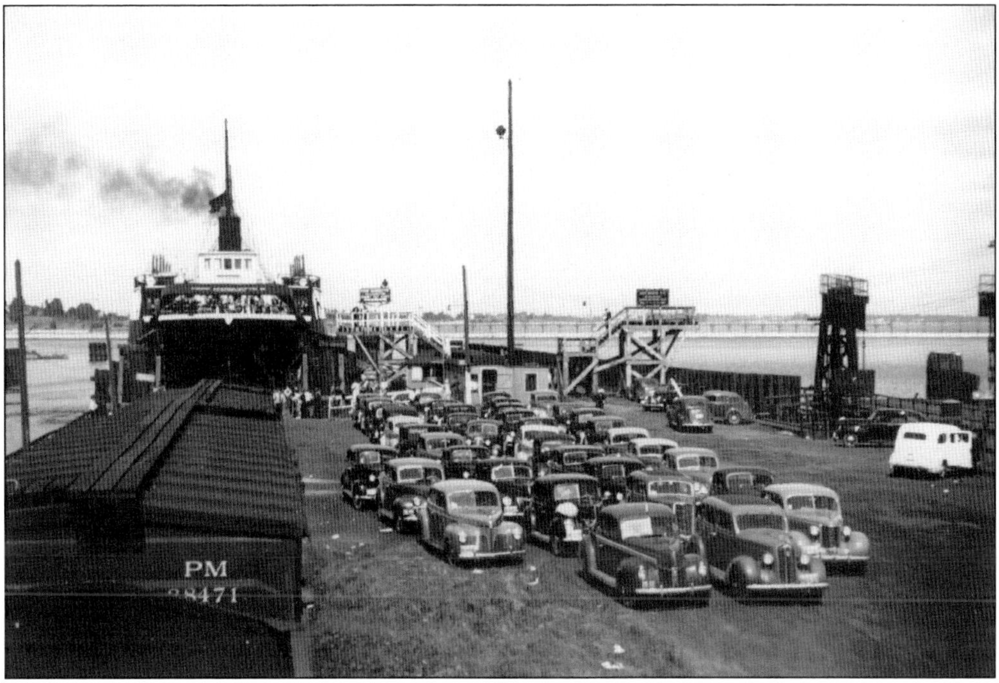

A load of summertime tourists and their automobiles await the switching of a cargo of freight cars at the west Chicago and Northwestern lakefront slip at Manitowoc, Wisconsin. The empty ferry slip on the right was used by the Ann Arbor Railroad fleet. Within an hour, *Pere Marquette 22* will be on its way to Ludington. (Photograph by Erhardt Peters, author's collection.)

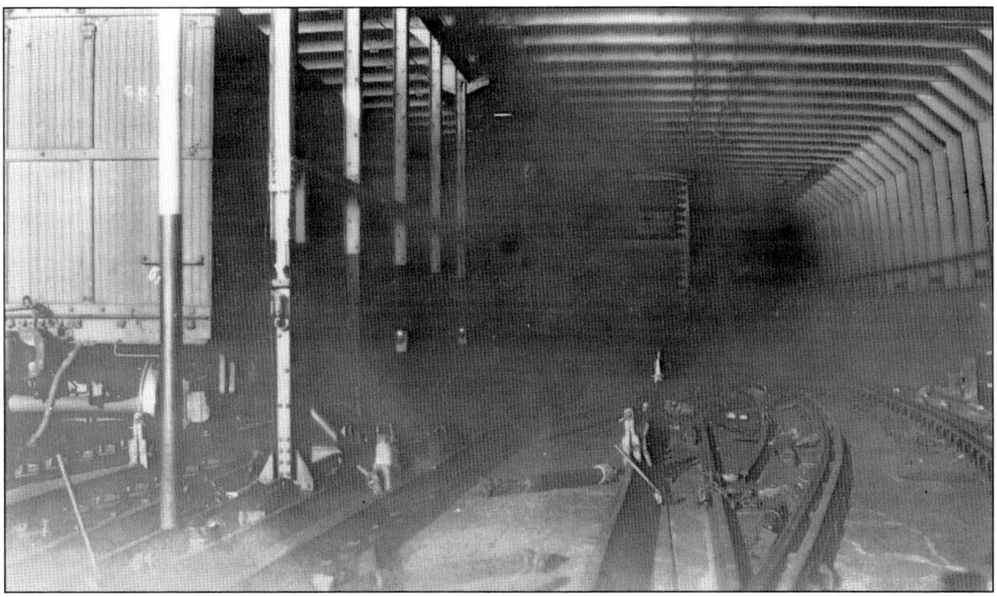

This collection of restraining gear is typical of that used to secure railroad cars to the deck of the car ferries during heavy weather. Clamps were used to prevent the cars from rolling fore and aft, and the screw jacks took some of the weight off the truck springs to prevent the cars from swaying independently from the ship's motion. (Photograph by Erhardt Peters, author's collection.)

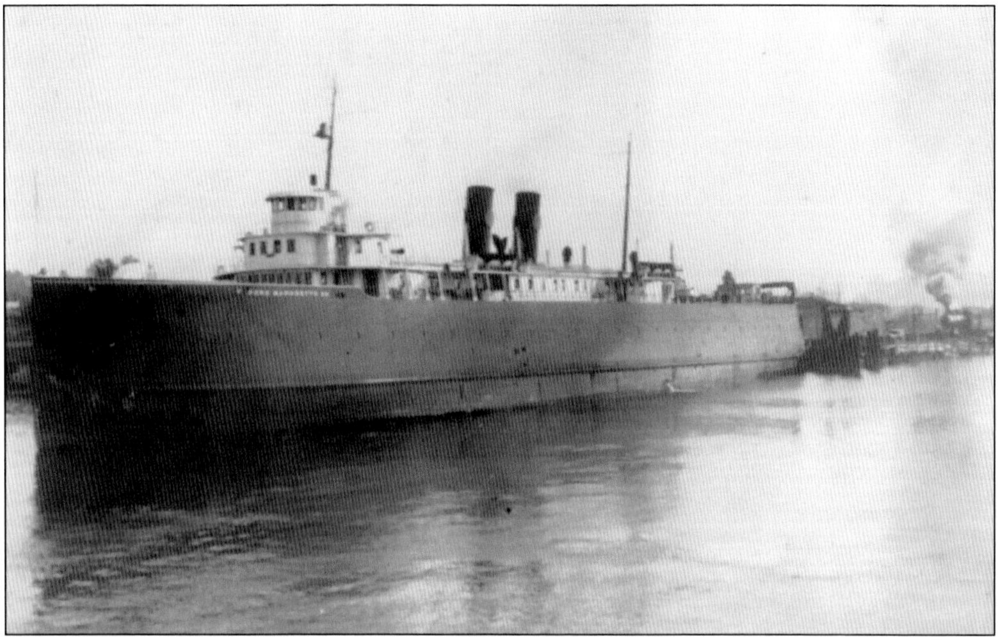

The *Pere Marquette 22* is backed up to the slip at Ludington to take on a load of railcars for the trip to Wisconsin. In the 1930s, a passenger could travel one way to Manitowoc for $2.50 or take a round-trip for $4; the family car could ride one way for $4.50 (Photograph by Erhardt Peters, author's collection.)

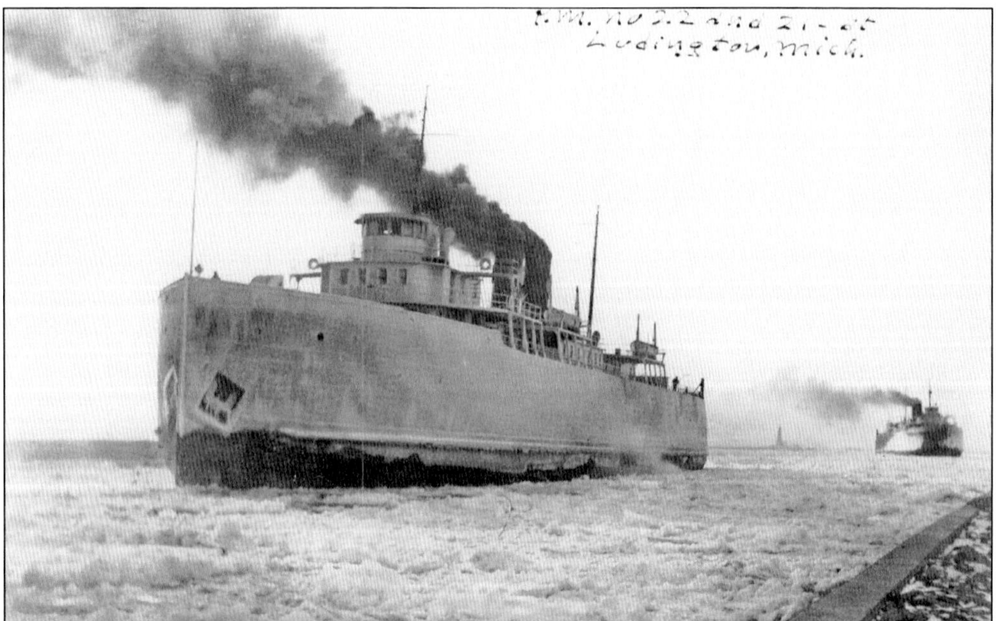

The twin car ferries *Pere Marquette 22* (foreground) and *Pere Marquette 21* are shown entering Ludington Harbor during a cold spell. They are struggling through a field of ice blown into the harbor by westerly winds. (Photograph by Erhardt Peters, author's collection.)

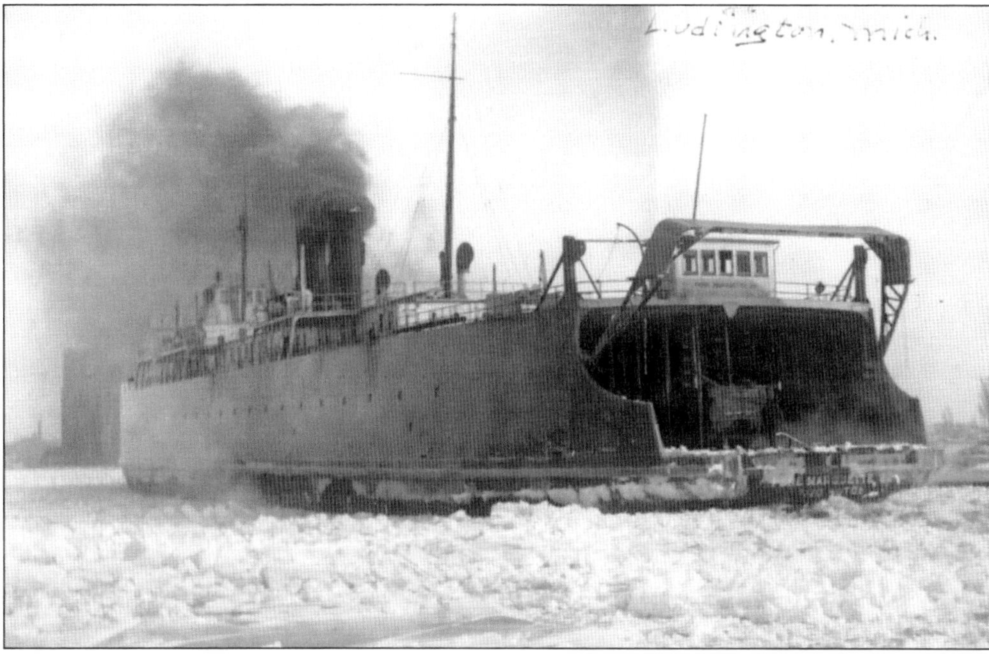

The *22* slowly works its way through a heavy ice field into the harbor at Ludington. To the left of the large grain elevator in the background is where the North Slip was located, right in line with the channel entrance. (Photograph by Erhardt Peters, author's collection.)

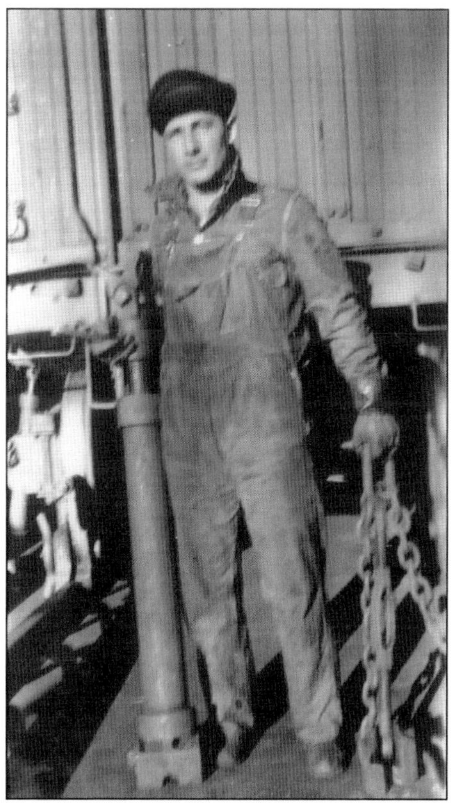

Erhardt Peters proudly displays the tools of his trade while working as a deckhand and car handler aboard the Pere Marquette car ferries. To the left is a 180-pound screw jack, and to the right are a short chain and turnbuckle. (Author's collection.)

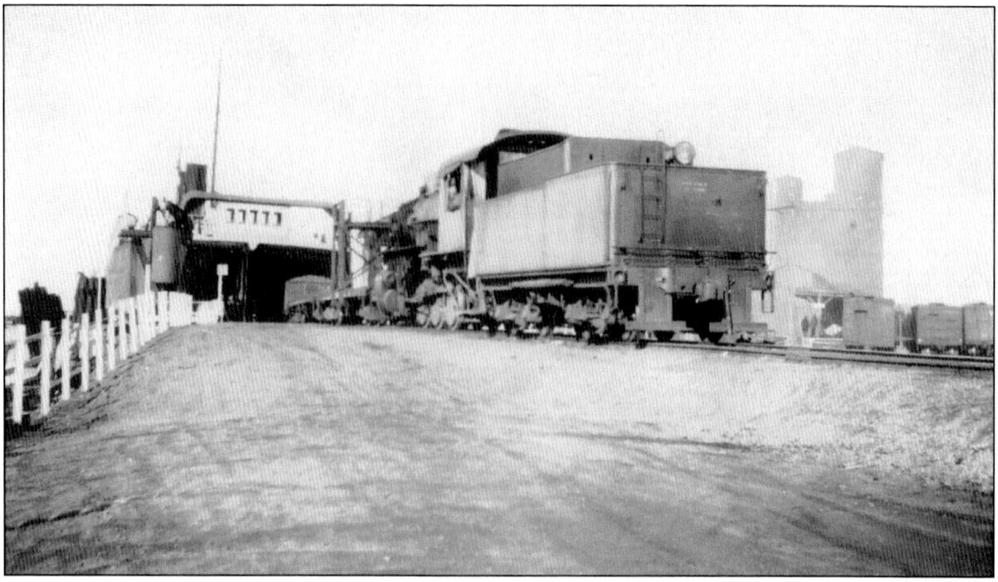

The seagate is up, the *Pere Marquette 22* is taking on a load of freight at the South Slip, later known as Slip No. 2, and the grain shed is to the right. Erhardt started taking pictures in his hometown of Leland, Michigan; his father was the chief engineer of the lightship *Manitou*, which may have influenced his desire to work on the lake. (Photograph by Erhardt Peters, author's collection.)

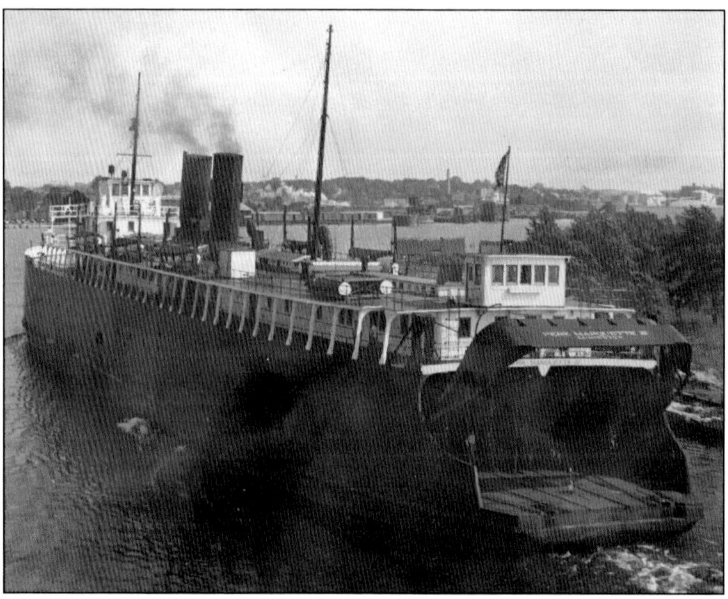

The *22* is shown entering Ludington Harbor after its 1936 cabin alteration, when its staterooms were increased from 12 to 40 rooms to provide more accommodations for the comfort of passengers. At that time, a larger lounge space and passenger dining room was also built. (Photograph by Erhardt Peters, author's collection.)

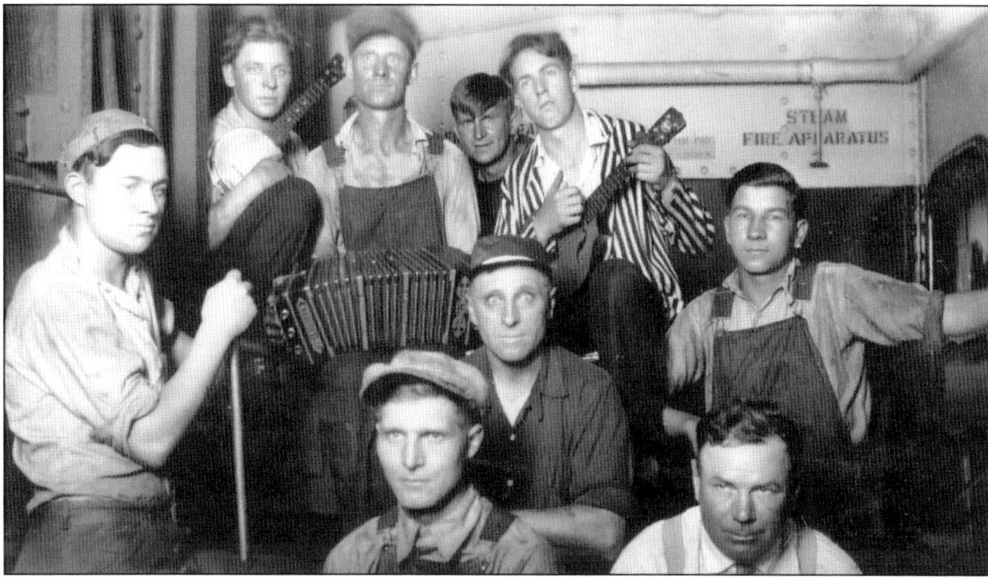

The car ferry crews were a tight-knit group that entertained each other by forming musical bands and boxing events during their off-watch hours. They also had nicknames for each other (such as "Jibber Jabber") that were used so commonly that they sometimes did not know one's given name. (Photograph by Erhardt Peters, author's collection.)

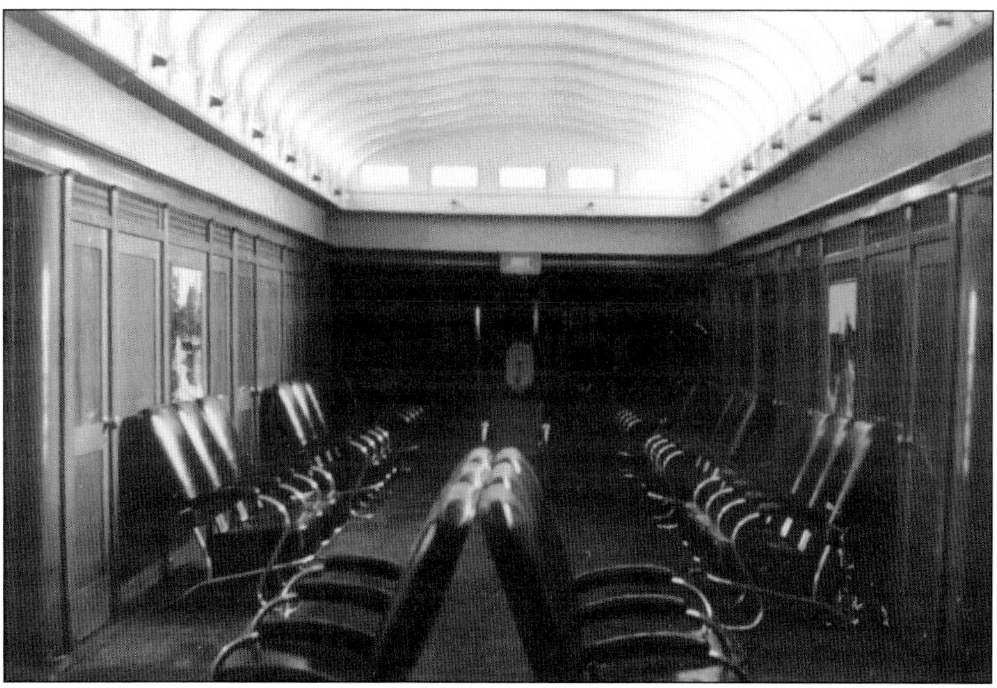

This view shows the main lounge of the *Pere Marquette 22,* where passengers could sit and read or relax on the cross-lake trip. The staterooms opened onto the lounge space, which was illuminated during the daytime by this impressive skylight. (Photograph by Erhardt Peters, author's collection.)

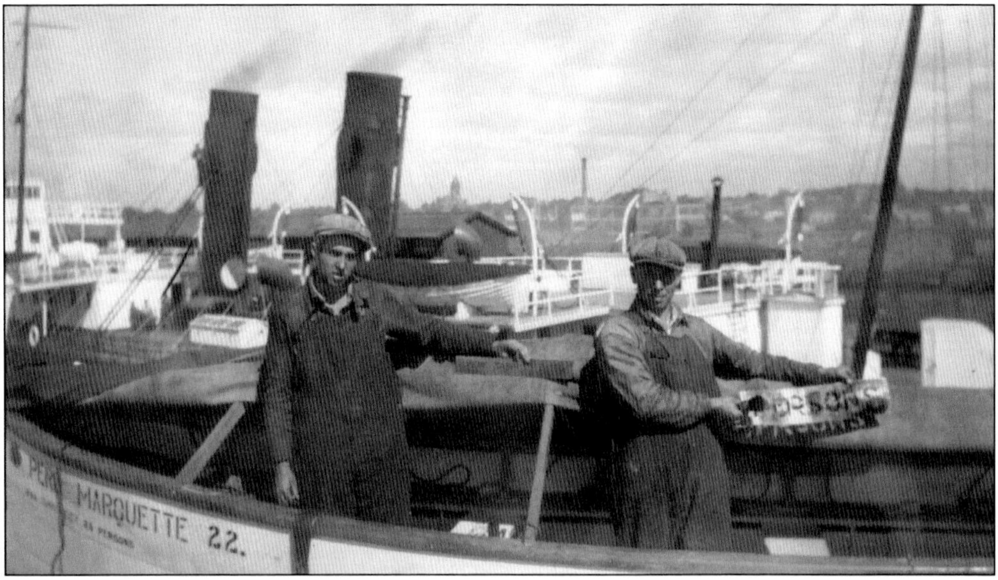

This photograph shows a work detail aboard the *22* labeling lifeboat information with stencils and paint. There were always jobs needing to be done aboard ship that crewmen could do while underway. During those days, shifts ran 21 days on and 7 days off. Crewmen might see family briefly on layovers, but it was a demanding job. (Photograph by Erhardt Peters, author's collection.)

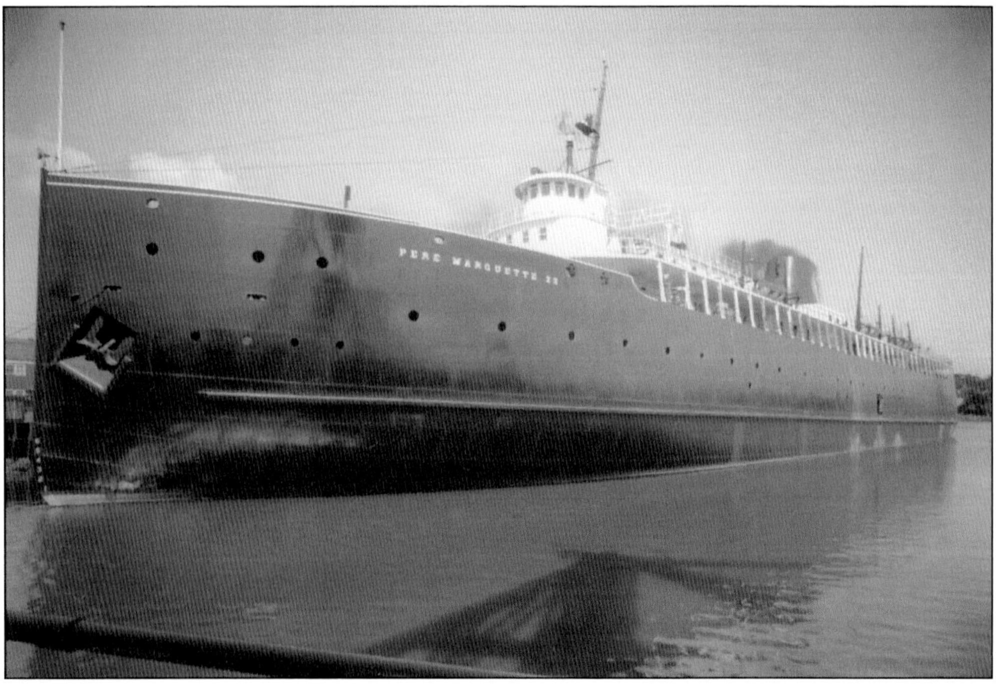

The Pere Marquette 22 and the *PM 21* were brought out together and were retired together in October 1971. The *Pere Marquette 22* was sold in 1973 for service in Panama and in 1978 to Jamaican interests. The *PM 22* was renamed the *Pegasus*, and its final disposition is unknown. (Author's collection.)

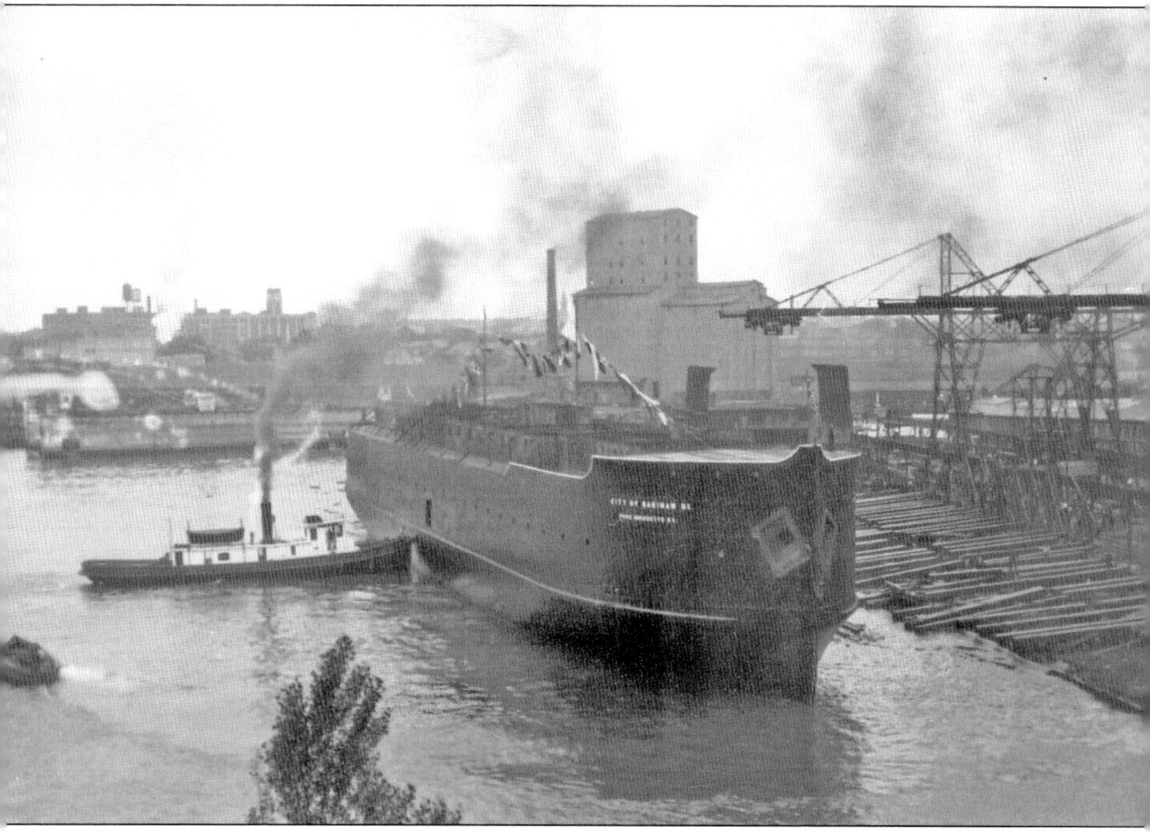

In 1929, the *City of Saginaw* was launched, followed in 1930 by the *City of Flint*. These had new turbo-electric propulsion that allowed them to reach speeds of 18 miles per hour. The *City of Saginaw* was sent to Wisconsin for an overhaul and caught fire while in Manitowoc. The damage was extensive and beyond repair. It was scrapped in 1973. (Author's collection.)

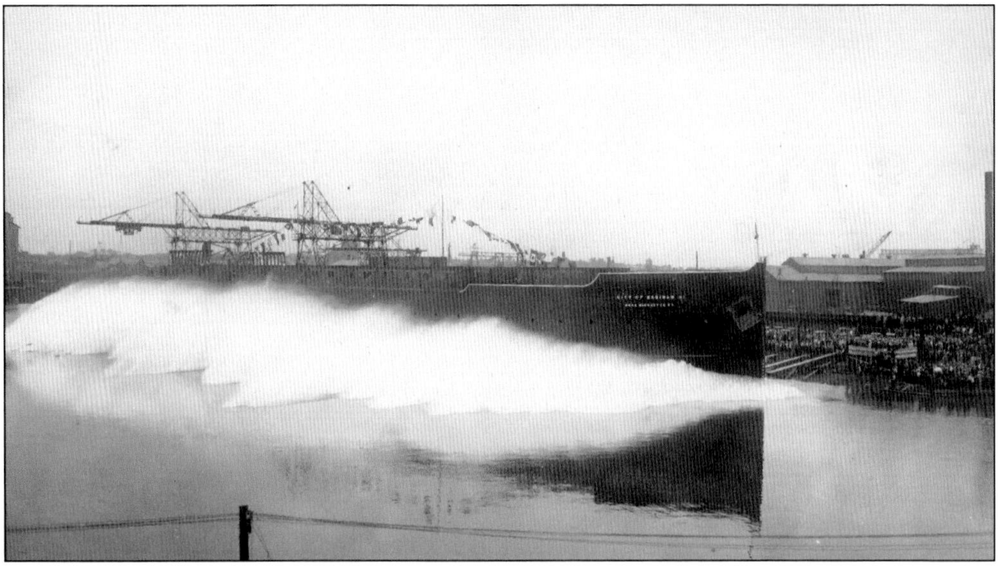

The *City of Saginaw 31* is launched; it was 381 feet in length and 57 feet wide. The *31* was one of the first commercial ships on the Great Lakes equipped with radar. Originally the *PM 23*, the designation was changed in recognition of the new turbo-electric propulsion system. (Photograph by Erhardt Peters, author's collection.)

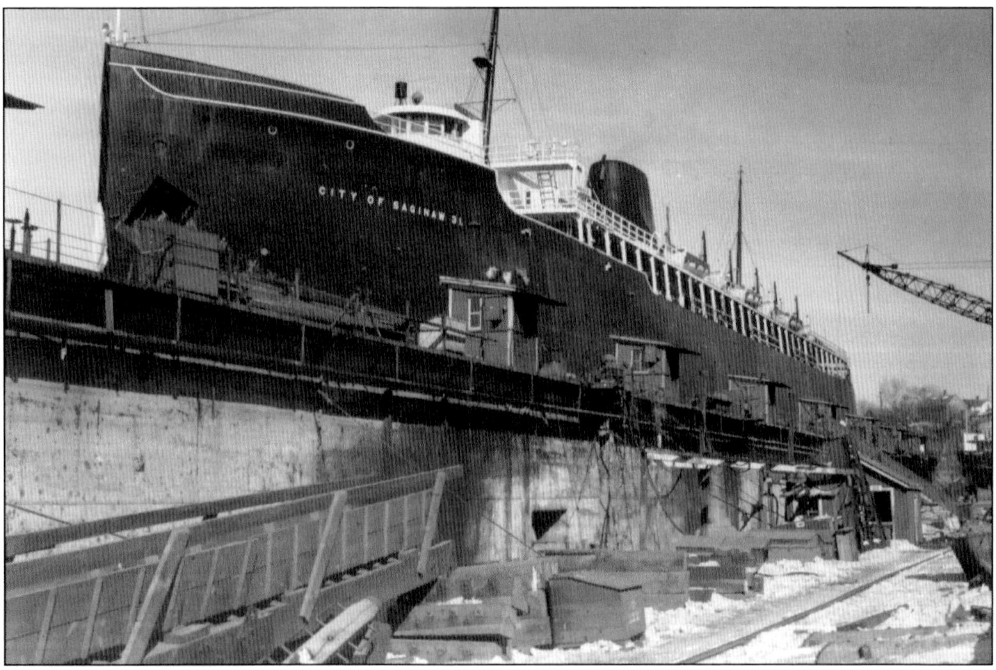

The *City of Saginaw 31* rides high and dry in a floating drydock at Manitowoc Shipbuilding Company during the 1940s. Commercial vessels are required to enter drydock for a thorough hull inspection once every five years to satisfy the safety requirements of the U.S. Coast Guard and the American Bureau of Shipping. (Photograph by Erhardt Peters, author's collection.)

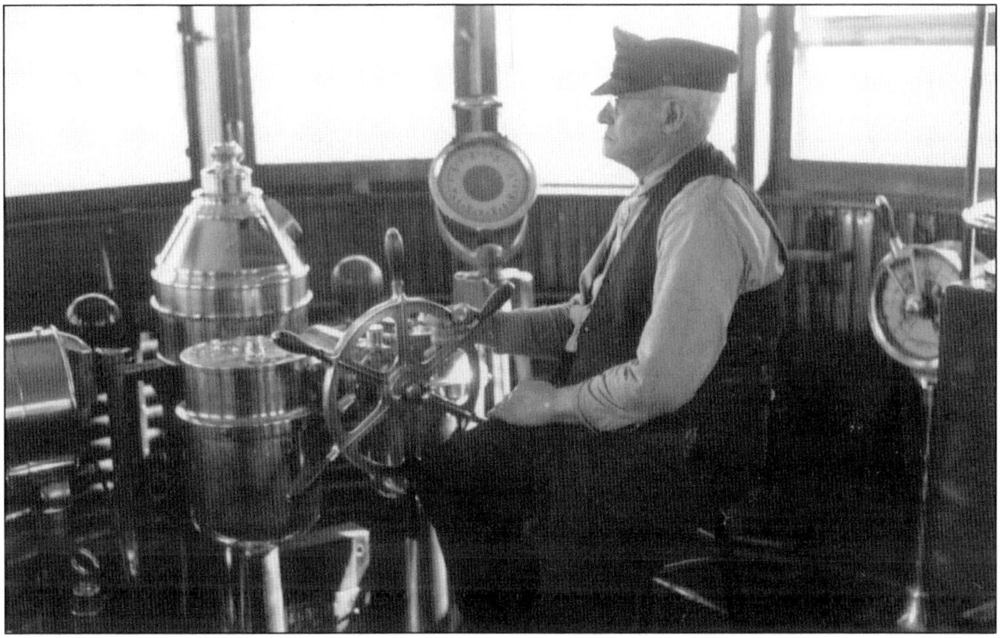

A wheelsman aboard the *City of Saginaw 31* watches the horizon as the newly launched boat steams along at 18 miles an hour. The *PM 31* and *PM 32* had small brass wheels as opposed to the older ships, which had larger wooden wheels in their pilothouses. (Photograph by Erhardt Peters, author's collection.)

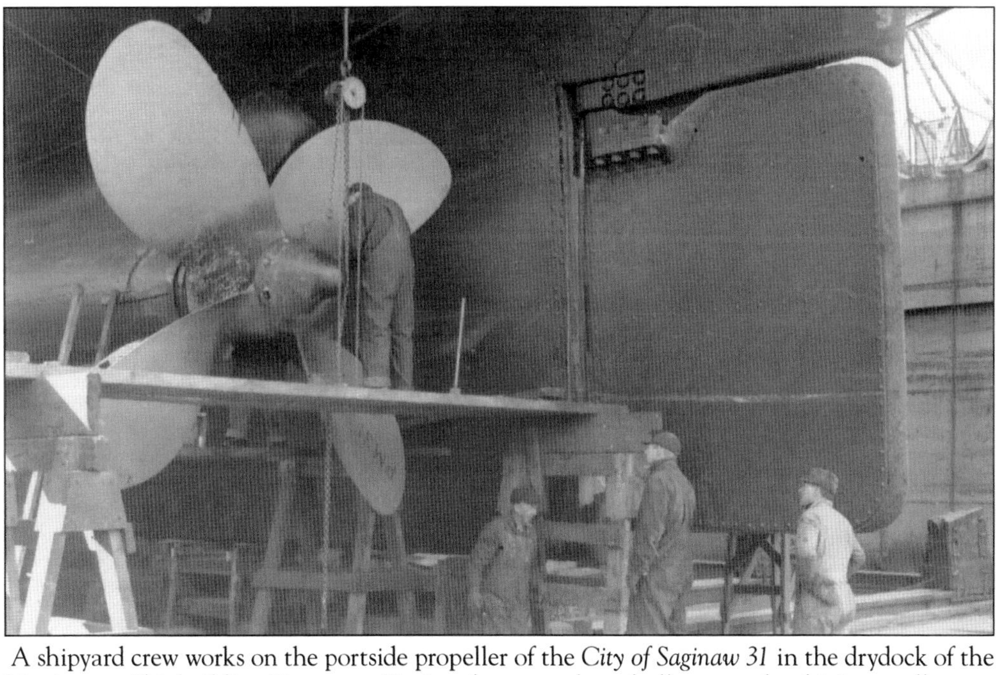

A shipyard crew works on the portside propeller of the *City of Saginaw 31* in the drydock of the Manitowoc Shipbuilding Company. During the compulsory hull survey, the ship's propellers are removed and the tail shafts and bearings inspected for deficiencies and normal wear. Note the size of the propeller and the rudder in comparison to the men inspecting the ship. (Photograph by Erhardt Peters, author's collection.)

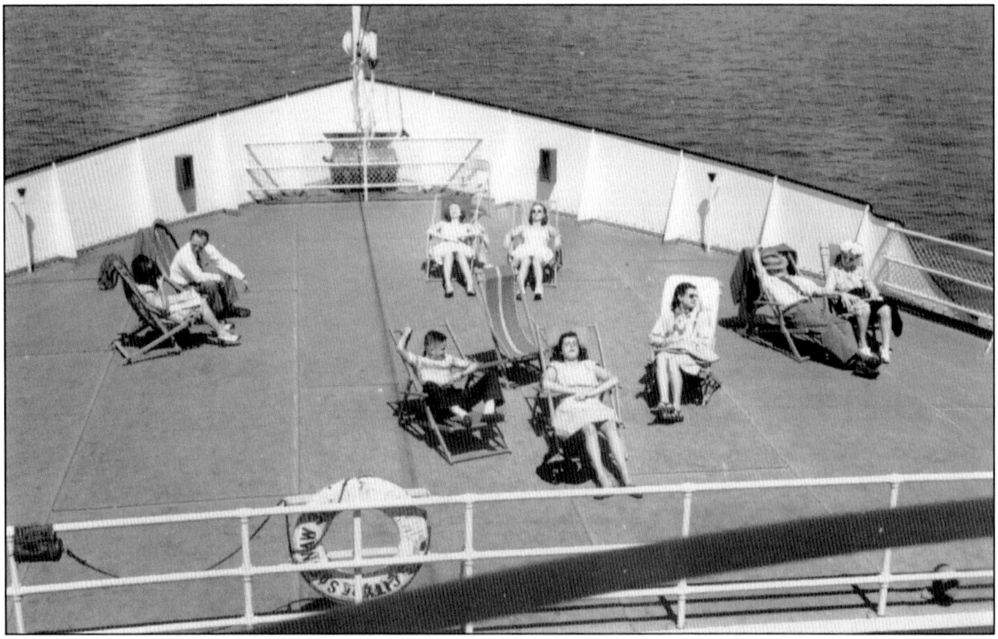

Looking down on the forward deck on a glorious summer day, passengers are enjoying the sun and the waves as they relax in the lounge chairs on the forecastle of the *31*. The Pere Marquette Railway and its successor Chesapeake and Ohio Railroad Company pursued the tourist business more vigorously than any of the other Lake Michigan car ferry operators (Photograph by Erhardt Peters, author's collection.)

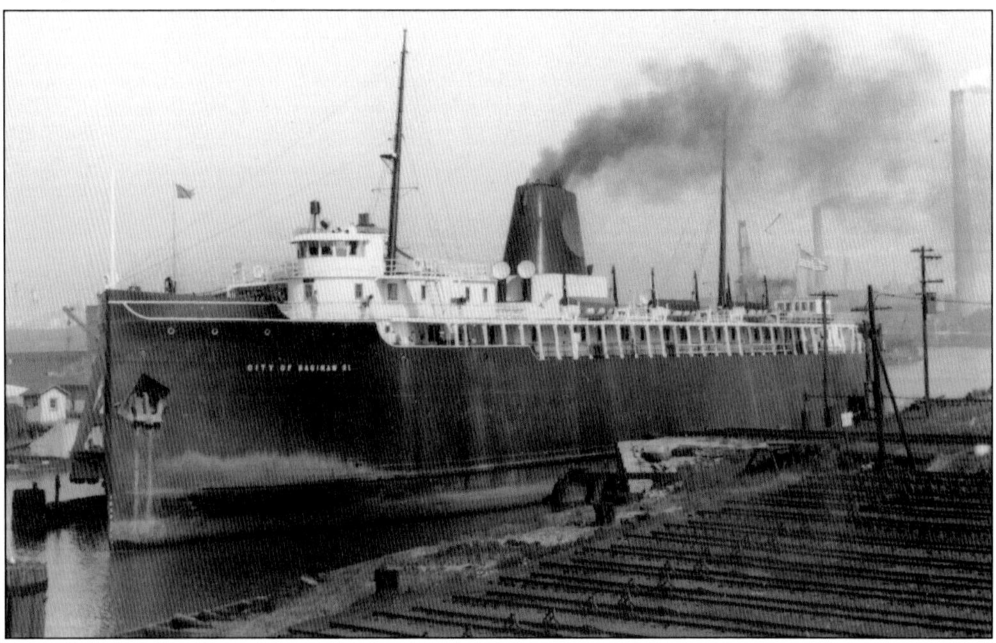

The *31* enters the open span of the Chicago and Northwestern Railroad swing bridge across Milwaukee's Kinnickinnic River on its way to the Maple Street car ferry dock. In 1942, the *City of Flint 32* and the *City of Saginaw 31* were modernized and took on an appearance more in the line of the *City of Midland 41*. (Photograph by Erhardt Peters, author's collection.)

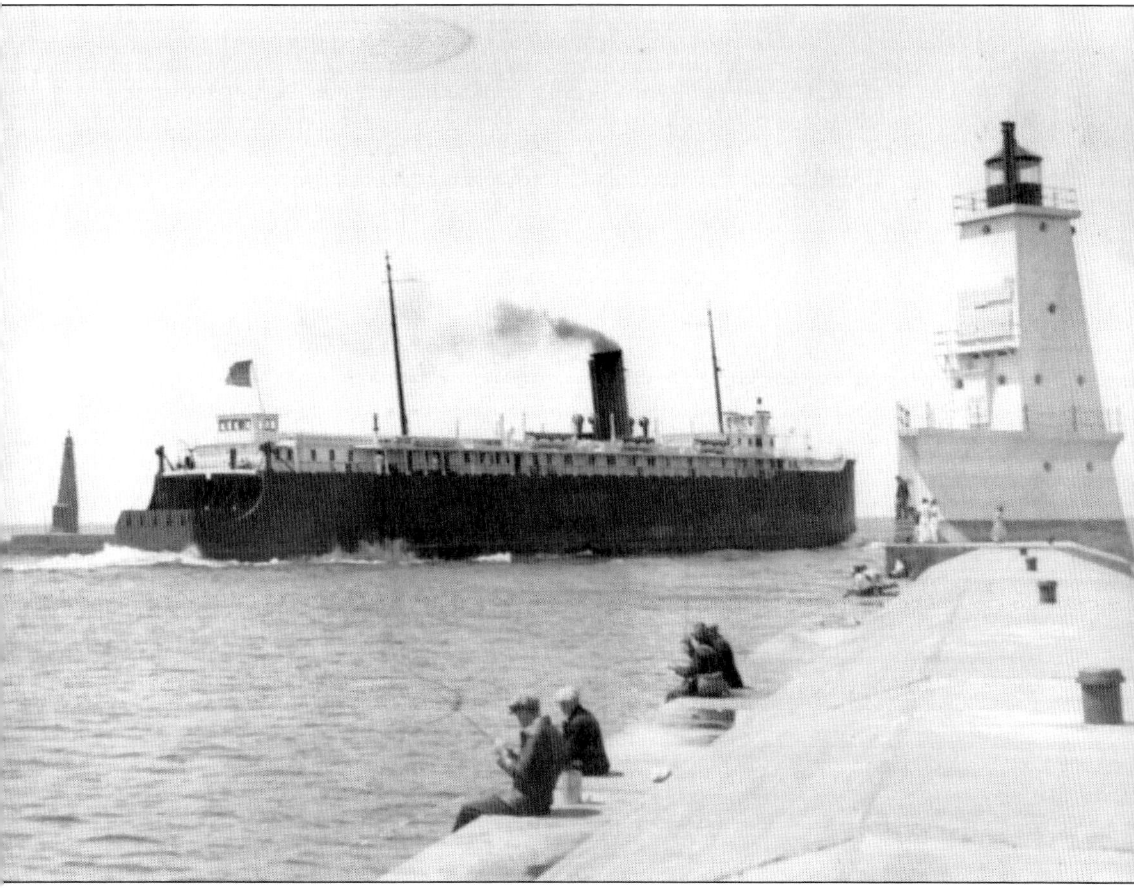

The *City of Flint 32* steams past the north break-wall lighthouse in 1939. Perch fishermen line the break-wall to bring in a stringer of some of the largest and best perch to be found along the lakeshore. Perch were so plentiful during the 1950s that Ludington ran a perch festival in July. (Author's collection.)

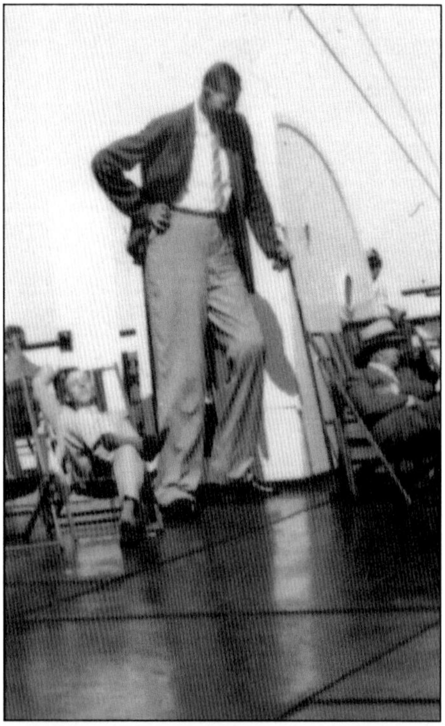

In July 1940, the Pere Marquette car ferries had their biggest passenger, Robert Pershing Wadlow. At 8 feet, 11 inches, the tallest man in the world arrived for his trip over to Ludington on his way to the Manistee Forest Festival. Known as the gentle giant, this young man had spent the previous three years traveling about the country with his father as a representative of the International Shoe Company. (Photograph by Ted Schultz, author's collection.)

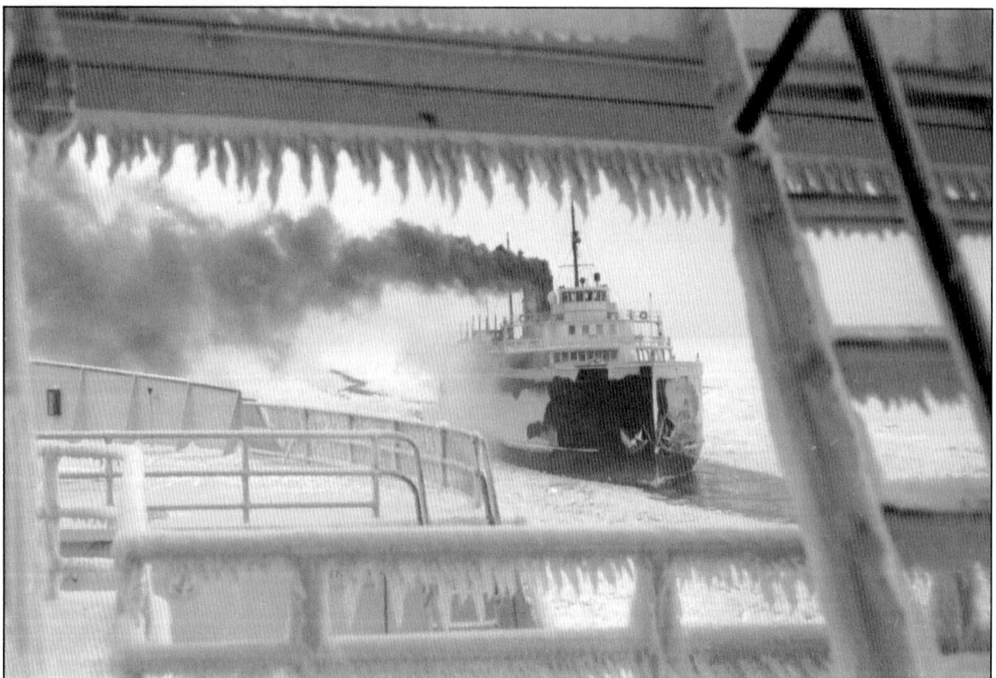

The *City of Flint 32* operated until 1967, was sold in 1969, and was converted to a barge by the Norfolk and Western Railroad. The *PM 31* and *PM 32* were the heart of the car ferry operations out of Ludington for the first part of the 20th century. They made thousands of trips across Lake Michigan carrying freight, families, railcars, and trailers. (Author's collection.)

The wheelhouse of the *City of Flint 32* shines in this picture taken shortly after it was placed in service. The car ferries played an irreplaceable role in the memories and lives of the families who worked the boats and the families who traveled on them. (Photograph by Erhardt Peters, author's collection.)

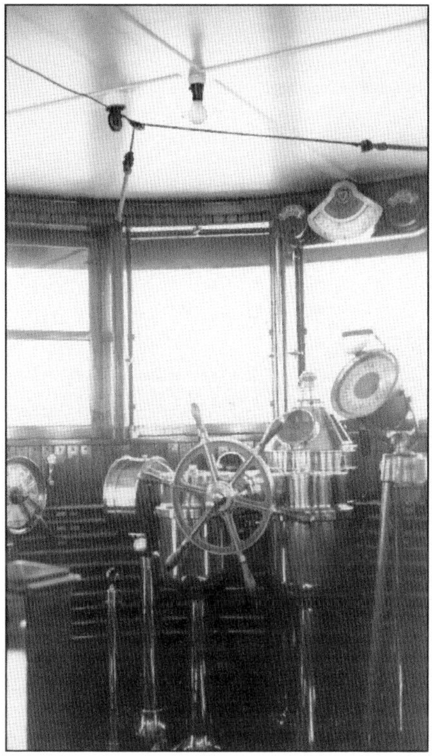

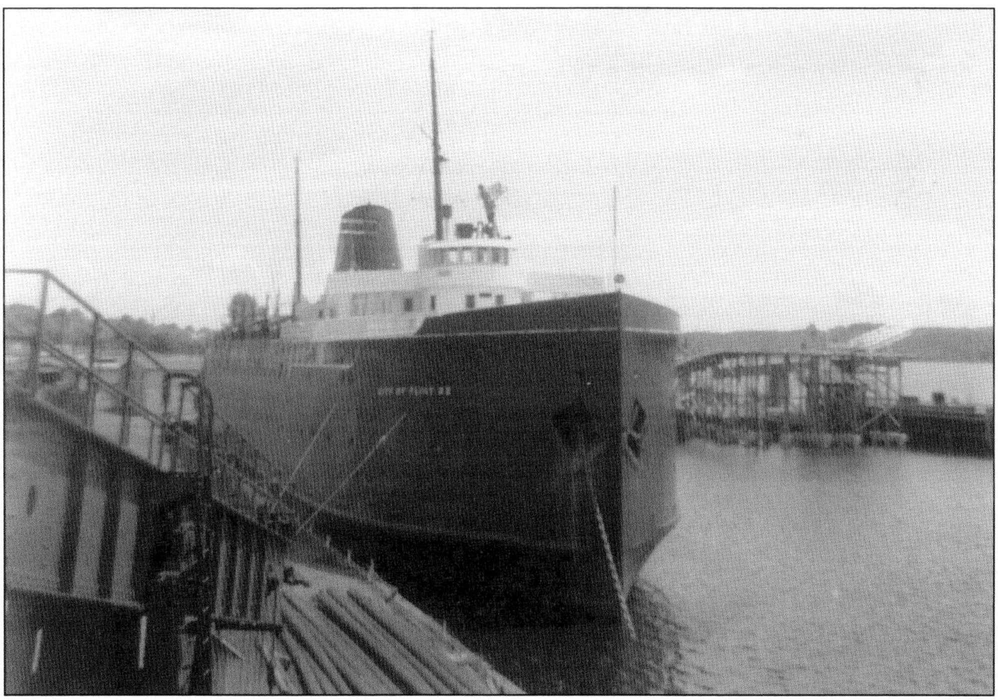

The *City of Flint 32* lies in Ludington's Slip No. 2-1/2, formerly known as Misery Bay. During the peak of operations, the ferries would use this slip for idle periods during annual inspection and minor maintenance. (Photograph by Erhardt Peters, author's collection.)

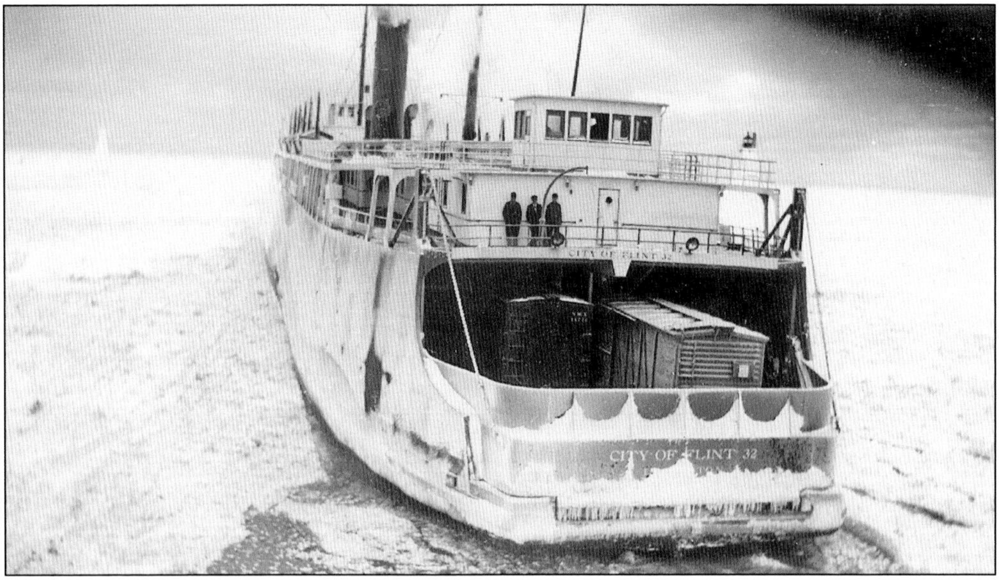

In 1929, after the sinking of the Grand Trunk car ferry *Milwaukee*, extensions to the seagates were added to improve safety, as seen in this view of the *PM 32*. When the wreck of the *Milwaukee* was found, it was discovered that the 5.5-foot seagate was bent in the shape of a "W" and ripped from one of its hinges. (Photograph by Erhardt Peters, author's collection.)

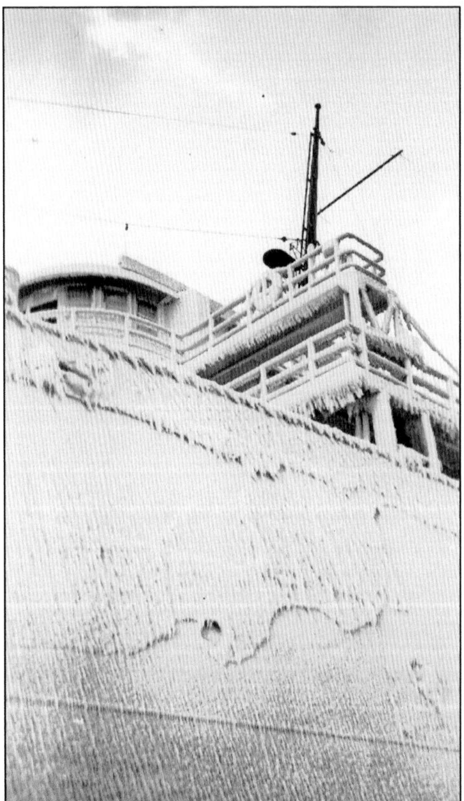

An iced-over *City of Flint 32* shows off the details of the open railings that surrounded the bridge wings and cabin. The *31* and *32* were the last ships constructed with traditional naval architecture such as this. Later ferries had steel plating instead of railings, which created a more modern, streamlined-appearing ship. (Photograph by Erhardt Peters, author's collection.)

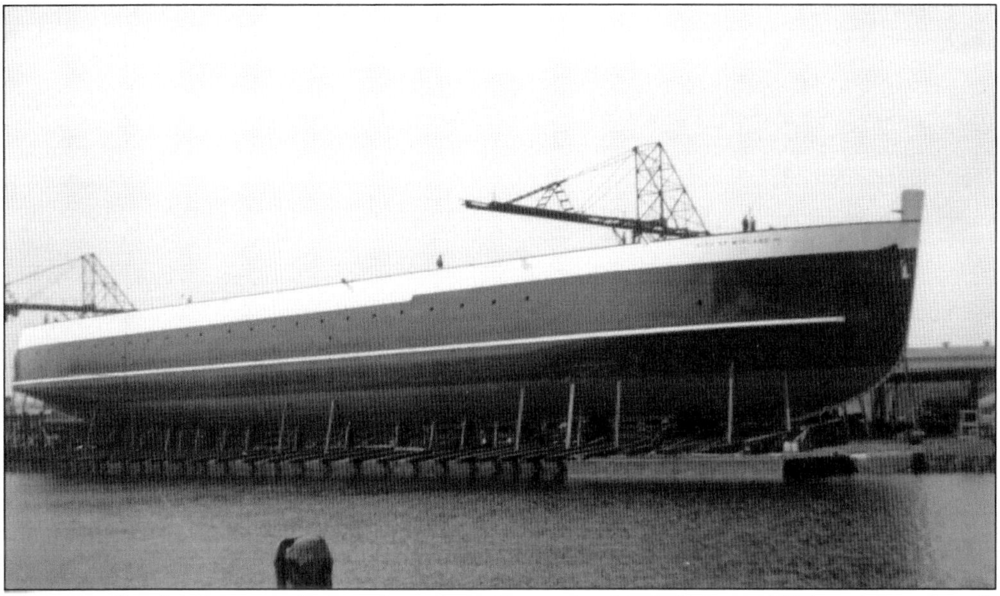

The *City of Midland 41* is ready for its launch on September 18, 1941. It was 406 feet in length with a beam of 52.2 feet. There were 60 staterooms, and the *Midland* was built at a cost of $2 million. The *Midland* was considered one of the finest car ferries ever built to serve on the Great Lakes. The creation of this ship marked a turning point in the modern era for the Lake Michigan car ferry fleet. (Photograph by Harold Holmes, author's collection.)

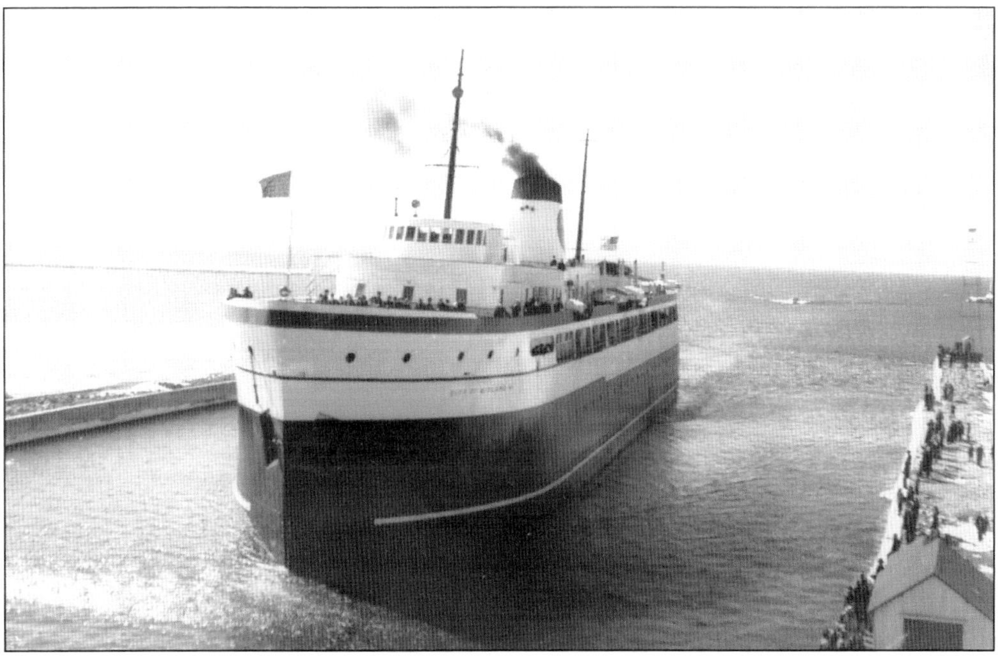

Schools and stores were closed in anticipation of the arrival of the new flagship the *City of Midland*, in command of Capt. Charles Robinson. Crowds were estimated to be in the range of 10,000 people on that Wednesday afternoon. As the *Midland* came through the channel, it was first greeted by the foghorn and then by a series of signal flags before being escorted by the Ludington Coast Guard. (Photograph by Harold Holmes, author's collection.)

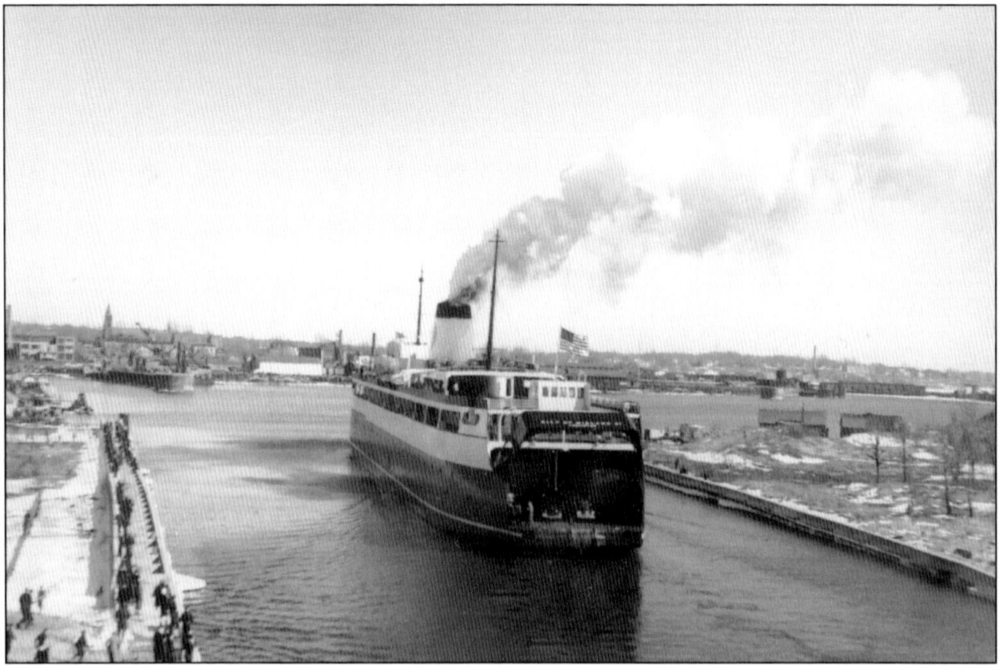

The *City of Midland* passes the lookout tower at the U.S. Coast Guard station, where Harold Holmes and other photographers have awaited its arrival. The stack is painted white, but after a couple of months, it was not possible to keep the stack clean, and it was painted black. (Photograph by Harold Holmes, author's collection.)

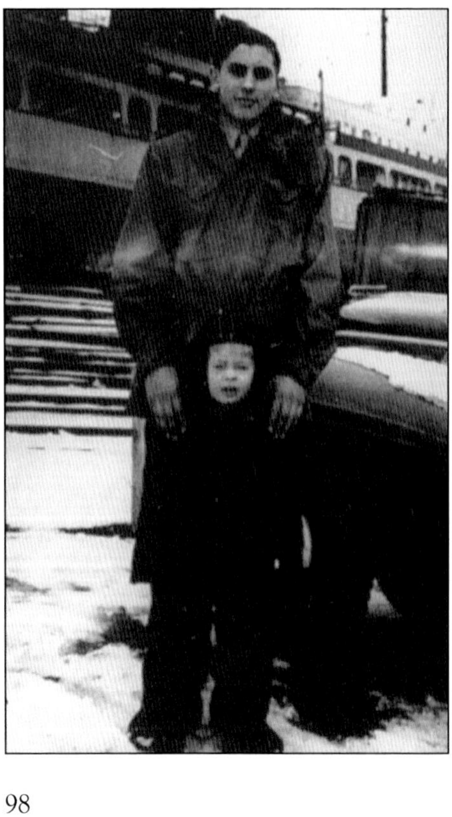

Richard Petersen is shown here with his young cousin Kirk Williamson as he prepares to leave aboard the *City of Midland 41* for training camp in Wisconsin in 1944. The car ferries provided an opportunity for training on the Great Lakes during this time of war. The *41* remained in service until 1967. (Author's collection.)

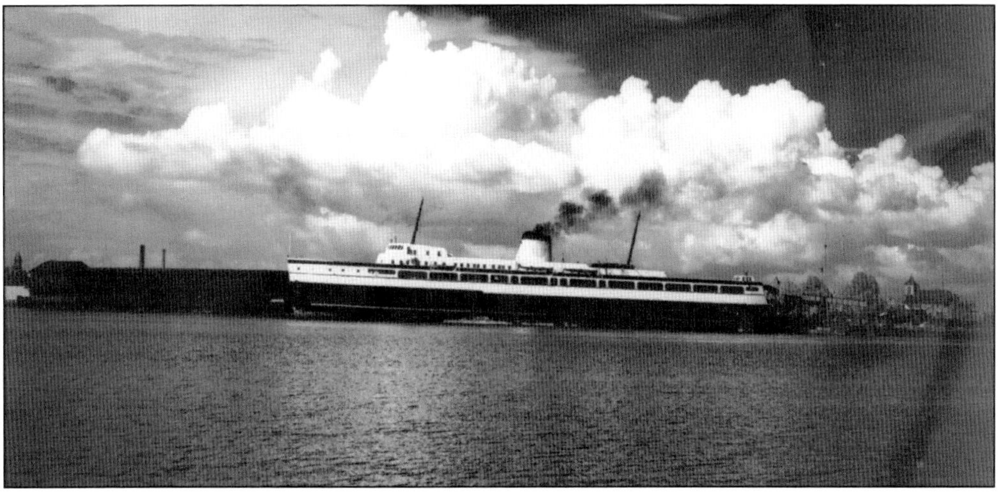

The *City of Midland* is framed against a magnificent background of cloud cover after its maiden voyage by Captain Robertson. The Holmes Studio housed several decades of magnificent photographs from a talented photographer. Unfortunately the studio caught fire in 1956, and most of the archives were lost. (Photograph by Harold Holmes, author's collection.)

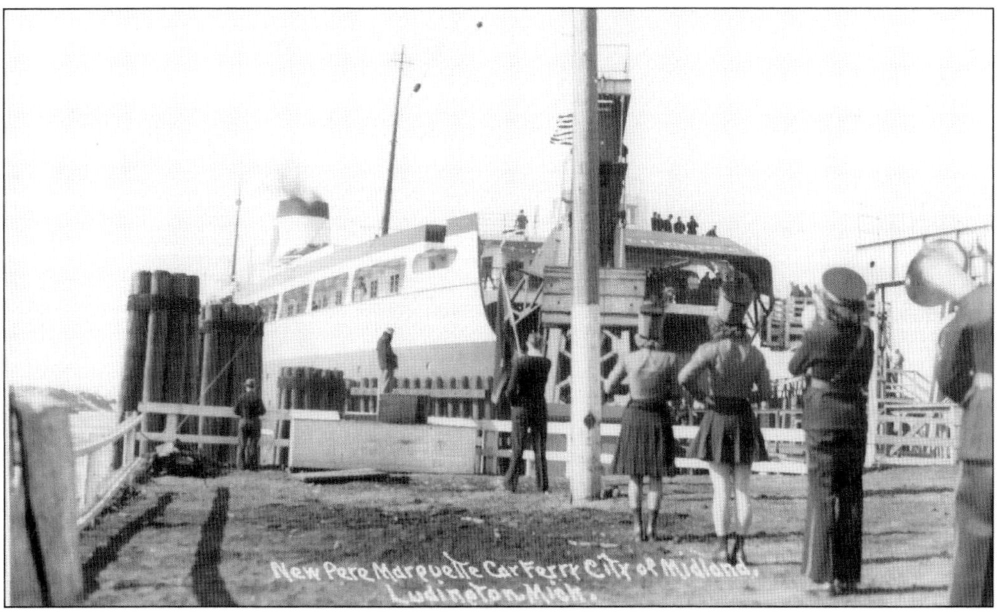

It was indeed a noisy welcome for the *City of Midland 41*, as every factory with a whistle, tugboat, and locomotive within earshot joined the welcome to the cheers of the thousands of people who lined the channel entrance. The Ludington High School Band was also at the dock to serenade the arrival of this new $2-million addition to the car ferry fleet. (Photograph by Harold Holmes, author's collection.)

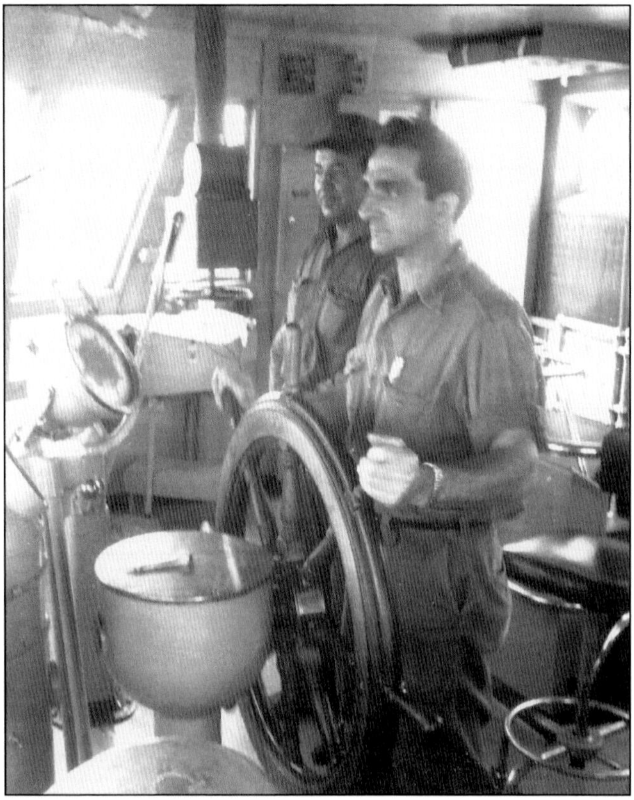

Frank Tavolocci documented different eras of the development of the car ferry service in Ludington. Frank, a longtime car ferry man, is at the wheel of the *41* about 1950. (Photograph by Frank Tavolocci, courtesy of James F. Fay.)

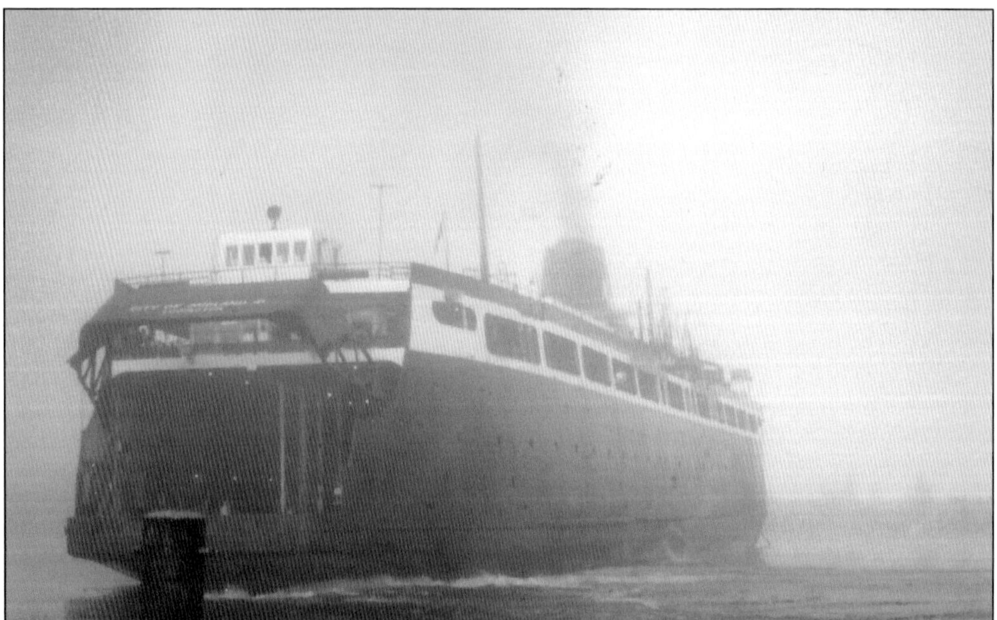

The *City of Midland 41* backs into the dock at Ludington in a shroud of fog. There were few options for the *41* to continue working on Lake Michigan. The decision was made to cut it down into a barge in 1997 for a new company by the name of PM Shipping, Inc. (Author's collection.)

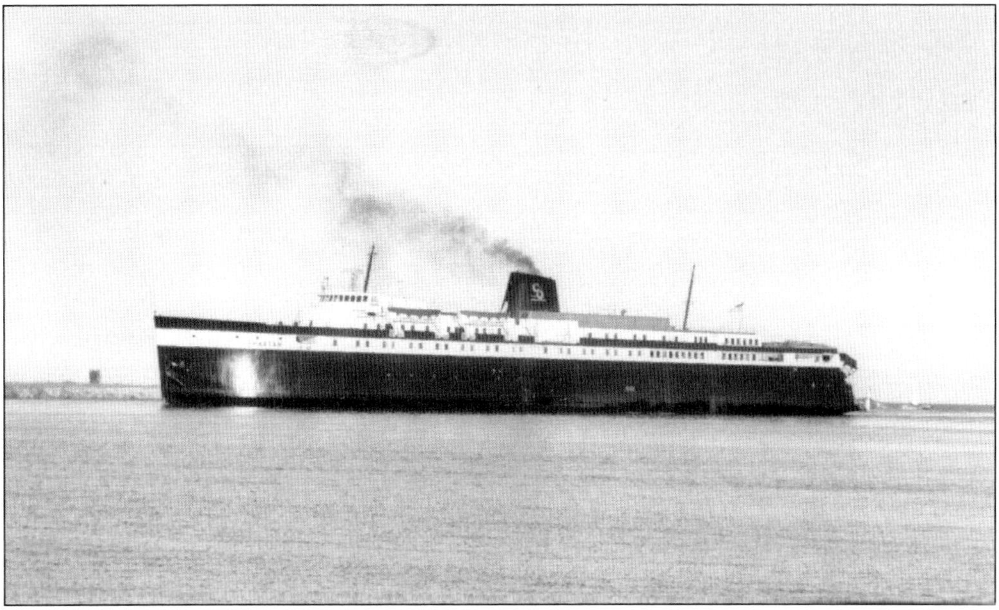

Arriving from Milwaukee, the *Spartan* makes the turn on its way to Slip No. 3 on Ludington's Pere Marquette Lake. The *Spartan* and its sister ship, *Badger*, were the last new car ferries built for service on Lake Michigan. (Author's collection.)

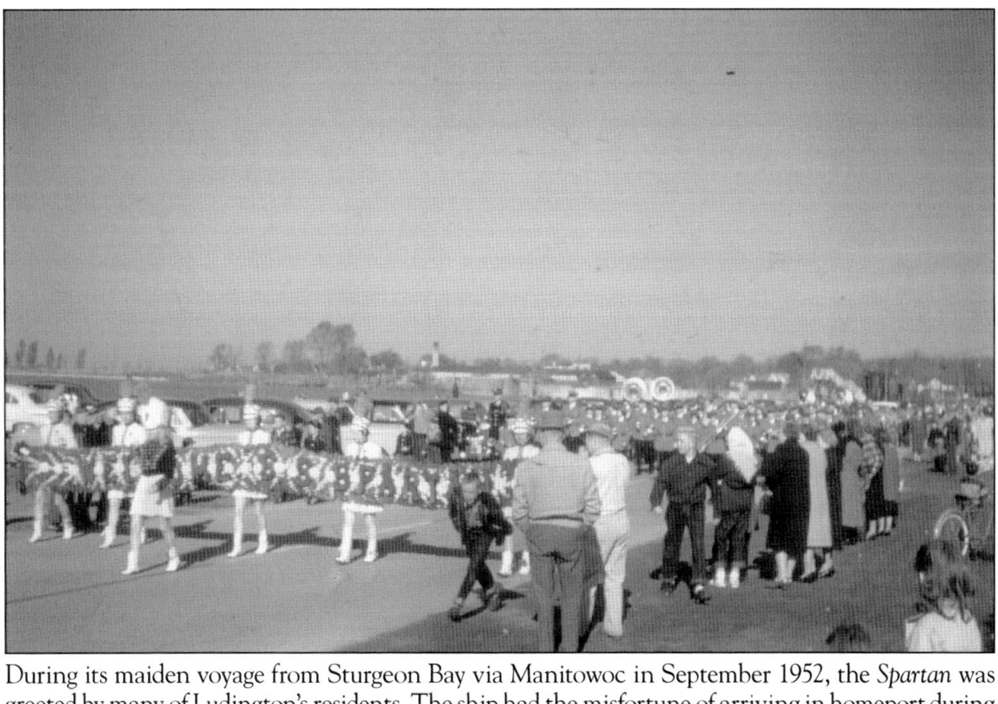

During its maiden voyage from Sturgeon Bay via Manitowoc in September 1952, the *Spartan* was greeted by many of Ludington's residents. The ship had the misfortune of arriving in homeport during the end of a summer-long labor strike by licensed officers aboard the ferries. (Author's collection.)

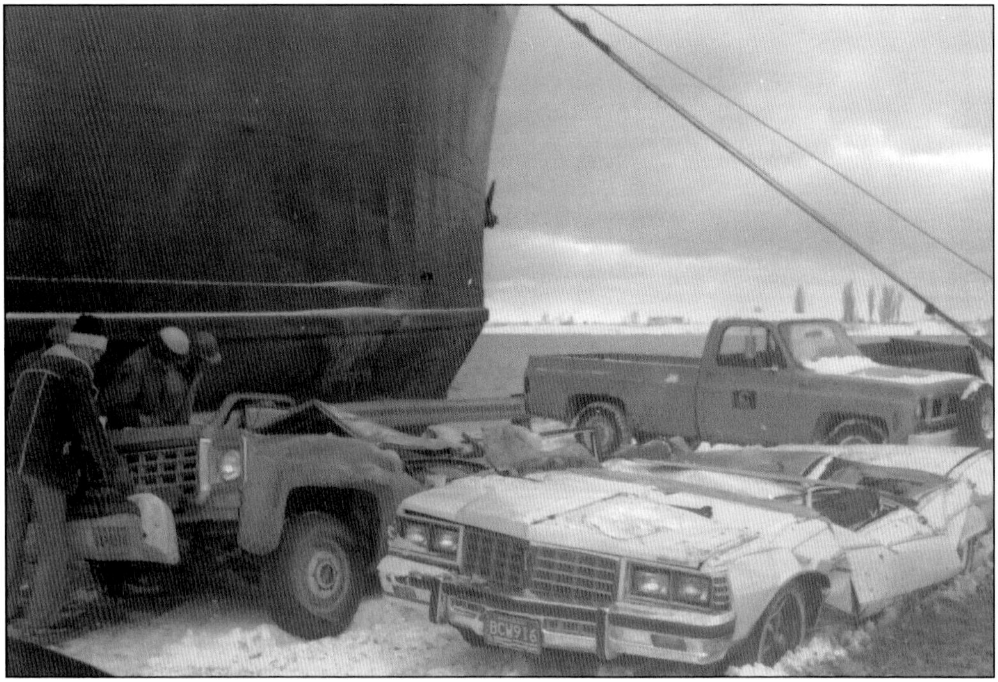

This scene shows two vehicles that were crushed by a railcar of calcium chloride that fell over in heavy seas on the aft car deck of the *Spartan*. No one was hurt, but the cars were a total loss. Such damage was rare but not unheard of. (Author's collection.)

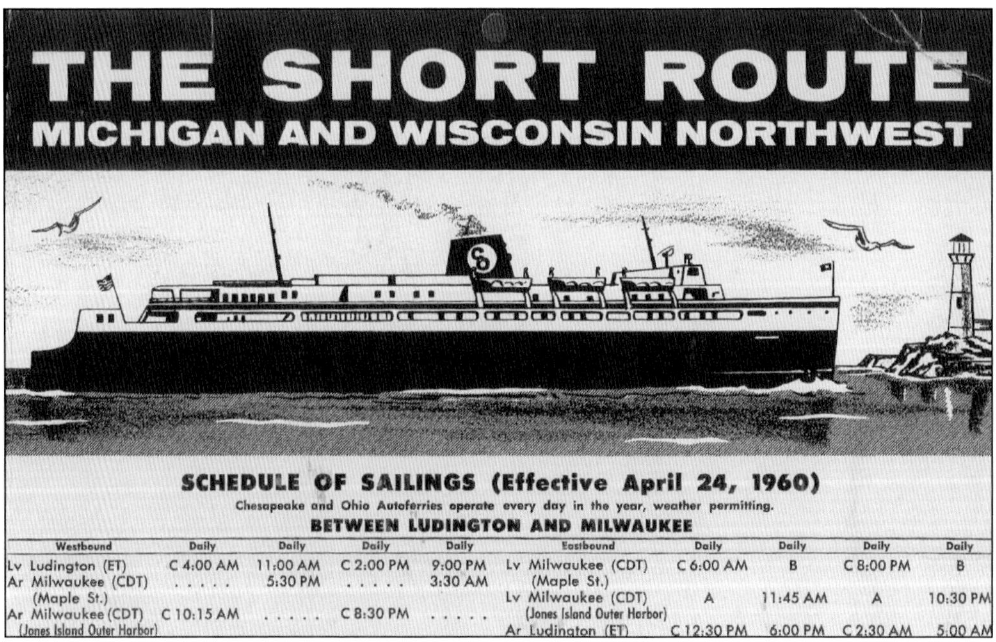

THE SHORT ROUTE

MICHIGAN AND WISCONSIN NORTHWEST

SCHEDULE OF SAILINGS (Effective April 24, 1960)

Chesapeake and Ohio Autoferries operate every day in the year, weather permitting.

BETWEEN LUDINGTON AND MILWAUKEE

Westbound	Daily	Daily	Daily	Daily
Lv Ludington (ET)	C 4:00 AM	11:00 AM	C 2:00 PM	9:00 PM
Ar Milwaukee (CDT) (Maple St.)	. . . . .	5:30 PM	. . . . .	3:30 AM
Ar Milwaukee (CDT) (Jones Island Outer Harbor)	C 10:15 AM	. . . . .	C 8:30 PM	. . . . .

Eastbound	Daily	Daily	Daily	Daily
Lv Milwaukee (CDT) (Maple St.)	C 6:00 AM	B	C 8:00 PM	B
Lv Milwaukee (CDT) (Jones Island Outer Harbor)	A	11:45 AM	A	10:30 PM
Ar Ludington (ET)	C 12:30 PM	6:00 PM	C 2:30 AM	5:00 AM

This 1960 Chesapeake and Ohio car ferry timecard shows four scheduled sailings daily between Ludington and Milwaukee. Ferries were dispatched as freight demanded on an unscheduled basis as well between all ports throughout the year. (Author's collection.)

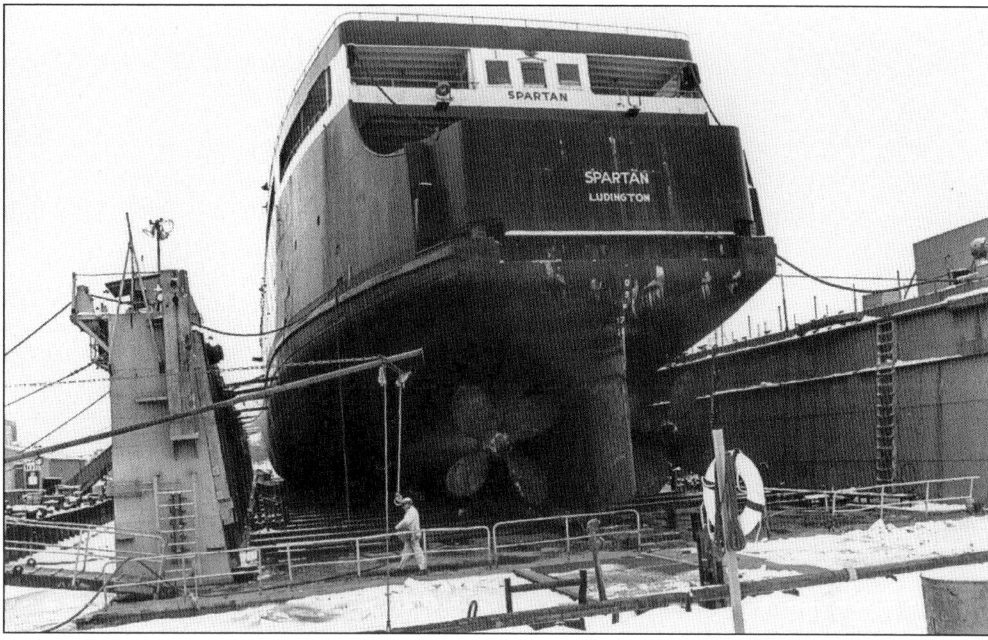

The *Spartan* is shown at Bay Shipbuilding Company's floating drydock during the 1970s. This dock and much of the equipment from Manitowoc Shipbuilding Company was moved to the site of the former Christy Corporation after the Manitowoc yard outgrew its ability to construct the largest freighters that were being ordered during the early 1970s. (Photograph by Frank Tavolocci, courtesy of James F. Fay.)

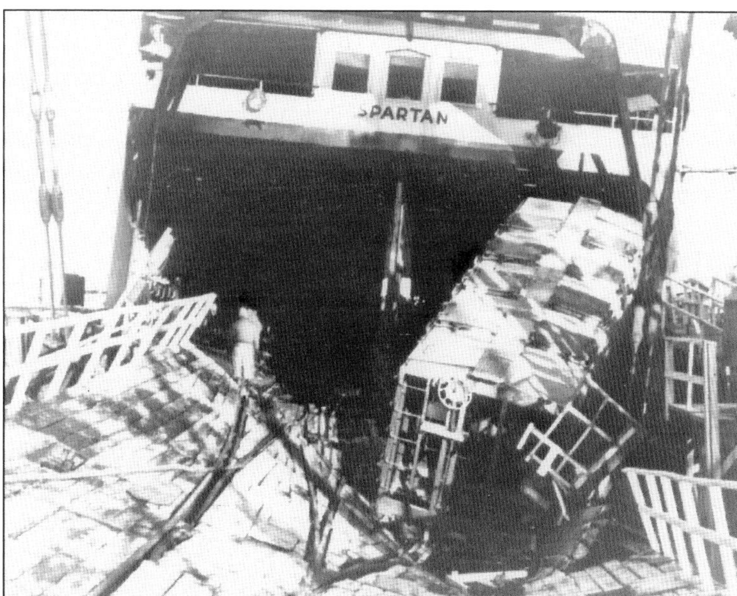

This view shows the aftermath of a collapsed loading apron during the 1970s. Such collapses were common throughout car ferry history. Several months of repair was required to repair the timbers and girder structure after such an accident. (Author's collection.)

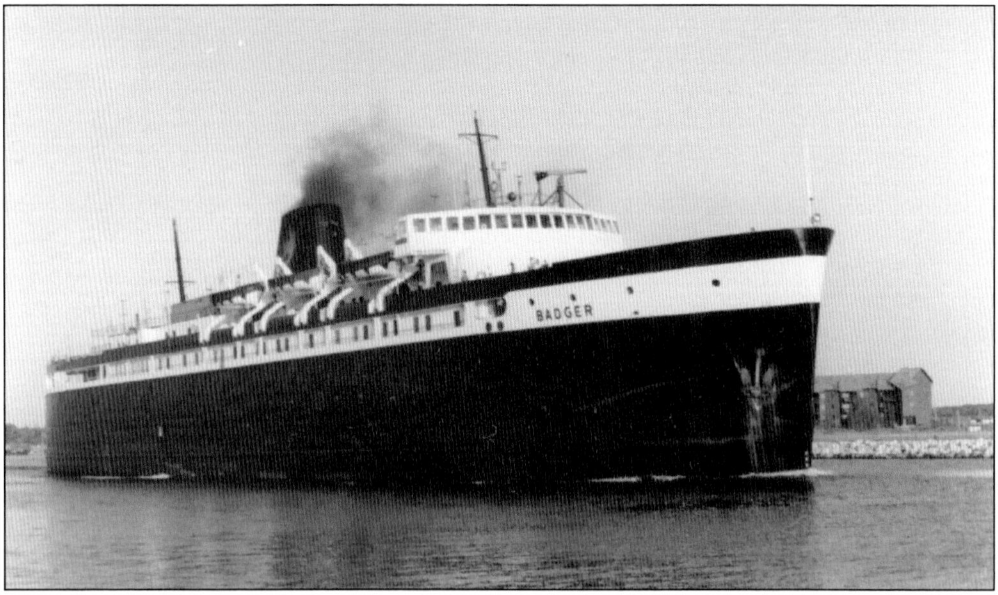

The *Badger* was built for the Chesapeake and Ohio Railroad by the Christy Corporation in Sturgeon Bay and launched on September 9, 1952, as one of two ships commissioned. Named for the University of Wisconsin's team, the *Badger* was equipped with 42 staterooms. They were considered luxurious accommodations at the time. At 410 feet in length, nearly 60 feet in width, and a cost of $5 million, it was designed with passenger comfort in mind. (Author's collection.)

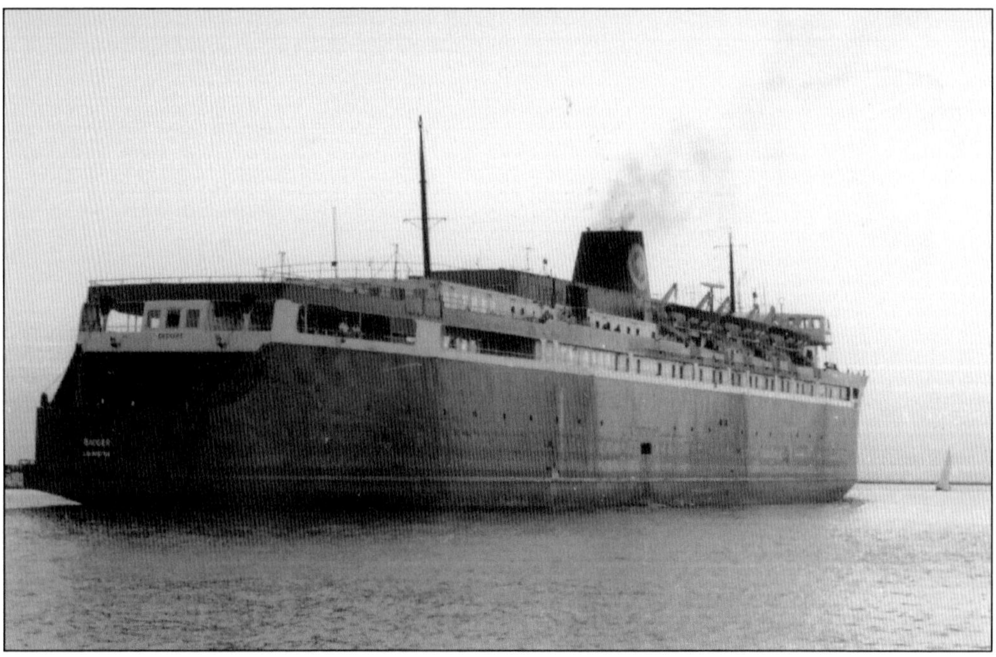

In the 1950s and in previous years, the kitchen served up a number of menu items for the passengers and crew. Served by white-clad waiters, passengers were seated at tables and ate their meals on china plates, which are now very collectible and valuable. On earlier ships such as the *Pere Marquette 32*, fine etched-crystal goblets were used for drinks, and Rookwood floor vases decorated the dining room. (Author's collection.)

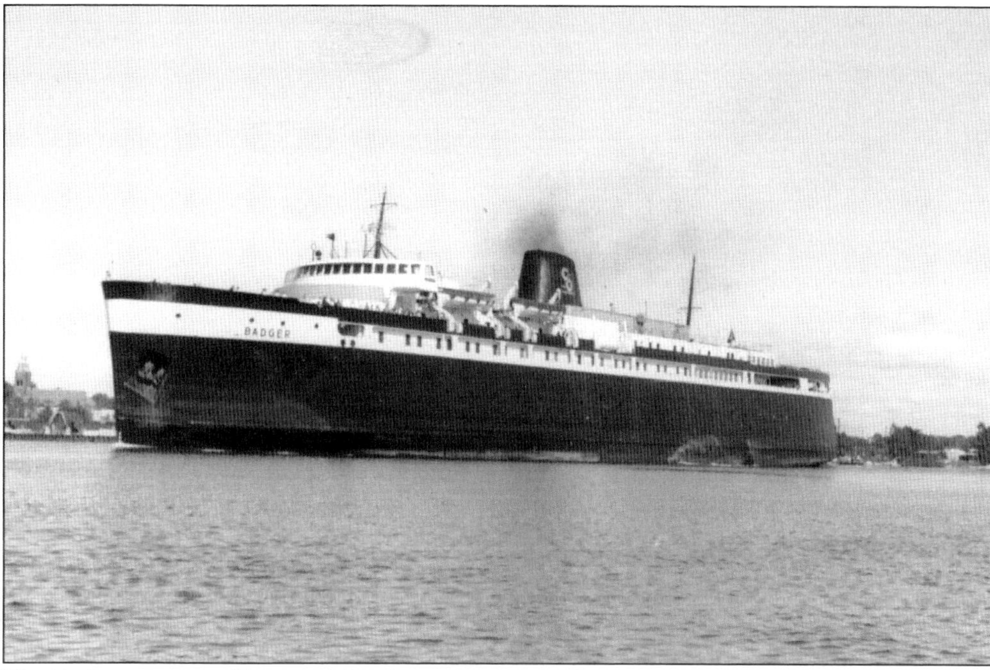

The *Badger* is powered by two 3,500-horsepower Una-flow engines built by the Skinner Engine Company in 1952. These engines were designated in 1996 by the American Society of Mechanical Engineers as a historic landmark. The *Badger* made its maiden voyage on March 21, 1953. (Author's collection.)

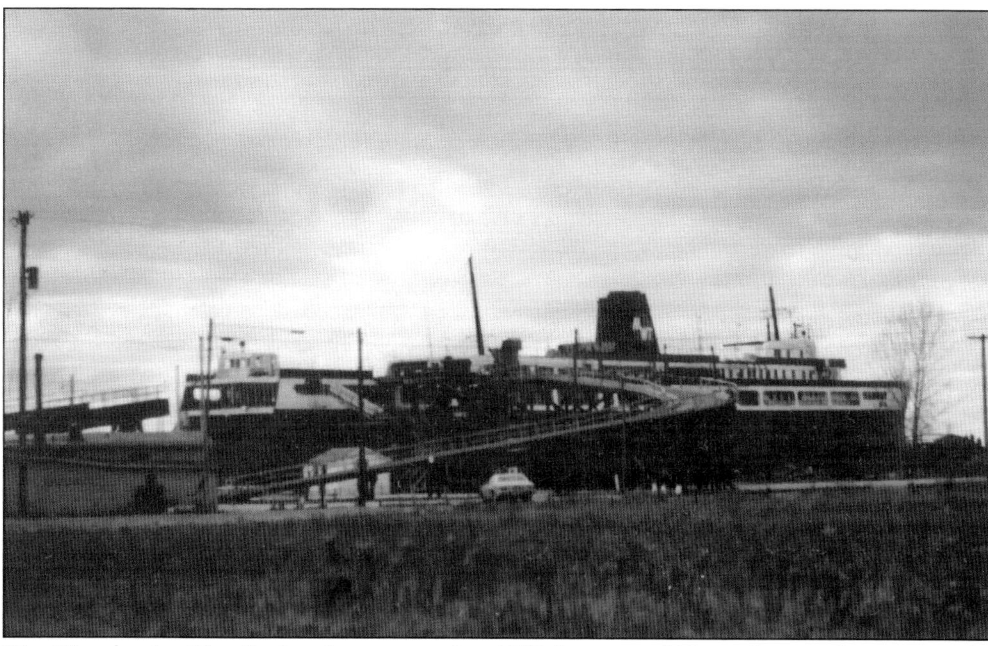

The Chesapeake Ohio Railroad announced in 1975 that it would be seeking to discontinue the car ferry service. At the time of the announcement, only the *Badger*, *Spartan*, and *City of Midland* remained in service; all of the older ships had been scrapped or converted to barges by that time. The Chesapeake and Ohio discontinued the operation at Ludington in 1982. (Author's collection.)

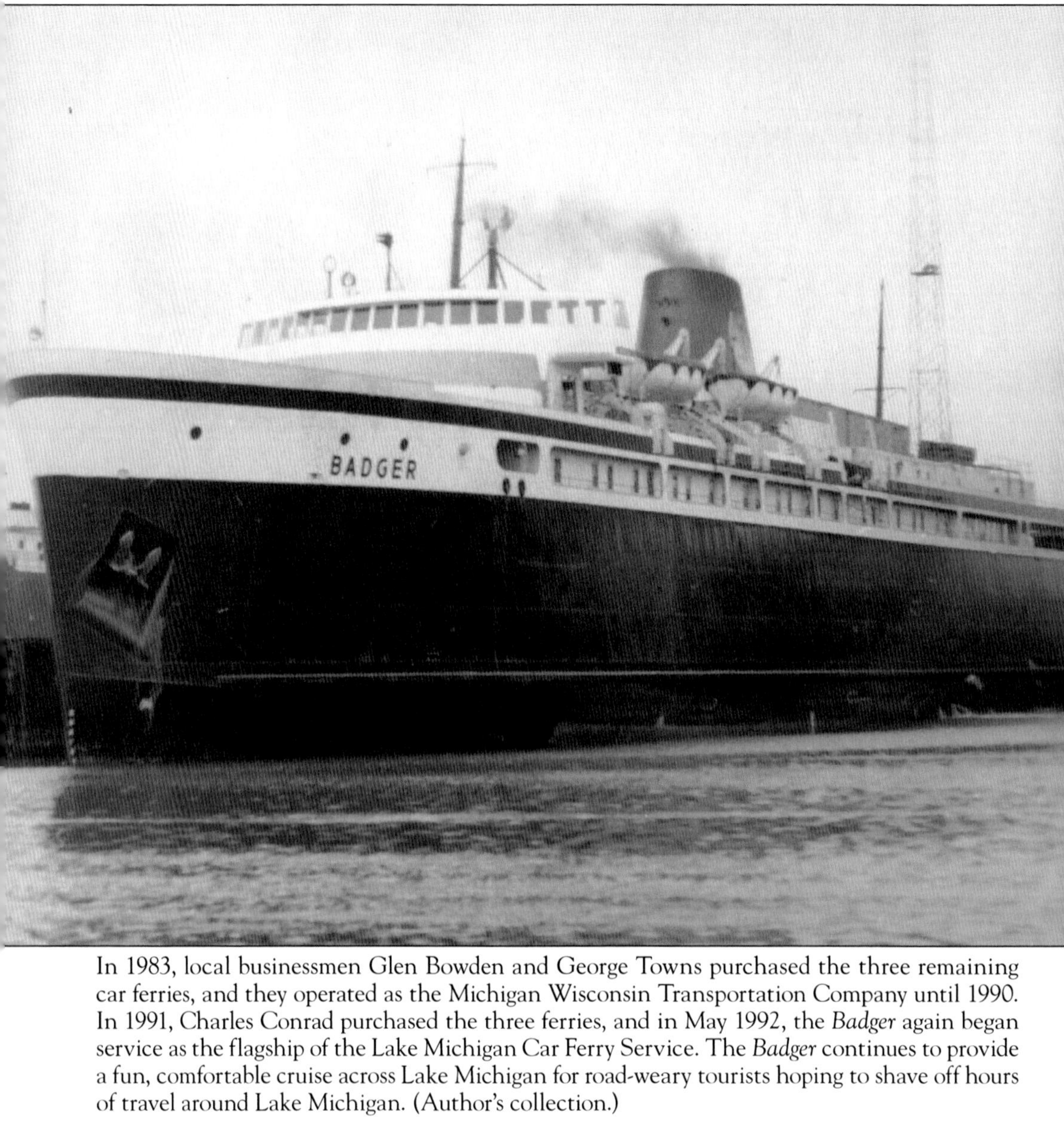

In 1983, local businessmen Glen Bowden and George Towns purchased the three remaining car ferries, and they operated as the Michigan Wisconsin Transportation Company until 1990. In 1991, Charles Conrad purchased the three ferries, and in May 1992, the *Badger* again began service as the flagship of the Lake Michigan Car Ferry Service. The *Badger* continues to provide a fun, comfortable cruise across Lake Michigan for road-weary tourists hoping to shave off hours of travel around Lake Michigan. (Author's collection.)

Three

Harbor and Maritime Traffic

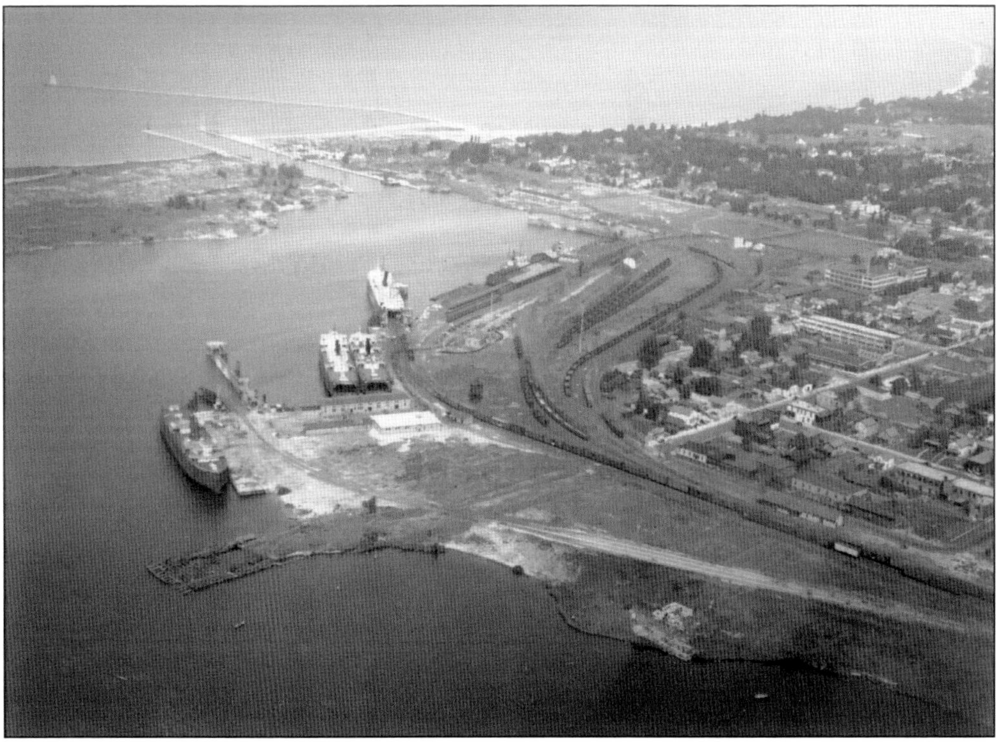

This aerial view of the harbor at Ludington shows very clearly the position of the slips and the layout of the channel and harbor. Three of the car ferries can be seen at dock, with one taking on a load of railcars in preparation for its crossing to Milwaukee. (Photograph by Harold Holmes, author's collection.)

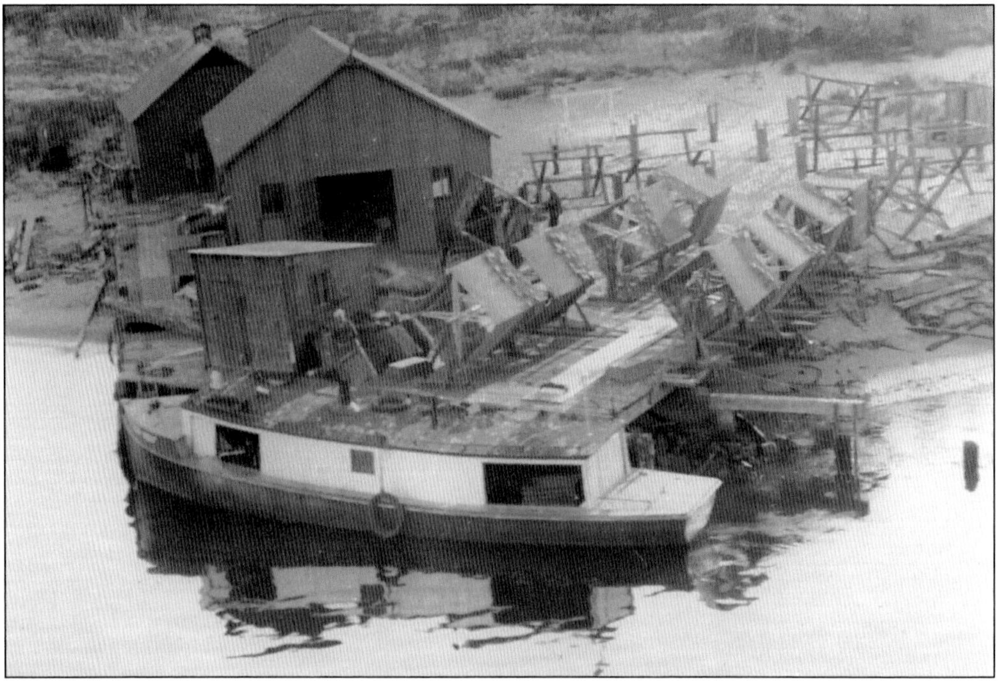

The spike of sandy peninsula that is referred to as Buttersville once had a small creek on the south end, hence the nickname "the Island." It was once several communities—Buttersville, Taylorsville, Seatonsville, and Finn Town—that are all ghost towns now but were once alive with activity from the sawmill, schooners at the dock, and fish tugs going in and out and were home to over 1,000 souls. (Photograph by Erhardt Peters, author's collection.)

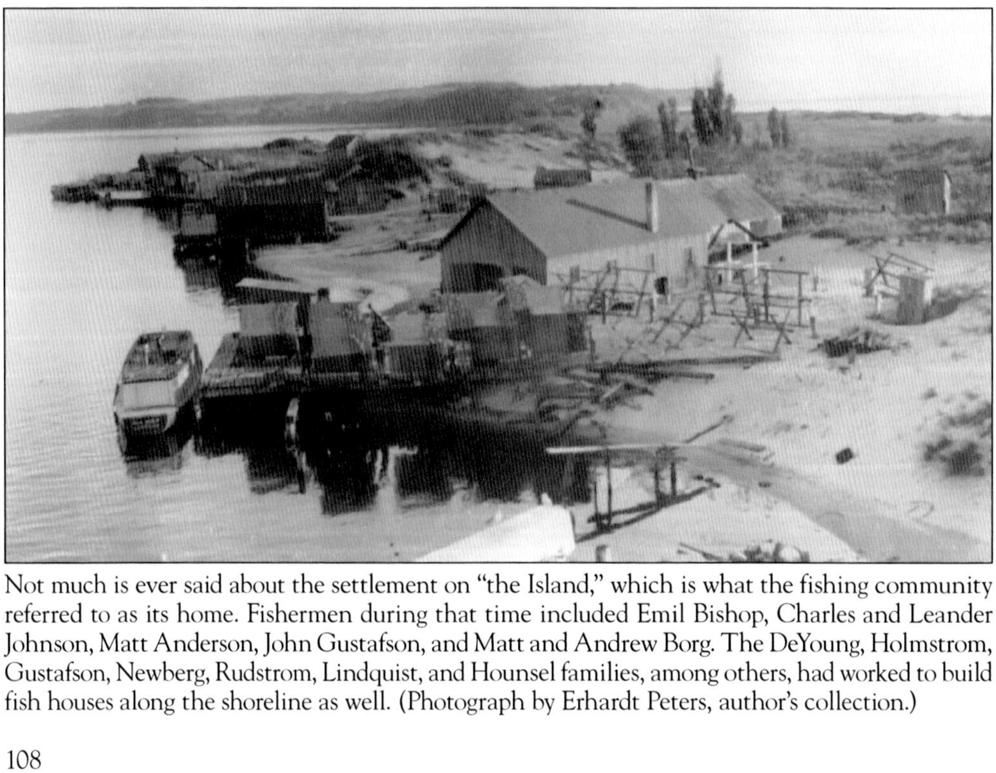

Not much is ever said about the settlement on "the Island," which is what the fishing community referred to as its home. Fishermen during that time included Emil Bishop, Charles and Leander Johnson, Matt Anderson, John Gustafson, and Matt and Andrew Borg. The DeYoung, Holmstrom, Gustafson, Newberg, Rudstrom, Lindquist, and Hounsel families, among others, had worked to build fish houses along the shoreline as well. (Photograph by Erhardt Peters, author's collection.)

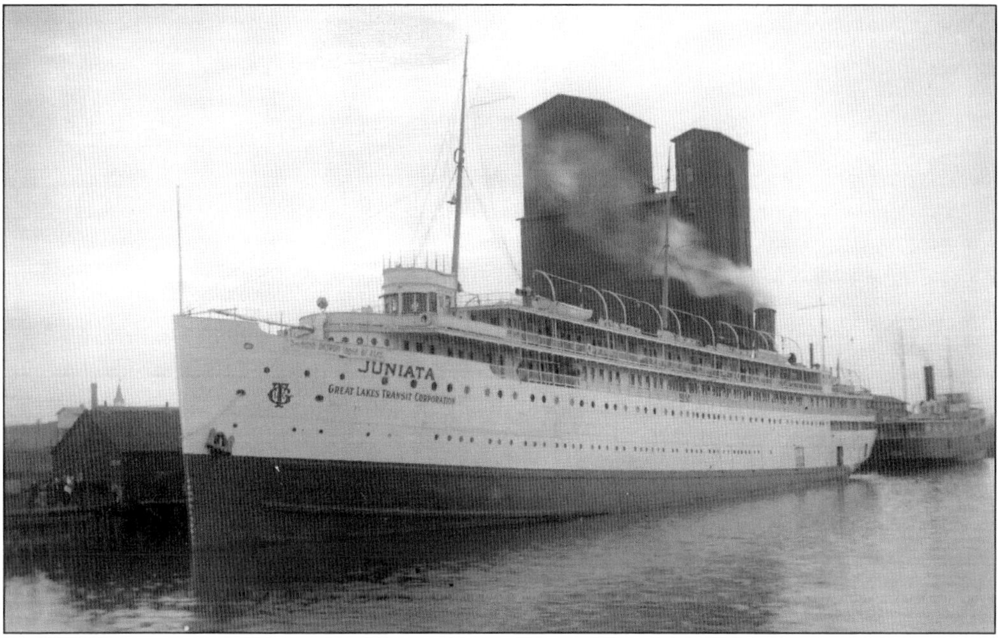

New regulations had docked the *Juniata* as wooden passenger ships were mothballed after the Morro Castle passenger ship fire. The *Juniata* was saved and redesigned to be fireproof. Part of the job of refitting the boat was the removal of the wooden superstructure and replacing it with steel. It is shown here docked in Ludington Harbor to take on passengers and freight. (Author's collection.)

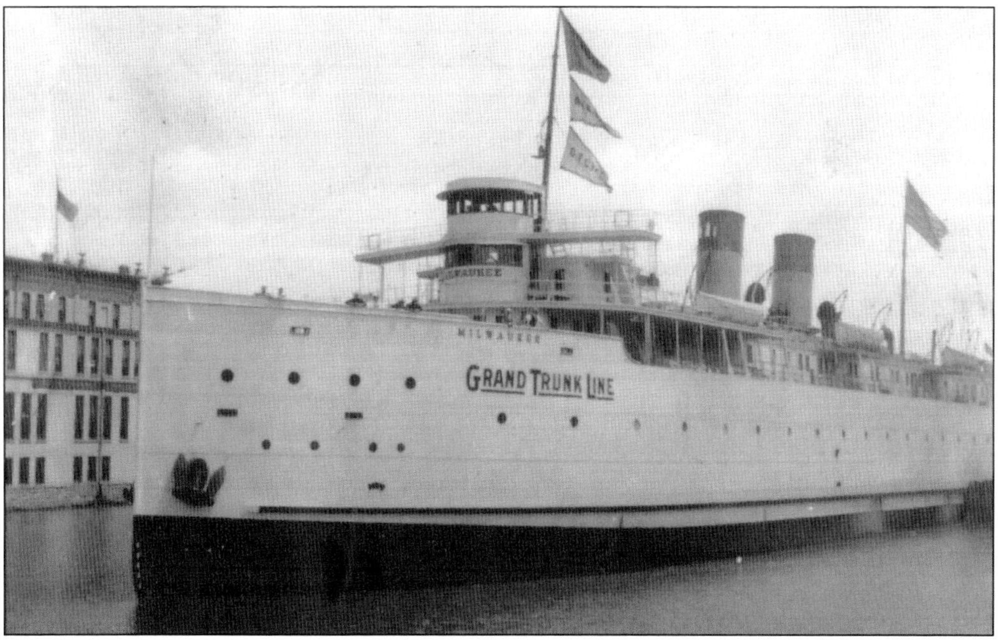

The ill-fated *Milwaukee* was lost with all hands during a storm on a regular run to Grand Haven. Capt. Robert "Heavy Weather" McKay was known for his lack of fear in tackling some of Lake Michigan's greatest gales, but he met his match on October 22, 1929, when the lake claimed the car ferry *Milwaukee* of the Grand Trunk Line. (Author's collection.)

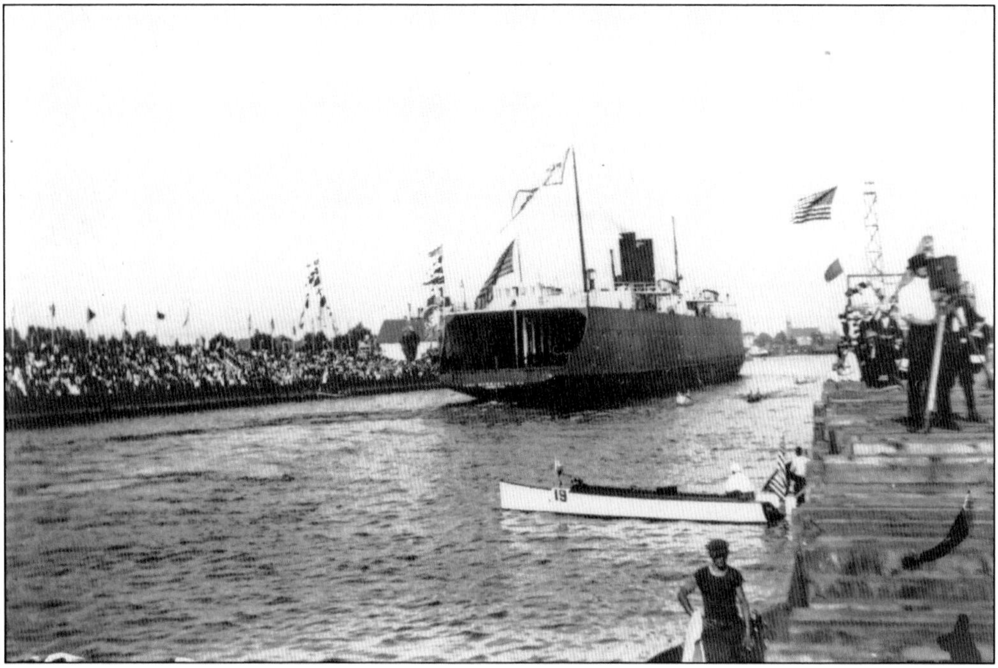

The development of the harbor and its improvements were crucial for the continued growth of the car ferry fleet and increased shipping traffic for the port of Ludington. The Million Dollar Harbor Project took about 10 years from proposal to completion and cost about $1.5 million to complete. The celebration was still named the Million Dollar Harbor Jubilee. (Author's collection.)

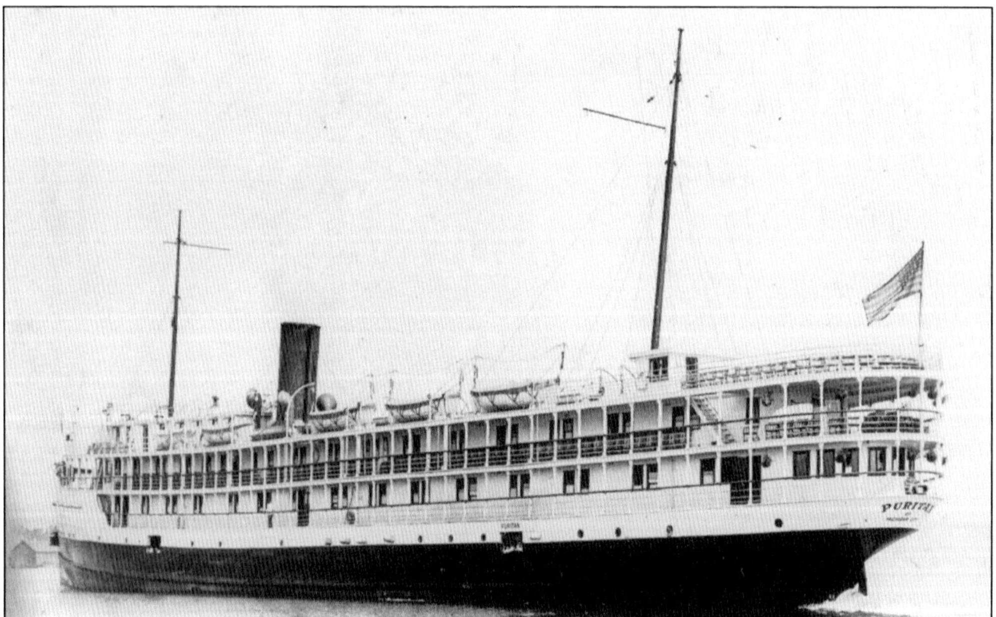

The *Puritan* was originally built by the Graham Morton Transportation Company in 1901, and like many commercial ships of the time, the *Puritan* was conscripted for service during World War I and returned to lake service in 1919. Eventually renamed the *George M. Cox*, this boat sank after striking the Rock of Ages in Lake Superior in 1933. (Author's collection.)

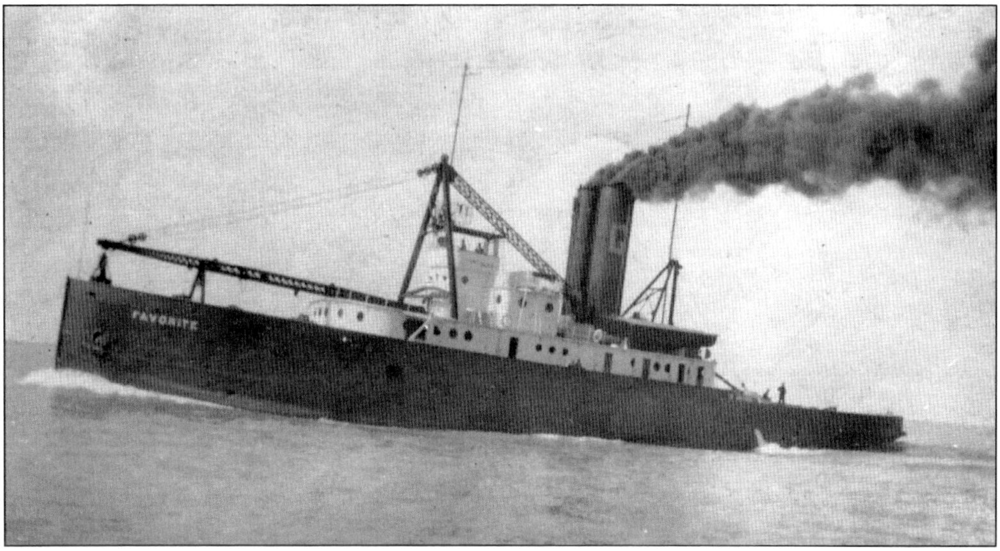

The *Favorite* really was; the ship was well known throughout the Great Lakes and the Ludington area as well. The *Favorite* was built in 1907 and at 180 feet in length was a powerful wrecking tug. The crane can be seen clearly on the deck. The *Favorite* is listed as owned by U.S. interests up until 1948, when it was purchased by Peru for the Peruvian navy in 1948. (Photograph by Erhardt Peters, author's collection.)

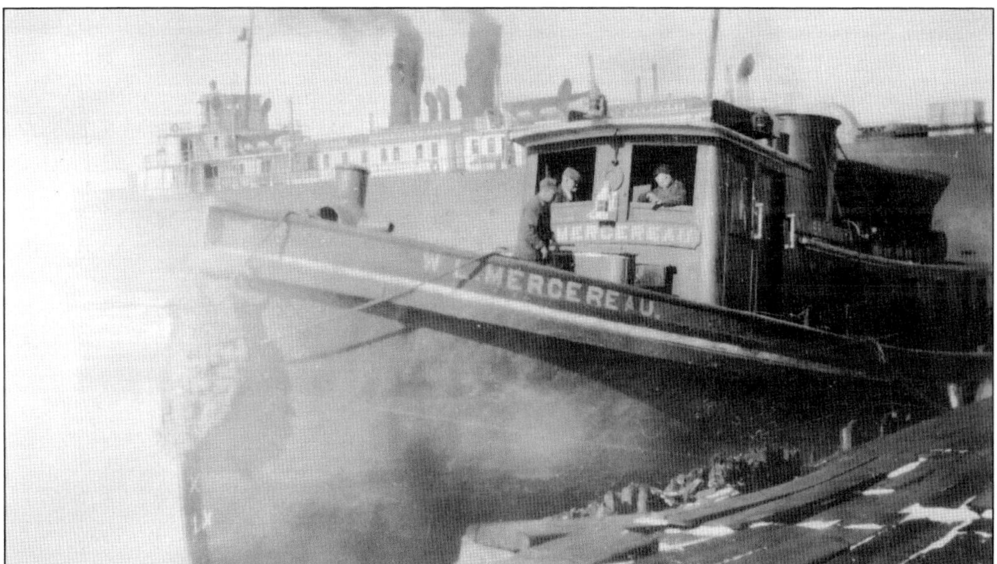

The tug *Mercereau* prepares to cast off at Ludington. The tug was chartered from the Great Lakes Towing Company during the winter months from 1911 to the early 1930s to keep the Ludington Harbor free of ice for the ferry fleet. Shortly after the fast and powerful icebreaking ferries *City of Saginaw* and *City of Flint* appeared, the tug *Mercereau*'s winter charter agreement was terminated. (Photograph by Erhardt Peters, author's collection.)

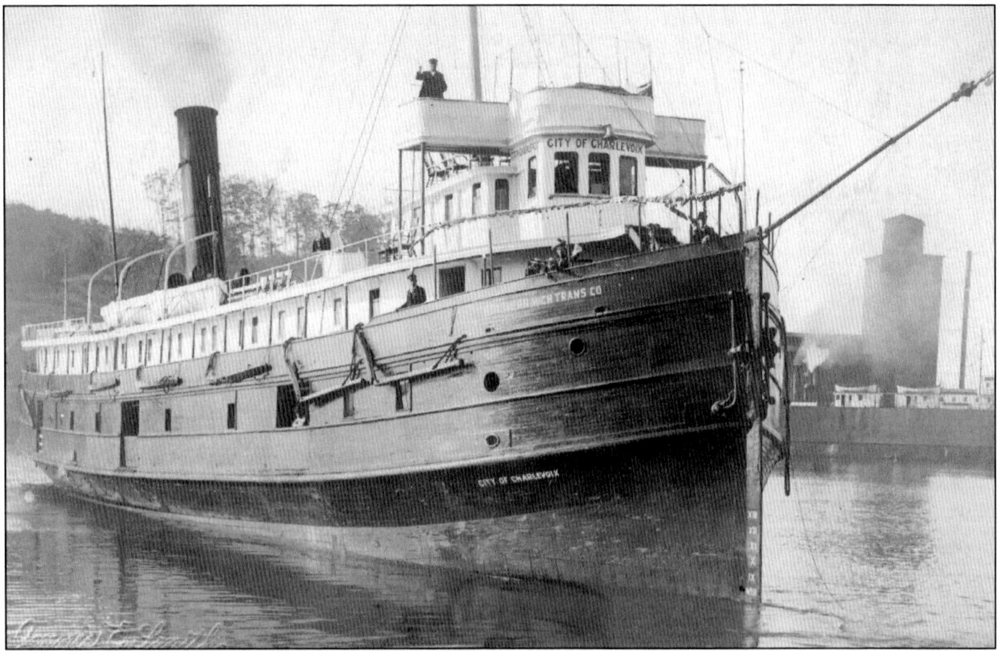

The *Kansas*, while not a part of the Pere Marquette Line, was nonetheless a frequent visitor to the port of Ludington and other stops along its Lake Michigan route. Built as the *Champlain* in 1870 by Daniel Keating of Ogdensburg, New York, it was renamed the *City of Charlevoix* in 1888 and the *Kansas* in 1904. Shown here under the Northern Michigan Transportation Company banner, the *Kansas* is coming out of the port of Frankfort. (Courtesy of James F. Fay.)

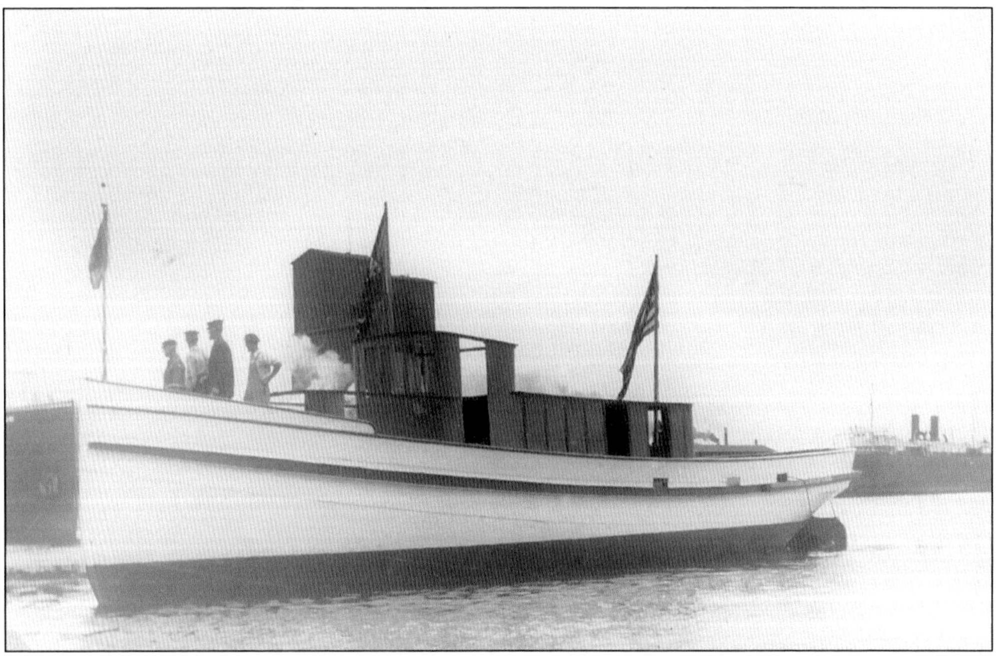

The fish tug *Arrow* was built in Ludington by the Giles Boat Works in 1914. Shown here are the newly launched *Pere Marquette 17* and the grain elevator in the background. The tug operated on the Great Lakes under a series of owners until being scrapped in 1987. (Author's collection.)

Built in 1873 by David Lester at Marine City, the *J. H. Rutter* is shown here in distress outside of Ludington Harbor on November 1, 1878. The *Rutter* had been driven into the shallows after its sails were blown out. The crew scrambled up the masts, clung to the rigging, and no lives were lost. The ship was declared a total loss but was raised the following year. (Author's collection.)

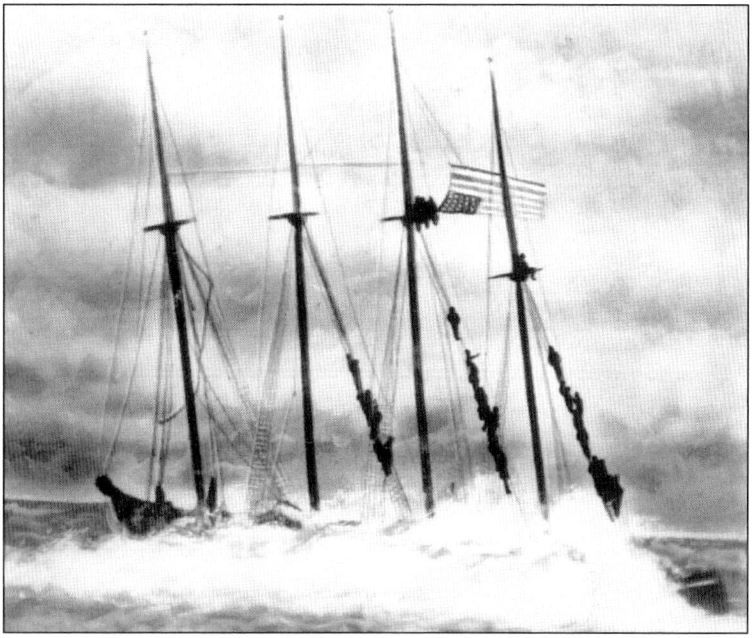

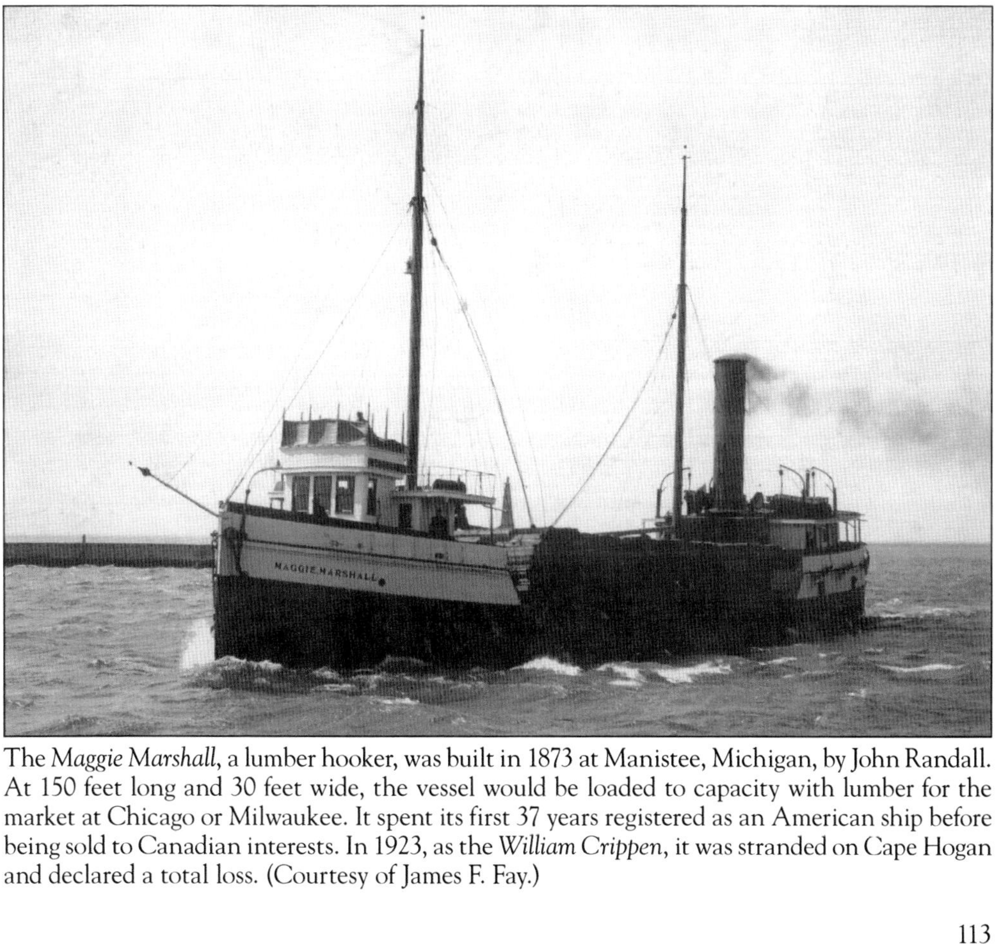

The *Maggie Marshall*, a lumber hooker, was built in 1873 at Manistee, Michigan, by John Randall. At 150 feet long and 30 feet wide, the vessel would be loaded to capacity with lumber for the market at Chicago or Milwaukee. It spent its first 37 years registered as an American ship before being sold to Canadian interests. In 1923, as the *William Crippen*, it was stranded on Cape Hogan and declared a total loss. (Courtesy of James F. Fay.)

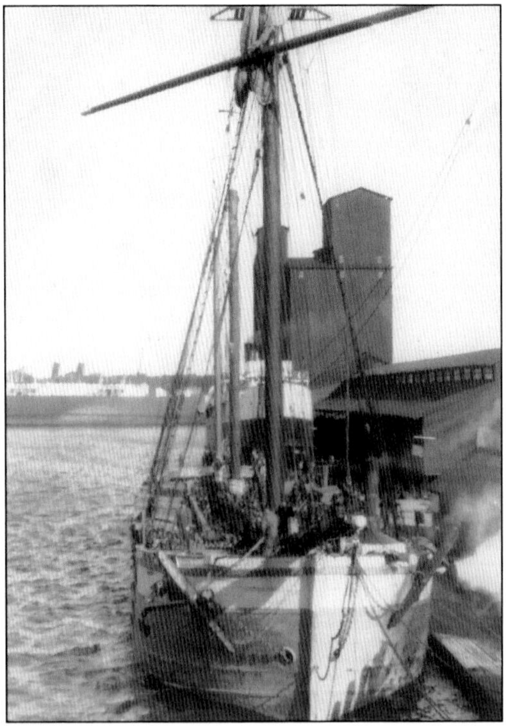

The last surviving commercial schooner on the Great Lakes was one that was familiar to Ludington as well. *Our Son* was built in 1875 at Black River (Lorraine), Ohio. The ship was named in honor of the son of Capt. Henry Kelly who fell from the ship while it was under construction and drowned. During its 55-year history, *Our Son* retained its name and its stature. The ship began its life as a three-masted schooner and ended its career on September 26, 1930, as the last commercial schooner on the Great Lakes. *Our Son* had a length of 182 feet, a 35-foot beam, and was capable of carrying over 1,000 tons of ore or 40,000 bushels of grain. (Photograph by Erhardt Peters, author's collection.)

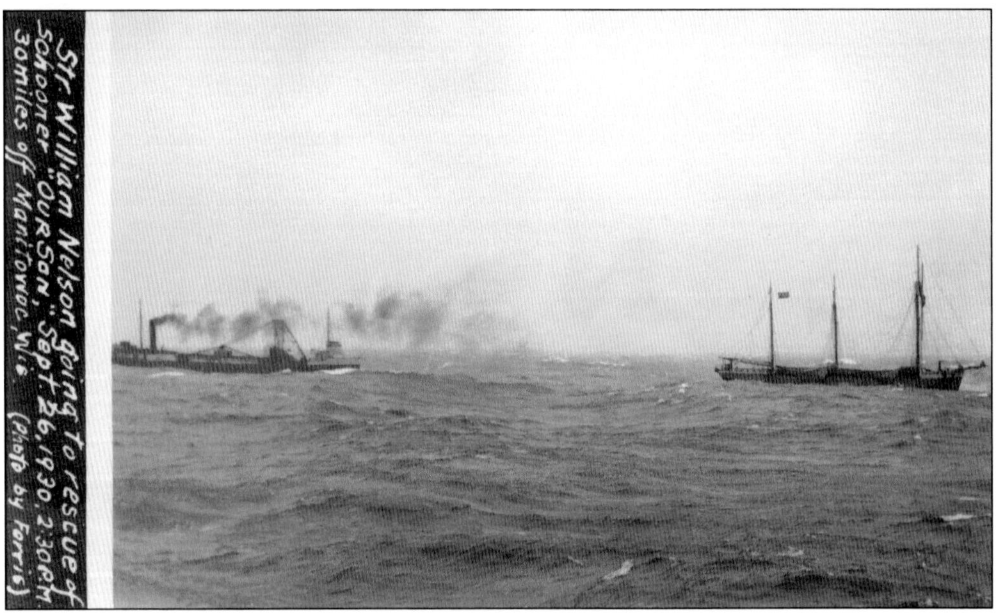

Our Son, carrying a load of pulpwood, had been fighting a gale about 20 miles northeast of Sheboygan and began filling with water. Capt. Fred Nelson ordered the Stars and Stripes to be flown upside down as a sign of distress, and the steamship *William Nelson* responded and removed the captain and six crewmen. The *Pere Marquette 22*, under the command of Capt. Wallace Henry Van Dyke, also responded. J. H. Ferris was aboard the *PM 22* with his camera and was able to take the last known photograph of the schooner *Our Son* with its flag flying in distress. (Photograph by J. H. Ferris, author's collection.)

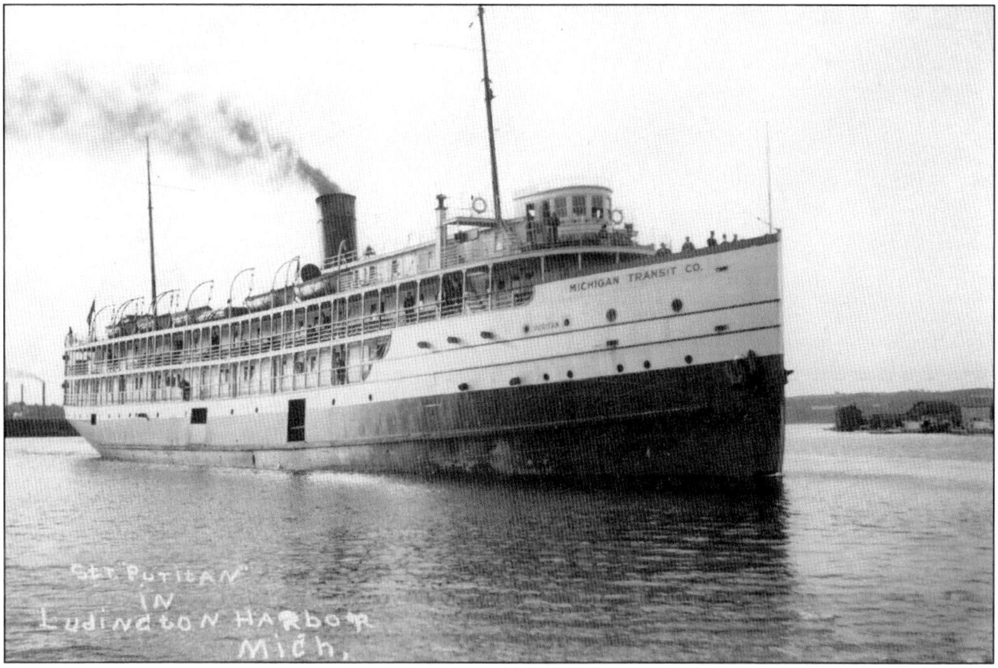

The steamer *Puritan* glides across Pere Marquette Lake on its way out to new ports along its service route. Some of the fish shanties and nets at Finn Town are directly to the right of its bow. Long since gone, the shanties were replaced by the Crosswinds Condominiums. (Courtesy of James F. Fay.)

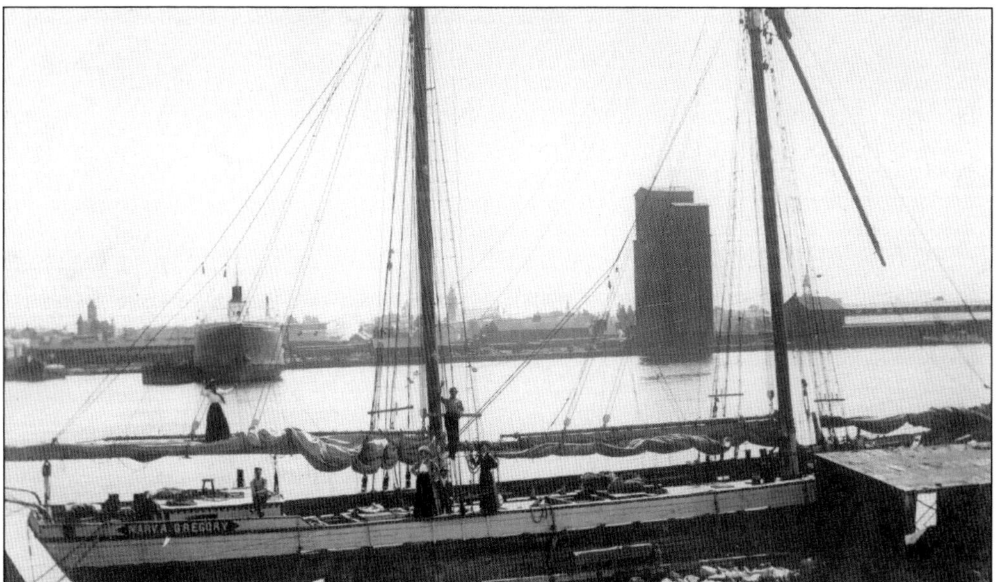

The schooner *Mary A. Gregory* is shown here docked at the Buttersville Peninsula at Finn Town. Several locals are shown standing on the beams to show of for the cameraman. Built in 1875 in Chicago by John Gregory, this schooner served on the Great Lakes until being abandoned in 1925. (Courtesy of James F. Fay.)

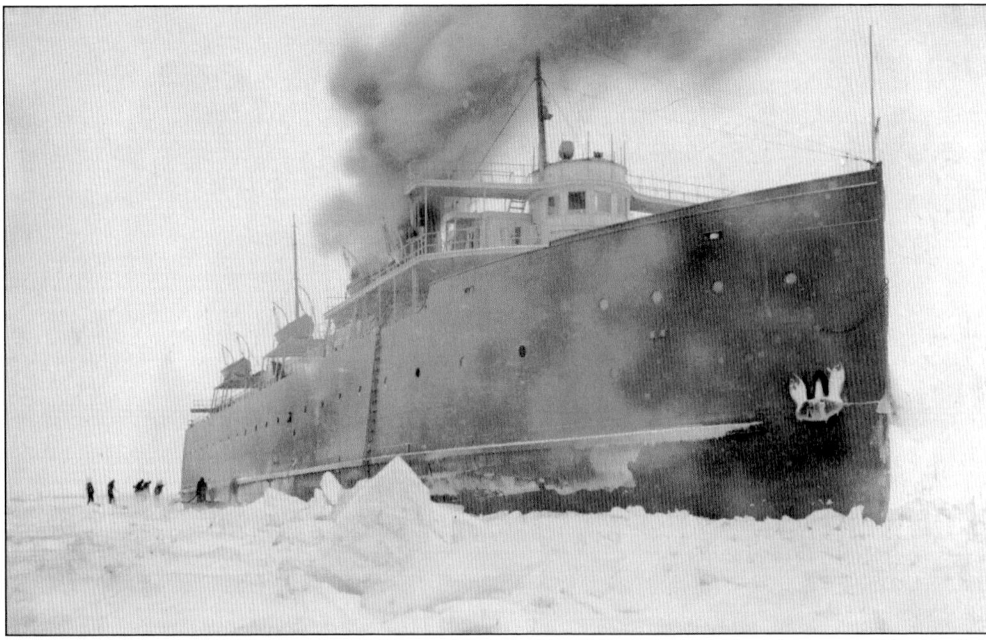

The *Manistique Marquette and Northern No. 1* was built in 1903 by the American Steamship Company. The Pere Marquette Railroad took over the Northport–Manistique ferry line in 1904, and the boat was scheduled for the Ludington–Manistique run in May. Purchased in 1908 by the Grand Trunk Milwaukee Car Ferry Line and renamed the *Milwaukee*, the boat operated until it sank in a storm on October 22, 1929, with the loss of all hands. (Author's collection.)

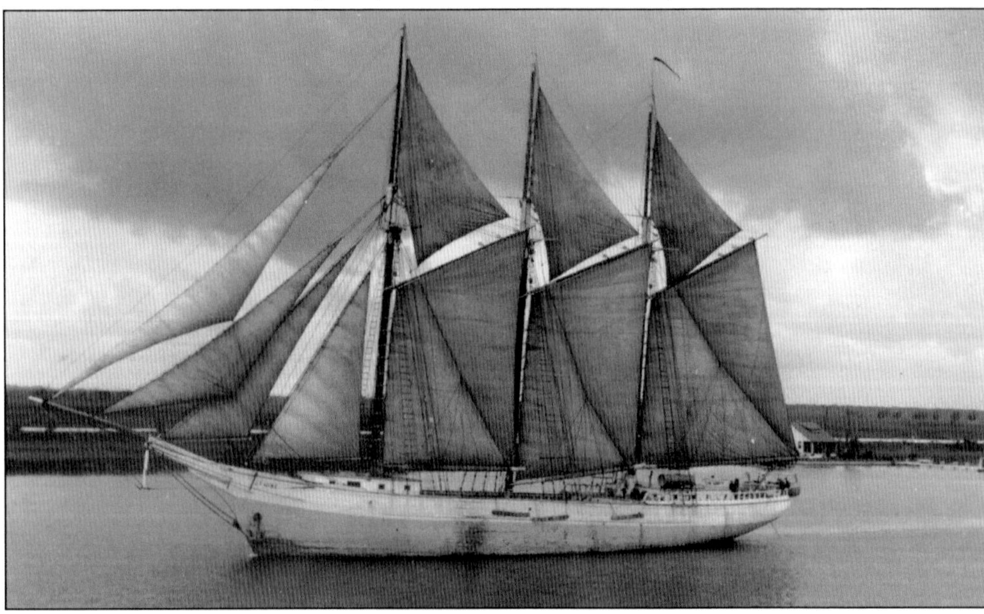

The three-masted schooner *J. T. Wing* is shown in Pere Marquette Lake under full sail about 1935. Built in 1919 at Weymouth, Nova Scotia as the *J. O. Webster*, the *Wing* had eight owners of record. After being purchased by the Detroit Historical Commission, the schooner was renamed *J. T. Wing*. The schooner traded the waters of the Great Lakes for a bed of gravel and served its final days as a museum on Belle Island near Detroit. (Author's collection.)

Four

Lighthouses and Lifesaving

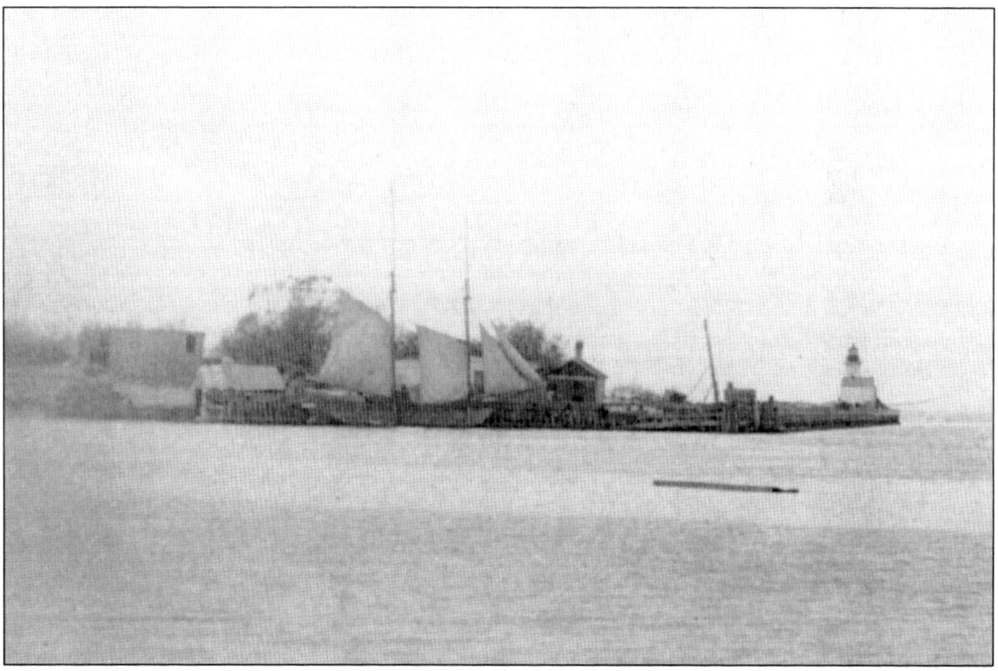

In this *c.* 1888 view looking westward from the harbor, the old south pier lighthouse can be seen. The first lighthouse was built in 1870 and was a white, framed structure that was only 25 feet tall and fitted with a red lens. The original structure was destroyed in a storm in 1876, and the new structure, which opened in May 1887, was a bit taller at 29 feet. (Author's collection.)

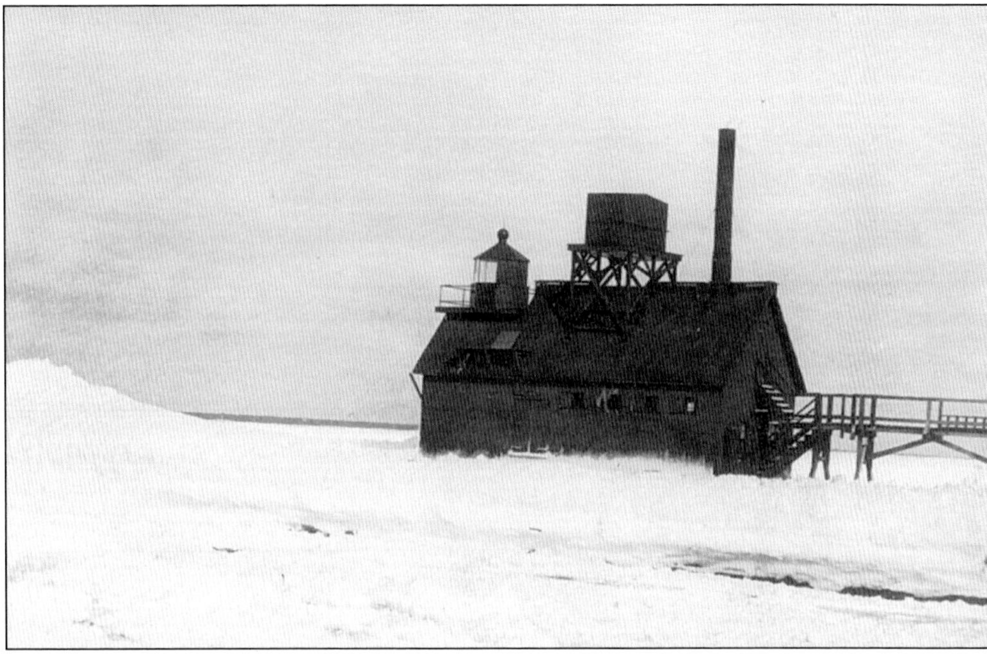

At one time, there were three lights on the two piers attended by one lighthouse keeper, Edwin Slyfield. Both the Ludington Lighthouse and the Manistee Lighthouse were built on the same design. The main light was located on the south break-wall in this photograph and in 1924 was moved to the north break-wall with the construction of the new lighthouse. (Author's collection.)

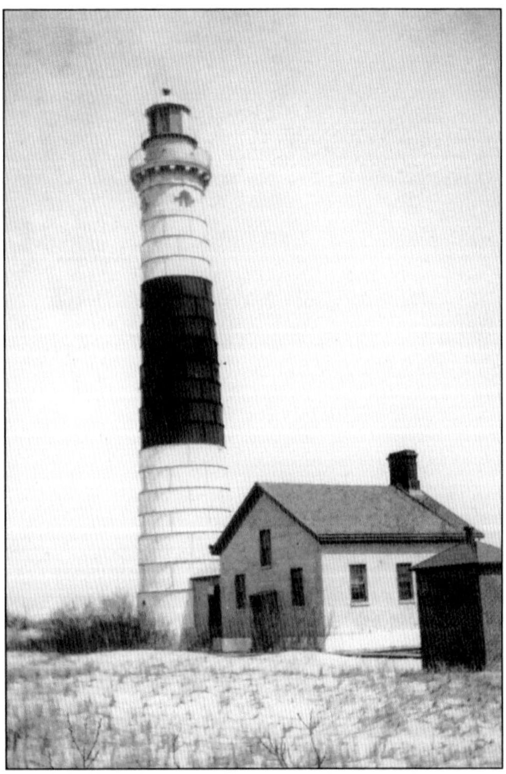

When the Big Sable Lighthouse was originally built in 1867, it was constructed of brick. It was not until years later, after many complaints, that a black and white steel outer casing was added to the structure to aid in its visibility by boats on the lake and to protect the bricks, which were deteriorating. (Author's collection.)

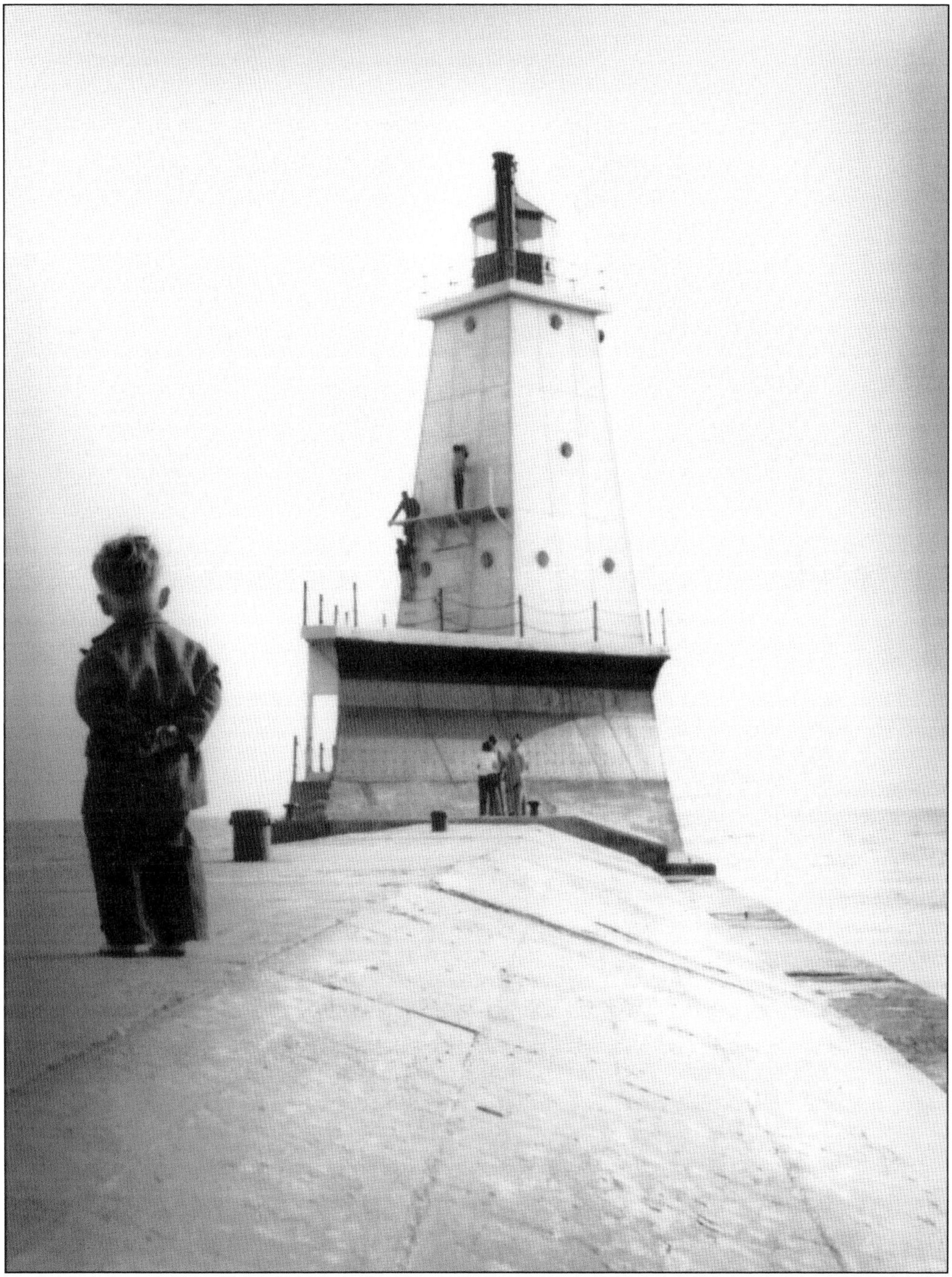

Young Thomas Holmes is surveying the current North Pier Lighthouse, which was built in 1924. The walk out to the lighthouse is a popular attraction for residents and tourists alike. In years past, the break-wall would be loaded with fishermen hooking their limit of perch, and in those years, Ludington hosted a perch festival. (Photograph by Harold Holmes, author's collection.)

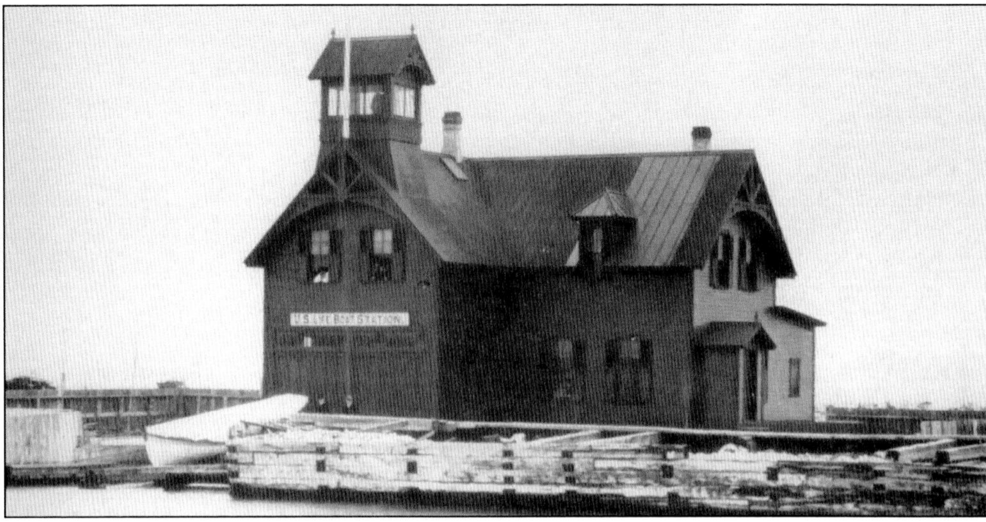

In 1883, the lifesaving station was moved from the Island (Buttersville Peninsula) across the channel by Charles Gatke and Andrew Turner. As of 1907, the room for the storage of the lifeboat and one apartment were from the original structure, the rest having been added at a later date. (Author's collection.)

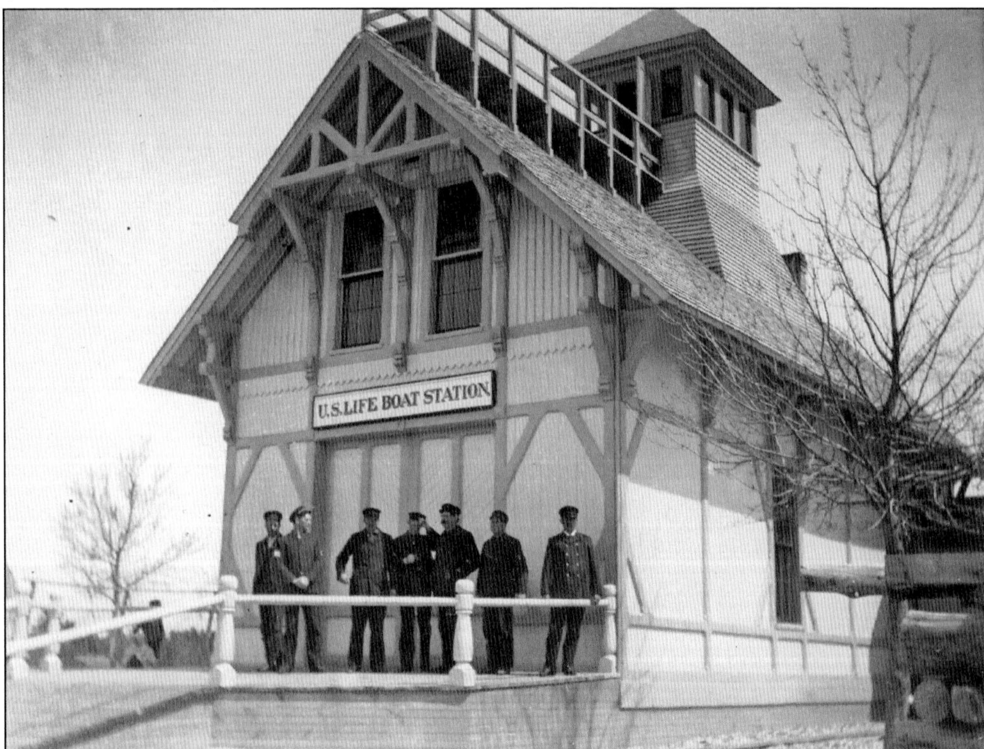

This is a c. 1888 view of the lifesaving station. In 1880, the lifesaving crew numbered seven men, which included Joshua Brown, captain; Jesse and Will Brown, surfmen (and brothers of the captain); Winnie Beaupre; Arthur Foster; Christopher Robson; and Arthur Goodrich. The station was located on the island (Finn Town) at the site of the Taylor Mills Salt Shed. (Author's collection.)

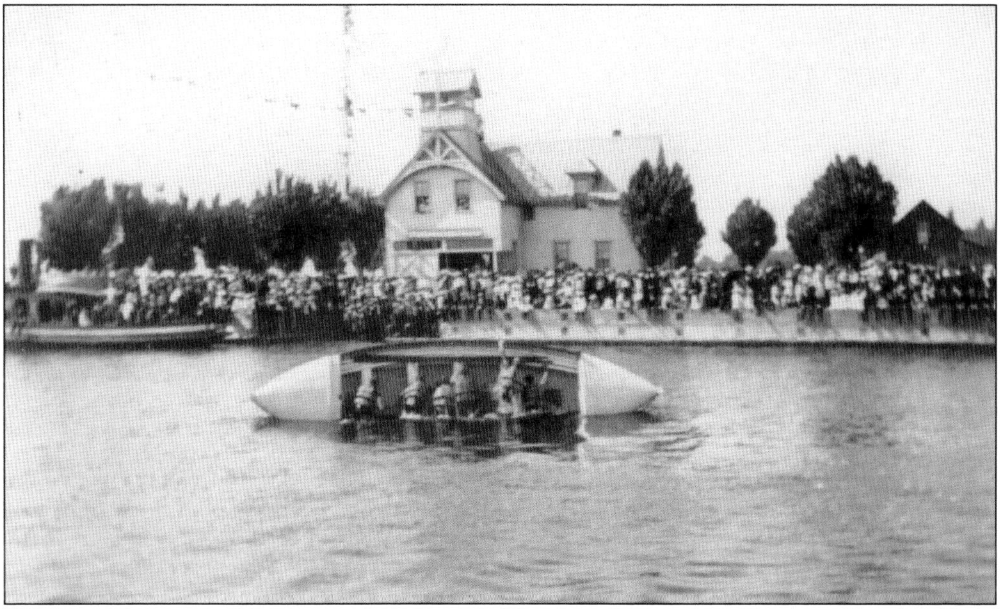

In 1892, the crew performed its regular drill practice as seen here for the inspector of lifesaving stations and impressed him so much so that the crew was picked as the best of the Great Lakes and asked to represent the lifesaving service at the Columbian Exposition in Chicago for eight months. The crew included Capt. Charles Tufts, Jason Pratton, Myron Grinnell, John Nelson, Peter Carlson, Berndt Carlson, Oscar Wilkenson, and Joseph Mitchell. (Author's collection.)

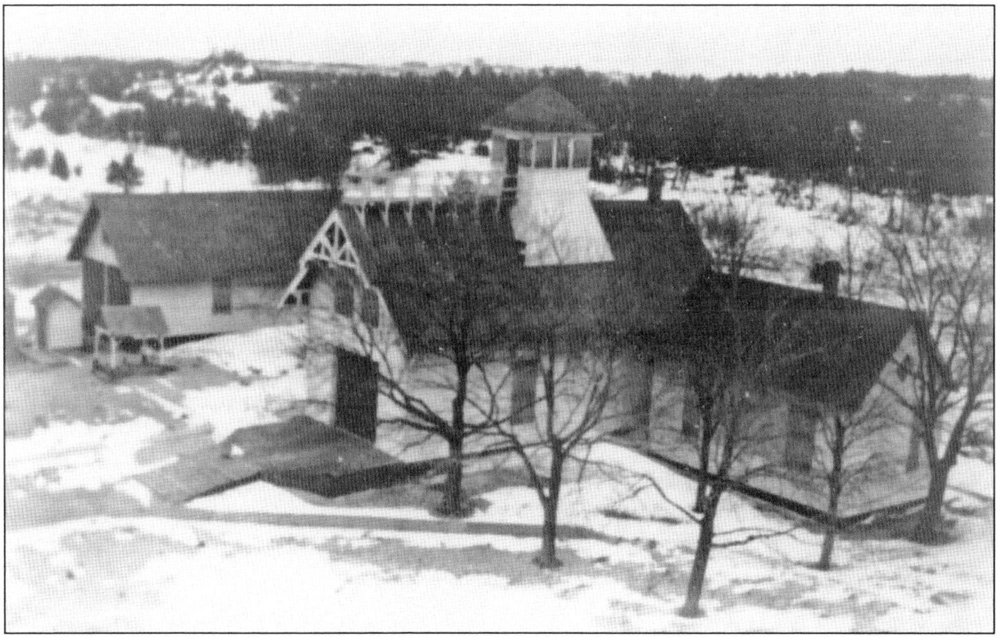

The Grande Pointe Au Sable Lifesaving Station, constructed in 1876 and opened for service in May 1877, was located about halfway between the Beach House at the Ludington State Park and the Big Sable Lighthouse. After the station was abandoned, there was a short-lived attempt to save the buildings for use as a maritime museum, and once that attempt failed, the buildings were eventually razed. (Author's collection.)

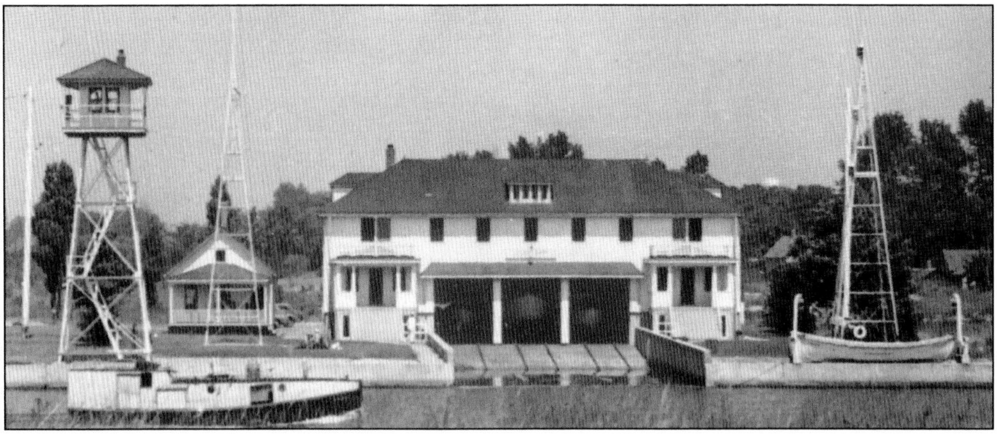

One of Ludington's fish tugs is coming home with the day's catch past the U.S. Coast Guard station at Ludington. In the 1940s, the boats used by the U.S. Coast Guard were housed inside the building at the ready to be launched down rails into the channel. The lookout tower and radio antenna can also be seen. (Photograph by Erhardt Peters, author's collection.)

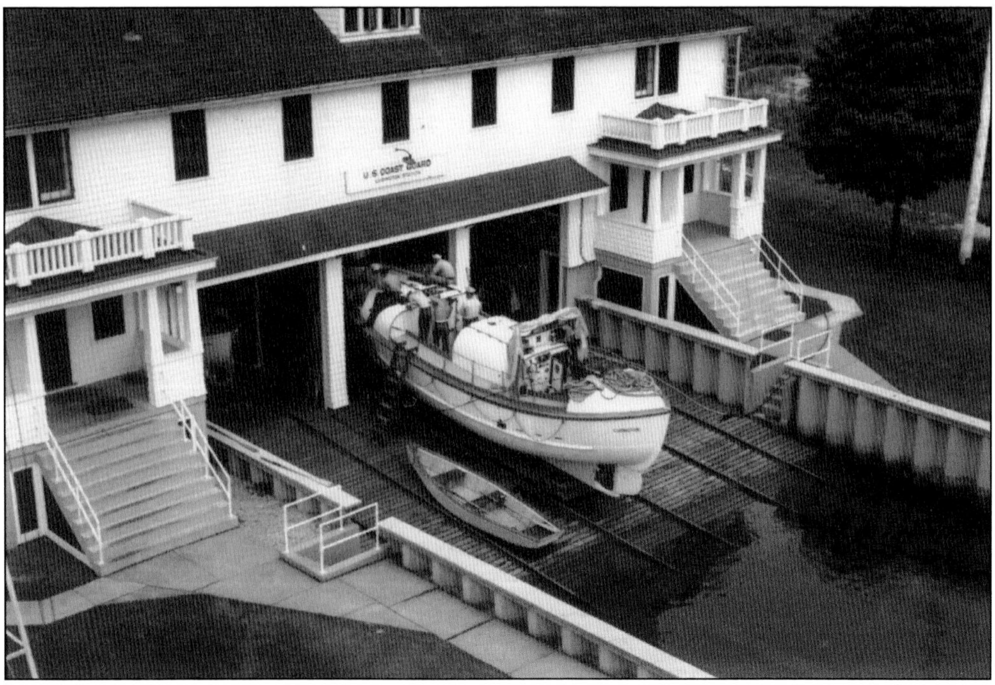

This view of the U.S. Coast Guard station at Ludington was taken from a passing car ferry. The station was a familiar sight to those traveling on the lakes and was an often-photographed landmark. Ironically, while thousands of pictures exist of the channel view of the building, none have been located of the street view to assist in restoration of the building as a maritime museum. (Photograph by Erhardt Peters, author's collection.)

Five

Armistice Day Storm of 1940

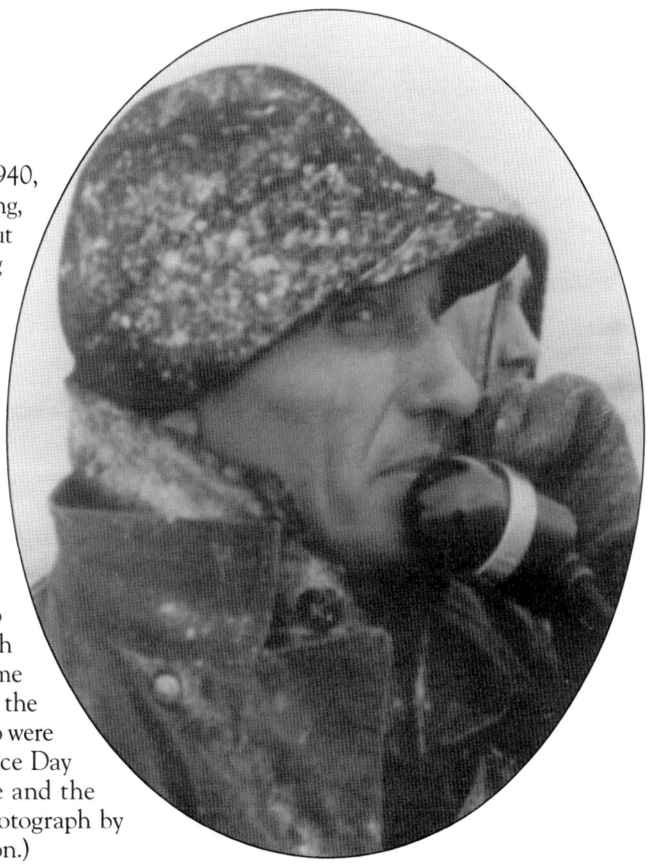

Armistice Day, November 11, 1940, started out as a mild late fall morning, one where people would venture out with no coat or went duck hunting with light gear in the marshes across the Midwest. The last forecast was a little colder with a few flurries. Chief boatswain A. E. Chrisotfferson had just come to Ludington in May 1940, and he is shown here calling in updates on the beached *City of Flint*. A storm came in fast with 50- to 80-mile-per-hour winds, rain, ice, and up to 26 inches of snow and drifts up to 20 feet deep in some places. Temperatures which had gone up to 70 degrees in some areas dropped to single digits. Like the tragedy of September 11, those who were old enough to remember Armistice Day 1940 remember where they were and the impact it had on their lives. (Photograph by Harold Holmes, author's collection.)

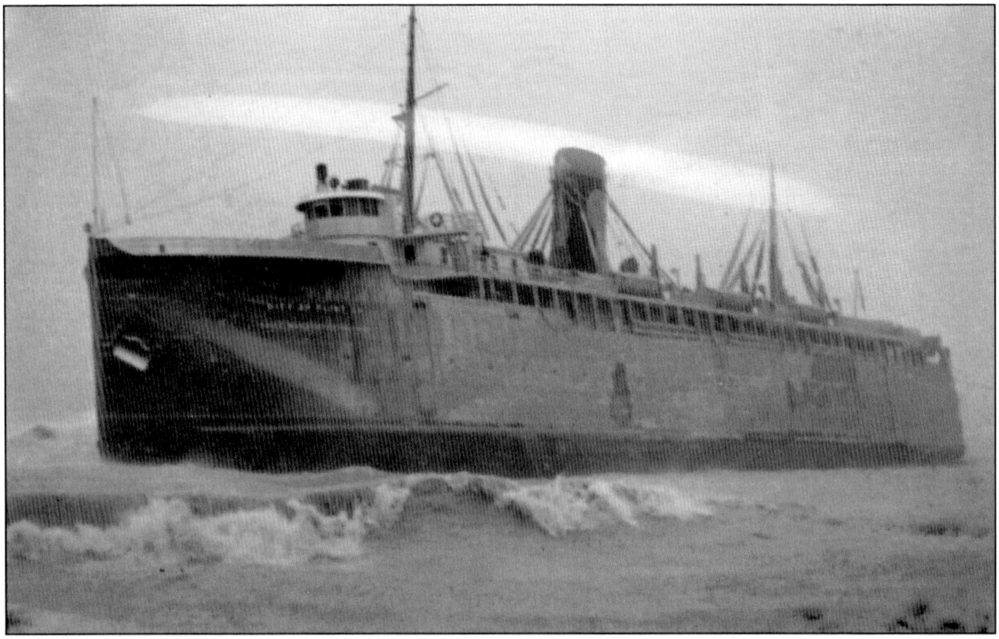

The *City of Flint* is shown being battered on the sandbar by the unrelenting action of Lake Michigan waves. They were unprepared for what some called the "Winds of Hell" that were barreling across the country and cutting a 1,000-mile-wide swatch of destruction. They did not see it coming. It was not that they did not have the technology; they knew a storm was coming, but the Chicago Meteorological Office was closed overnight, and no one was watching. (Photograph by Harold Holmes, author's collection.)

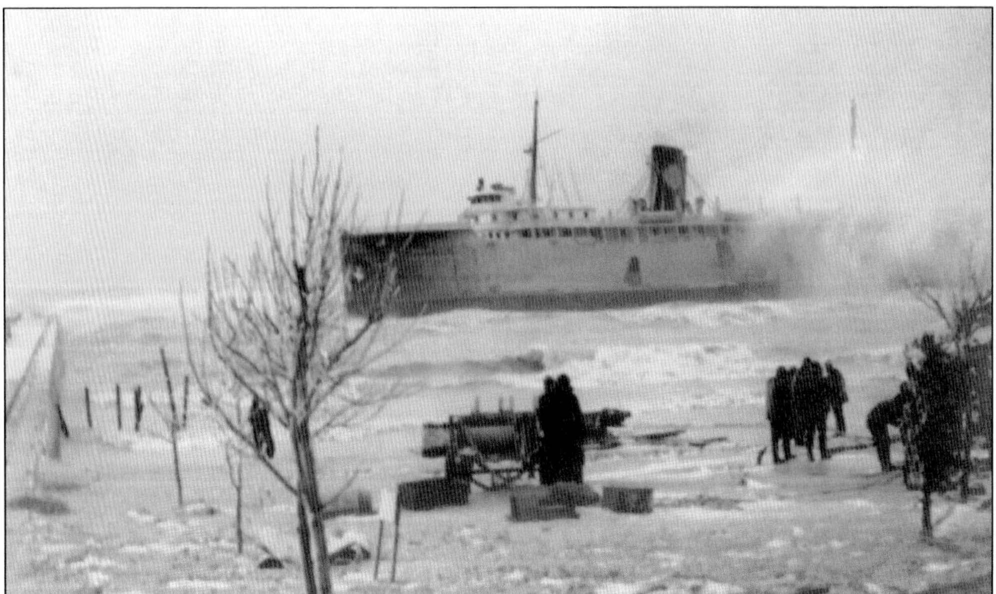

The U.S. Coast Guard felt it had its hands full in trying to help the *City of Flint* at Ludington. It attempted to remove two of the crew from the ship but abandoned the idea of removing all of the crew and the three passengers that were on board. (Photograph by Harold Holmes, author's collection.)

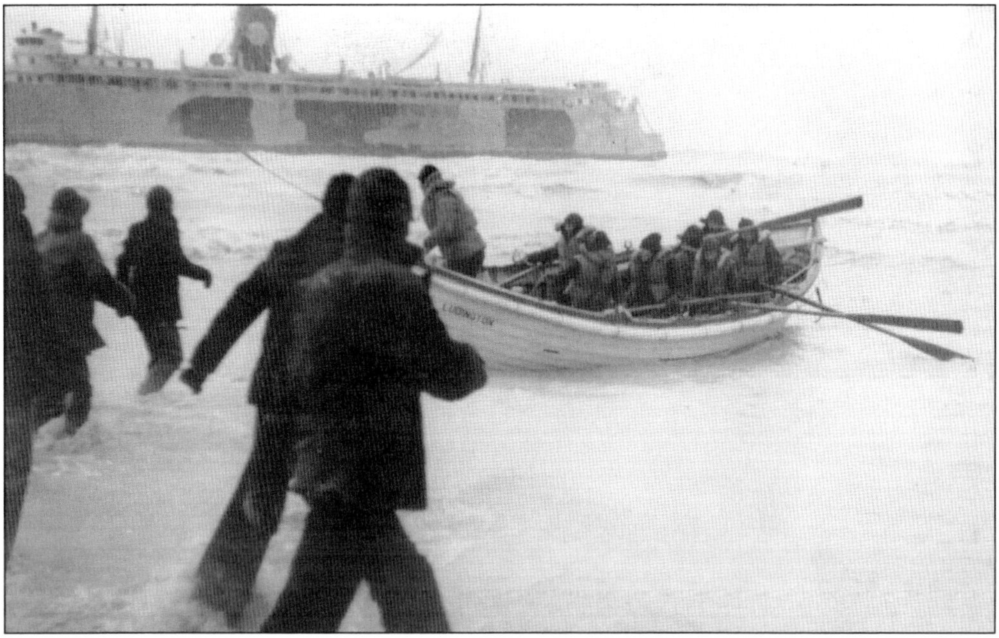

Men of the Ludington Coast Guard are coming back to shore after retrieving a body that had been spotted in the surf. Of the 13 bodies that washed ashore in Ludington during and after the storm, 11 of them were from the *Anna C. Minch* and two from the *Novadoc*. (Photograph by Harold Holmes, author's collection.)

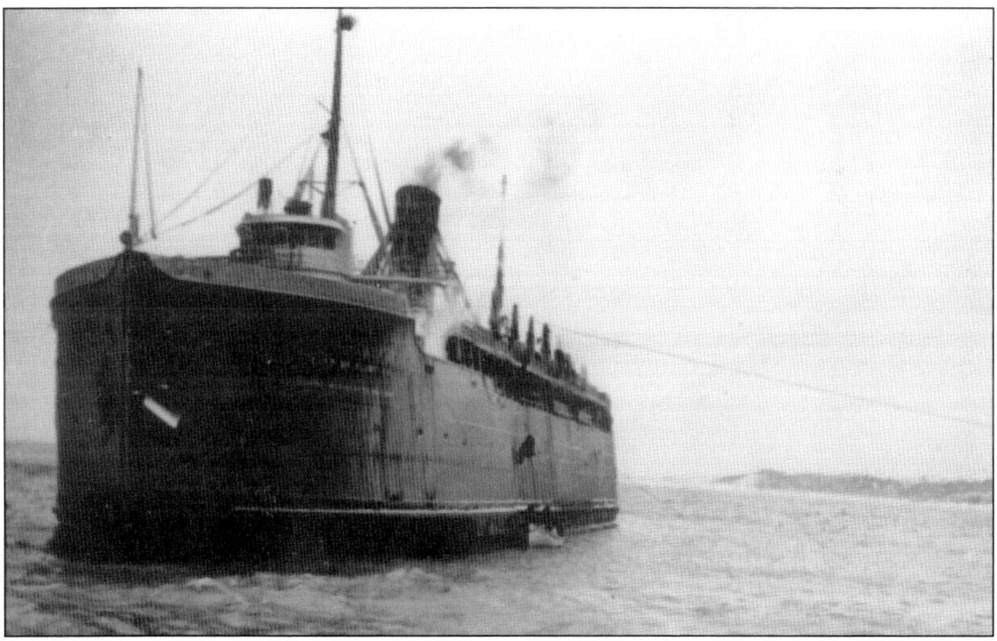

Wilfred Abrahamson recalled, "Moving the *City of Flint* off from the sandbar was no easy task, the ship was drawing 17 feet of draft while sitting in 12 feet of water, the *21* did not have any freight on board and was drawing 14-2 feet of draft. In addition to the *PM 21* the tug *John F. Cushing* of Chicago was brought in to assist and was drawing 17.6 feet of draft." (Photograph by Harold Holmes, author's collection.)

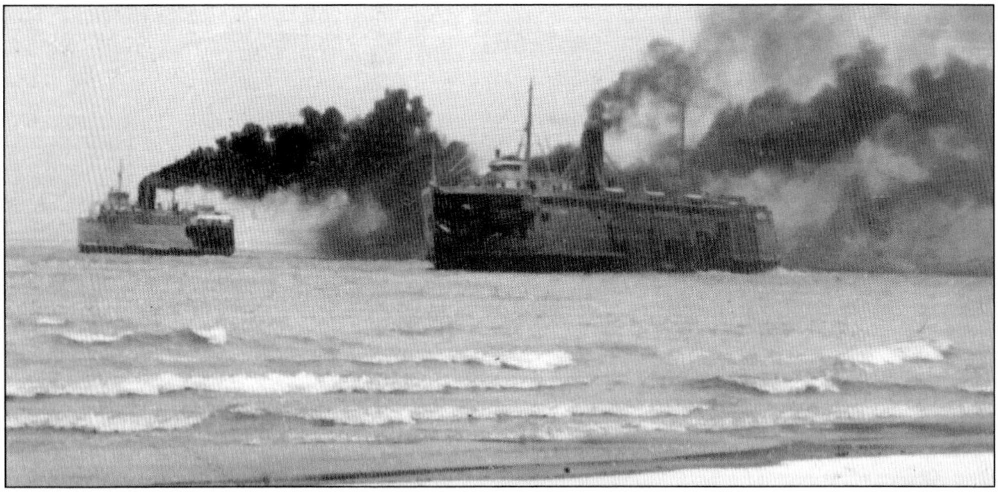

Abrahamson continued, "A line was placed from the *21* to the *32* and the tug *Cushing* had a line on the bow of the *PM 21*. For 26 hours these boats ran at full throttle before the *City of Flint* pulled free from the sandbar. After being freed the *PM 32* was towed to Manitowoc by the tug *John F. Cushing* to have 2000 tons of ice removed." Although local lore reports that an inspection showed virtually no damage to the *PM 32*, there was some significant damage uncovered. (Photograph by Harold Holmes, author's collection.)

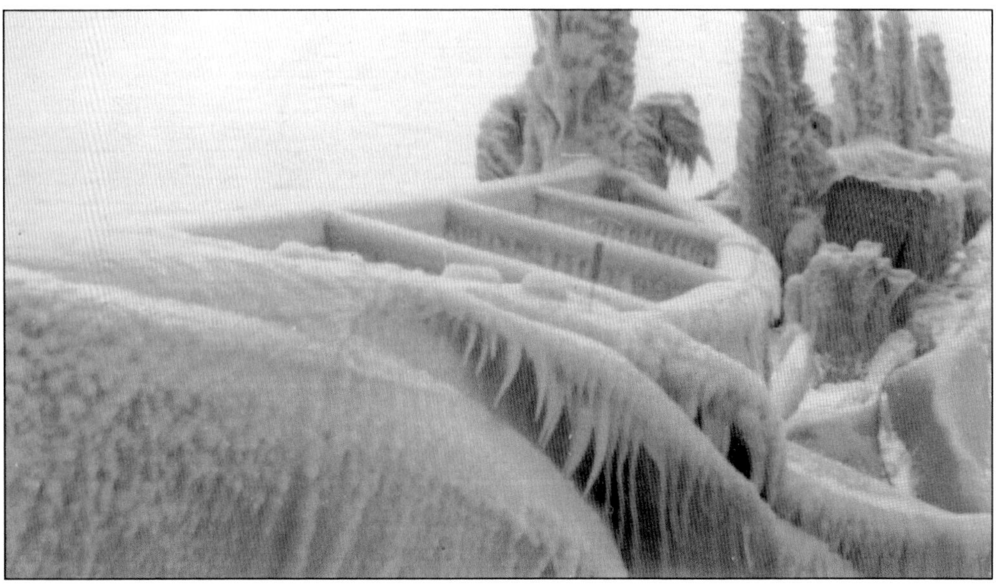

On the *William B. Davock*, all hands were lost; the *Novadoc* was broken in two off Pentwater; the *City of Saginaw* was six hours overdue but made it to Milwaukee safely; and the *City of Flint* failed to navigate the harbor entrance and beached off the shore. The last car ferry to go aground had been the *Pere Marquette 19* near Big Point Sable in 1916. (Photograph by Harold Holmes, author's collection.)

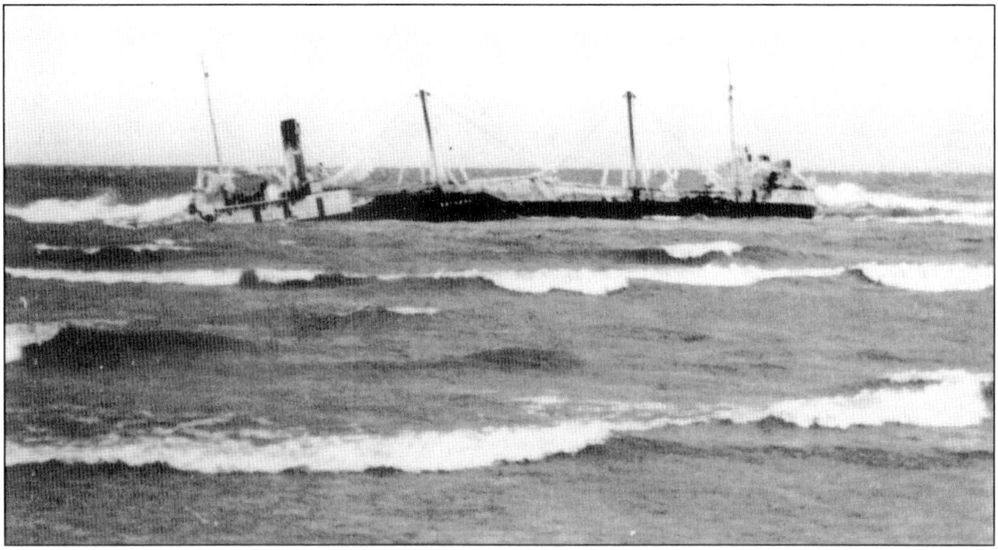

The *Novadoc* is seen here outside of Pentwater after the Armistice Day storm put it on the sandbar and broke the ship's back. The U.S. Coast Guard delayed in its response to assist the *Novadoc*, and the rescue of the crew was left to local fisherman Capt. Clyde Cross and his tug, *Three Brothers*. (Photograph by Harold Holmes, author's collection.)

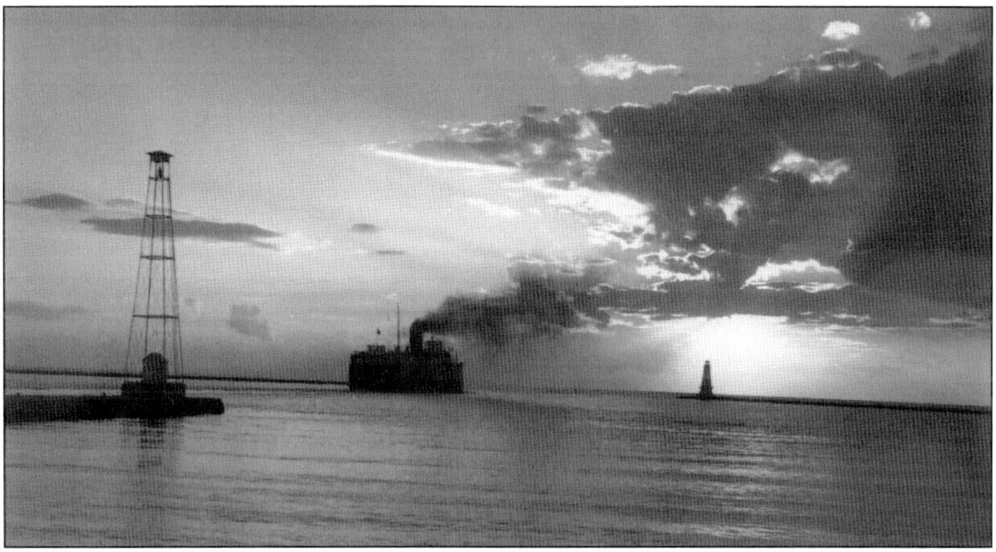

A lone car ferry sails through the Ludington channel on its way out to Manitowoc, Wisconsin. The *Badger* remains alone as the last coal-fired car ferry sailing on the Great Lakes. There have been several close calls, and others have stepped in to save the car ferry service. First it was Michigan Wisconsin Transportation (MWT), incorporated by Glenn Bowden and George Towns, who took over after the Chesapeake and Ohio abandoned the ferries. Charles Conrad successfully resurrected the car ferry service a year after MWT closed with the creation of a new company named Lake Michigan Car Ferry (LMC). The *Badger* continues to sail today and hopefully for many long years to come. Car ferries are synonymous with Ludington. They are part and parcel—an important piece of the local landscape, history, and culture of the area. They define the identity of Ludington, the place where the car ferries are and will hopefully always be. (Photograph by Harold Holmes, author's collection.)